Aberdeenshire Library and Information Service
www.aberdeenshire.gov.uk/libraries
Renewals Hotline 01224 661511

HEADQUARTERS

2 3 JAN 2007

1 7 MAR 2007

2 7 APR 2007

-9 AUG 2007

-5 SEP 2007

-2 JUL 2009

-6 OCT 2007

1 3 NOV 2007

-9 JAN 2008

3 1 JAN 2008

1 8 FEB 2008

-6 MAR 2008

-5 APR 2008

2 6 MAY 2008

26. JUL 08

2 6 AUG 2008

1 3 OCT 2008

-1 NOV 2008

06. JAN 09

-3 FEB 2009

02. MAR 09

2 5 APR 2009

-2 JUN 2009

DAVIES-SCOURFIELD, Gris

In presence of my
foes

IN PRESENCE
OF MY FOES

IN PRESENCE OF MY FOES

A Memoir of Calais, Colditz and
Wartime Escape Adventures

by

Gris Davies-Scourfield

Pen & Sword
MILITARY

First published in Great Britain in 1991 by Wilton 65,
Republished in 2004 by
Pen & Sword Military
an imprint of
Pen & Sword Books Ltd
47 Church Street
Barnsley
South Yorkshire
S70 2AS

ISBN 1 84415 197 2

The right of Grismond Davies-Scourfield to be identified as Author
of thi   dance
with   .988.

All rights   roduced or
transmitted   r mechanical
including pho   n storage and
retrieval syst   er in writing.

Typeset in 11/13 Sabon by
Phoenix Typesetting, Auldgirth, Dumfriesshire

Printed and bound in England by
CPI UK

Pen & Sword Books Ltd incorporates the imprints of Pen & Sword
Aviation, Pen & Sword Maritime, Pen & Sword Military, Wharncliffe
Local History, Pen & Sword Select, Pen & Sword Military Classics
and Leo Cooper.

For a complete list of Pen & Sword titles please contact
PEN & SWORD BOOKS LIMITED
47 Church Street, Barnsley, South Yorkshire, S70 2AS, England
E-mail: enquiries@pen-and-sword.co.uk
Website: www.pen-and-sword.co.uk

To my wartime comrades in the Defence of Calais, in the Polish
Resistance and in Colditz Castle, especially those,
the bravest of the brave, who gave their lives.

Yea, though I walk through death's dark vale,
Yet will I fear none ill;
For Thou art with me, and Thy rod
And staff me comfort still.
My table Thou hast furnished
In presence of my foes;
My head Thou dost with oil anoint,
And my cup overflows

Contents

Acknowledgements

I must first say a very big thank-you to my many friends, who have long been urging me to set down this tale of travels, travails, excitements, frustrations and disasters which made up my rather unusual adventures in the Second World War. Without their encouragement the tale would never have been told.

My thanks are also due to my old Colditz friend, Kenneth Lockwood, for supplying me with pictures and photographs of the castle, from which came Geoffrey Mead's drawing and to Tana Riviere who drew for me the map, without which some of my wanderings would be meaningless to many of my readers.

I am most grateful to the following for allowing me to quote from other works: from *The Colditz Story*, (Hodder and Stoughton Ltd), and Mr S. H. R. Jeal the Executor of the estate of the author, the late Major Pat Reid; from *The Flames of Calais* by the late Airey Neave (republished by Pen and Sword Books, 2003); from *Colditz Recaptured*, edited by the late Reinhold Eggers, (Robert Hale Ltd); from *Colditz the Full Story* by the late Major P. R. Reid, (Macmillan, London Ltd); and from *Tunnelling into Colditz*, by Jim Rogers (Robert Hale Ltd).

I also want to thank the following for permission to use photographs from their books: Henry Chancellor and Hodder and Stoughton Ltd. (*Colditz – The Definitive History*); Robert Hale Ltd. publishers of Reinhold Eggers' *Colditz – The German Story* and *Colditz Recaptured*; and Jon Cooksey, author of *Calais – A Fight To The Finish, May 1940*, Pen and Sword Books Ltd.

I am extremely grateful to my publishers, Pen and Sword Books Ltd., and in particular Brigadier Henry Wilson, who also served in the 60th, for all their help, advice and encouragement for their production of this book in its new form. My sincere thanks also go to the late Lord and to Lady Holderness for its initial publication through their firm Wilton 65.

Last, but by no means least – indeed most of all, I thank my wife, Diana, whose idea it was in the first place that I should make the effort and who read and criticized (often severely but always constructively) my manuscript, then typed it all and, when I changed its form and scope, typed it all over again with never a word of complaint! For this, as in all things, my debt to her is incalculable.

Introduction

I was born in 1918 just as the First World War was drawing to a close, the third surviving son of Gwyn and Helen Saunders-Davies. Soon afterwards, when my father unexpectedly inherited the Mote Estate in Pembrokeshire, our name was changed to Davies-Scourfield.

We five children had a marvellous upbringing on the Sussex Downs, then untouched by the plough and, as my father was a trainer of racehorses, there were always ponies to ride and the local hounds to follow.

My pre-war existence culminated in a wonderful year as a young officer in the 60th (The King's Royal Rifle Corps). However, the horrific memories of the War, with its heavy casualties in the trenches, continued to dominate my generation's early years.

My prep school library, for example, was full of war books, often tales of excitement, glamour and heroics but also, now and then, of mud, blood and misery. People said that there must never be another war; it was too horrible to contemplate, nay totally unthinkable.

But of course there was another war. Indeed ominous signs were not long in coming but failed to spoil the pleasures of my early years, even when sabres started rattling again beyond the Rhine. For me the months passed all too quickly and, as the spring of 1939 turned into summer, time was running out. It was a case of 'eat, drink and be merry'. The unthinkable was actually going to happen. Another war was about to begin.

When at last it came, most people took it calmly. We young officers actually found the prospect exciting rather than awe-inspiring, but my Company Commander, who had fought with distinction in the previous war, reacted with little enthusiasm. 'War is no picnic,' he said. My mother's comment was typical of her generation, 'Must we have another war? We have only just recovered from the last one.' Nevertheless she sent me a splendid letter which helped me many times during the coming years. 'Wherever you go,' she wrote, 'I know that you will always do your duty'. This book tells of my efforts to comply.

When the war began I was just twenty-one years old. They had been marvellous years for me and I succeeded in making the most of them. This was just as well for, within nine months, I would be launched into five years of bleak and dismal contrast.

This book is principally about battle, imprisonment and escape. It also attempts to highlight the enormous courage of the Polish people in their resistance to German occupation and repression and to keep alive the memory of many marvellous individuals whom I have been privileged to call my friends.

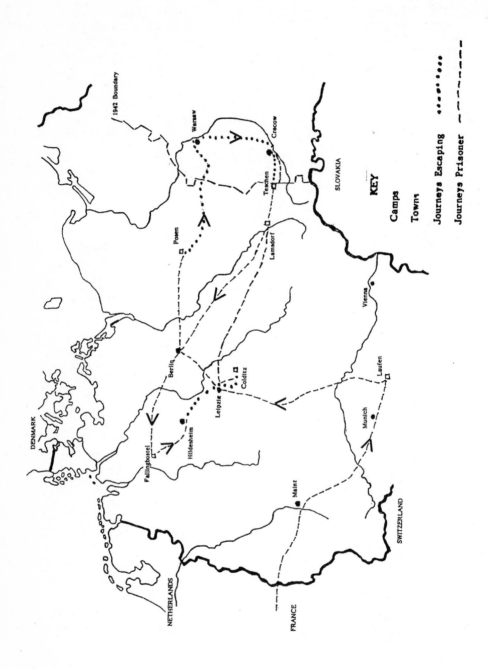

The Author's Travels 1940–45

1

SOUND OF STRIFE

In 1940 the main road to Boulogne left Calais at the Pont Jourdan: then it plunged through the town's ancient battlements into open country towards the village of Coquelles. On the left (or southern side) of the road stood the remains of Bastion 9, once a strongpoint of the old fortifications but, at this time, little more than a high semicircular mound with blocks of stone and concrete round the crest of its circumference.

It was on the top of Bastion 9 that I was standing when dawn broke on 24 May of that calamitous year. Round me riflemen were preparing defensive positions. We were waiting for the Germans to arrive: they had broken through the French positions at Sedan, swept forward to the Somme and captured Boulogne. They were now said to be advancing up the road towards Calais. I had got to the war at last!

It had taken me quite a long time to get there, over eight months in fact, since the war had begun, when those cosy pre-war peaceful days had indeed 'gone with the wind'. My mind drifted back to the excitement of those early days and the following months of preparing and waiting, sometimes with great impatience, for the opportunity of getting to grips with the enemy, the opportunity which had now at last arrived.

We and our sister regiment, The Rifle Brigade, were the two mechanized infantry battalions (known officially as Motor Battalions) of the 1st Armoured Division. Sections were carried in trucks (not yet armoured) but each company also had a scout platoon, mounted in Bren-gun carriers, which resembled tiny little tanks without roof or turret and only lightly armoured. I commanded B Company's scout platoon and was intensely proud of it.

Unfortunately the units in our division had not been fully equipped at the time so we could not go to France with the British Expeditionary Force. Instead we bustled about, closing down our barracks at Tidworth, sending home most of our private possessions and generally preparing for our move to billets in Dorset. As we drove from Bhurtpore Barracks for the last time (I was not to enter the Mess again for over thirty years) we could scarcely have struck terror into the hearts of any enemy able to see us. We were so short of transport that some of the riflemen had to travel in specially hired buses, and all officers' cars were needed. I drove at the head of my platoon in my old Standard 10, which I had bought while still at Sandhurst, as my first ever car, for the princely sum of £52. My platoon sergeant, Sergeant King sat beside me, and my batman, Rifleman Smith, buried under piles of luggage, was in the back!

As a battalion, we were quite well trained and had successfully maintained our traditions, which we shared with The Rifle Brigade, of being the best shooting regiment in the Army and the winners each year of most of the Bisley trophies.

As the armoured regiments were still in process of being re-equipped we were unable to do much training with them, which was a pity. Instead we concentrated on our own infantry training, map reading and (inevitably) shooting on the ranges back in Tidworth. The long marches and driving through the beautiful Dorset country-side gave me special pleasure that autumn. At one point I attended a divisional gas course and thus became, in addition to my duties as a platoon commander, the battalion Gas Officer. I learnt not only all about the old gases – chlorine, phosgene, lewesite and mustard – but also about the latest horror, a nerve gas known as arsene, which the Germans were said to be moving forward on the western front. To cope with arsene all gasmasks had to be hurriedly fitted with a special attachment. It was an interesting course, and the knowledge I acquired was to prove unexpectedly useful during the Calais battle.

B Company was billeted in the village of Stalbridge. A small house in Gold Street became our officers' mess, and I had a nice bedroom in a local business man's rather luxurious house at the top end of the village: later I lived with the local parson and his wife, the Reverend and Mrs Merriman, where I was also very comfortable. Often, when I came in at night for bed, he would ask me to his study for a glass of port. Three members of my platoon married Stalbridge girls as soon as the war was over, and made their homes there after the war.

Just outside the village lived Miss Guest who had her own pack of foxhounds, and one day when I was exercising my platoon we joined the hunt, careering madly along in our scout carriers, and we actually viewed the fox away! My riflemen entered enthusiastically into the spirit of it all, though most of them had never seen anything like it before. It was also Blackmore Vale country, and some of us managed to hire local horses: I had a day with them, but my horse was very slow, and I got badly left behind when hounds went streaming away. A little later I managed to get a day back with the Old Crawley and Horsham during weekend leave. Actually I nearly missed it because my car was on its last legs, which was hardly surprising as I never bothered to have it properly serviced. Fortunately my usual good luck came into play, and my kind businessman host, in whose house I was still billeted, insisted on lending me his beautiful new Citroen: I remember it had a free-wheel system which seemed very modern and exciting, and my mother was both amazed and impressed when I swished up the drive in this sleek and gleaming car.

Towards the end of October two of my brother officers (Henry Scott, our company second-in-command, and Dick Scott – they were not related) and I hired some horses and had a day with the Sparkford Vale Harriers. This turned out to be one of the best day's hunting I have ever had, and I sent my mother a vivid and detailed description which I found among her papers when she died in 1973. As we rode back in the late afternoon I could not know it would be nearly six years before I would see hounds again.

Early in November, following a special Intelligence report, our division was suddenly ordered 'post-haste' to East Anglia to guard against enemy landings. We were billeted around the Braintree area and remained there over Christmas before returning to Dorset. It was a pleasant interlude. We trained hard in extremely cold weather (the coldest winter, it was claimed, for many years) but there was time for relaxation too. Henry Scott organized a small shoot locally which boasted a few pheasants and partridges, and we did some wildfowling on Northey Island, in the estuary of the River Blackwater, near the home of the veteran writer and pacifist, Sir Norman Angell. We called on him to ask about the shooting, and he greeted us most charmingly in his dressing gown. It was very cold that winter, and there was a lot of snow about. It was here I discovered (new to me anyway) a useful trick when I had fallen in the snow and my gun barrels became frozen with ice which no amount of blowing and heavy breathing would shift; nor could I find anything to serve as a probe. It happened at a crucial moment when the evening flight was just starting, so I 'spent a penny' down the barrels which cleared the ice away at once! I called this trick 'useful' but have never had to use it since that day!

One evening I dined with the officers of the Welsh Guards Training Battalion in Colchester as guest of my brother David. The Commanding Officer at the time was Lord Glanusk. David had been with his 1st Battalion in Gibraltar when the war started, moved with it to France and then came to Colchester on promotion to major. It was, I remember, a very formal occasion, starting (suitably enough for Colchester) with oysters which I had never liked and doubt if I have ever eaten them since that evening. Someone told me that oysters were usually alive when one ate them, and that finished them for me once and for all. On the way back to Bocking I wondered if I should ever see old David again. As we three brothers were regular serving officers, it was highly unlikely that all three of us would come through the war unscathed.

I was living in Bocking with some very delightful people called Delph. Mr Delph held a senior chemist's appointment in Courtauld's. He and his wife were exceedingly kind to me and pampered me for several days when I was in bed with flu. While lying in bed I was able to hear on the wireless the fantastically exciting broadcast from Montevideo about the scuttling of the German pocket battleship *Graf Spee*, our first big success of the war.

Back in Dorset life continued as before. Sergeant King, who had looked after me since I first joined the Regiment eighteen months before, left for Headquarter Company, leaving Sergeant Wall as my righthand man. John Robinson, 6 Platoon commander, also departed (alas to be killed in North Africa at the beginning of 1943) and was succeeded by Dick Scott. Coming to join us were Wally Finlayson (the actor Wally Douglas) and Martin Willan who took 7 and 8 Platoons respectively. Rawlinson became Company Sergeant Major. Later a splendid chap called Jack Poole arrived and was attached to our company.

Major J.S. Poole, DSO, OBE, MC had served with the 4th Battalion of the Regiment in the First War, being wounded and captured, escaped successfully through Holland, then joined The Royal Flying Corps, later was with General Ironside at Archangel, became a Lloyds underwriter, tried unsuccessfully to make his fortune in Rhodesia, then became a District Officer in the Sudan. Back in England he met, while in hospital, a very attractive young nurse whom he married, becoming in his spare time a major in a territorial army anti-aircraft unit in Sussex. Nevertheless, in accordance with War Office policy, whereby all officers on the Regular Army Reserve, including those serving with the Territorials, must return to their regiment. Jack who was over forty had to revert to the rank of Captain and was posted to our Training Centre at Chisledon.

He should never have been with us but Eddie Campbell, who was commanding at Chisledon, sent him along to find out about up-to-date motor battalion tactics. 'As soon as you think you have learnt enough come back and give me a hand', Eddie had told him. Unfortunately (as it turned out), our company commander, 'Puffin', suddenly became Battalion second in command, and the Colonel asked Jack to stay and take over B Company until a new and younger major could be appointed. In the event his relief was only nominated after we had left for France and, in view of the situation at the time, was unable to follow. This unlucky turn of events was to cost Jack five years' loss of liberty, permanent damage to his health and the destruction of his marriage.

The joys of our peaceful existence were tempered for many of us by a very real anxiety that somehow the war would be won before we got to it. It was embarrassing enough that the Regiment had missed the Battle of Waterloo, all our battalions having been overseas at the time, so that to miss Hitler's war would be frustrating to say the least!

Thus we were still at Stalbridge on 10 May when the German offensive on the western front began. The Norwegian campaign, which had started early in April, had failed to involve us but now, with everyone 'Battling away like billy-o' as Henry put it at breakfast that morning, we all became very excited. Indeed we were quickly on the move, orders coming through late that night. As duty officer I had to rouse the whole company. Jack later recalled in his autobiography *Undiscovered Ends*.

Audrey woke me up. 'The telephone's ringing: I'll go and see what it's about.' It was one of my subalterns, Grismond Davies-Scourfield. 'Tell Jack we're moving within two hours. . . Yes, I'm afraid he'll have to come straight away.' It was about one o'clock in the morning.

In the early hours the battalion, together with 1 Rifle Brigade, became the newly formed 30 Infantry Brigade under Brigadier Claude Nicholson, a 16/5th Lancer, and off we went.

But not alas to France. Once again our destination was Essex, and we were soon busy preparing to defend the coast against possible invasion or at least landings of some kind or raids by air or sea. My platoon's task was to defend Canvey Island, rather a derelict area in those days. The sudden arrival of my eleven scout carriers and five motor cycles caused some mild surprise among the few inhabitants to see us: our steel-helmeted warlike appearance seemed quite out of place in those dingy but wholly peaceful surroundings.

Almost immediately we were withdrawn to Bury St Edmunds and occupied a large tented camp in nearby Fornham Park. This became a base for reconnoitering the whole Suffolk and Essex area and for swimming and sunbathing in truly gorgeous weather.

Meanwhile a great battle was raging across Holland, Belgium and Luxembourg and a crucial point was reached when the Germans crossed the Meuse.

'That really is very bad news,' said our Colonel, Euan Miller, (later to become Lieutenant General Sir Euan Miller KCB, KBE, DSO, MC, DL), who had been on the headquarters staff in France until he came to us in January, and on Tuesday, 21 May we got at last our proper marching orders.

Jack Poole later wrote:

The news from France was dark but not sufficiently black to deter me from asking for a day's leave to go racing at Newmarket. Euan Miller, my commanding officer, evidently did not think my presence indispensable and granted me leave. I had hardly packed my bag when orders arrived for the battalion to move at once. That night we drove through Newmarket – a map replaced my Race-Form – and arrived at Southampton the next morning.

We left Fornham Park just before midnight. We moved in two columns, wheeled and tracked. The latter consisted of the four Scout platoons commanded by Mike Sinclair (A Company), me (B Company), Phil Pardoe (C Company) and Richard Warre (D Company), the whole column under Mike's command as he was the senior of us.

That last drive has always remained vividly in my memory. Swinging right-handed in Bury we took the road to Newmarket, and, as we passed through it, I thought of myself as a small boy staying there with my grandfather and watching the racehorses file past on their way to the Heath. On the high ground south of the town we came up with the rear of the wheeled column which had halted, and a dispatch rider appeared with the orders for us to proceed without lights. The cancellation of this order was sent out shortly afterwards but never reached us, so that we drove through the night with all lights extinguished, which was dangerous on the London road and slowed us up considerably. Mike and I stood together on the road, waiting to move on. Away to our left search-lights near Harwich swept the sky. As we approached London dawn began to break and with it rain which started gently but steadily increased. Men and equipment were soon soaked, yet it was not on the whole unpleasant, and the trees and hedges gliding past provided us with a last look at our English countryside.

When we eventually swung onto the North Circular the rain had become a deluge. We were met by the Adjutant, Alick Williams, who directed us into a large petrol station where we all filled up. Some locals produced tea for us which was highly popular: soldiers loved their tea in those days and used to say 'If the tea is good, then the whole meal is good'. On ahead with the wheeled column B company were having an uneventful journey except for Wally Finlayson (7 Platoon) whose truck had broken down close to where we now waited. The recovery vehicles travelled last of all, and before they arrived Wally had managed to devour eggs and bacon in a café, summon his father by telephone to bring him some money (which he did) and phone his wife to say goodbye! Phil Pardoe had also managed to communicate with his parents. He sent them a telegram saying 'Cook the ducks for dinner,' his pre-arranged codeword for 'We're going overseas'.

Still in the pouring rain we rumbled on. It was a fitting drive for my last moments in England, filled as it was with nostalgic memories of happier days. Staines and Egham reminded me of London trips with the Sandhurst fencing team; Sunningdale of pleasant visits to Holm place, staying with one of my school friends, Mervyn Mansel – I actually saw the house looking grey and silent in the falling rain as we rumbled by; and on through Camberley, past Sandhurst's gates, the Regal Cinema and the Wayside café where I had spent so many convivial evenings with my Sandhurst friends. I wondered where they would all now be, some already perhaps in action in France and Belgium.

On the Hertford Bridge Flats, south of Camberley, we again caught up with the wheeled column and had a belated and very welcome breakfast, always my favourite meal. The rain had ceased and heavy clouds were being blown from the sky. How well I knew this flat heath country stretching around us where I had attended my first Sandhurst exercise; commanded a platoon for the first time, hunted with the beagles, and, on Barossa Common, plainly visible in the rising distance, had ridden on happy afternoons.

Dick visited us as we munched our breakfasts and brought bad news: advanced units of the German army were only six miles from the Channel Ports, and there were rumours that Boulogne had actually fallen. It sounded as though we might be landed at Brest or Cherbourg where, Dick understood, our own Division had already arrived.

On we went past Basingstoke (as if returning to Tidworth from some London outing) and skirted Winchester, where I could see the landmarks of my schoolboy years. The new bypass, along which we were then driving, had been under construction when I was in the school. Sometimes with my friends (where were they now?) I had climbed about its half-built bridges and slid in Sunday tails and top-hat down its chalky embankments. Little did I think I would one day drive along it on my way to battle. I remembered – it seemed long ago – hearing in one of Budge Firth's[1] famous sermons of Old Wykehamists going to the front in the Great War, how they would lean from the train to catch a glimpse of the school buildings and the clump on St Catherine's Hill; perhaps they had heard the bells that echoed through the ancient town. Now, once more a new generation of Wykehamists might be told of us driving to yet another war to hold the Germans back. I thought again of the day I had left the school for the last time, with such high hopes for the future. It did not look so good now, and we would soon be in the thick of it all;

some of us no doubt already wondering, as we came to a halt on the outskirts of Southampton, how we would make out when the real bullets began to fly around and shells began to burst. It was the morning of Wednesday, 22 May.

Note:
1. The Reverend J. De E. Firth, Chaplain and later Housemaster at Winchester College.

2

INTO BATTLE

Apart from Dick Scott's BBC News report, few of us can have had much idea of what was going on and certainly nothing of the extent of the Allies' military disaster then unfolding. It was just as well. Nor did we yet know our destination. Indeed the decision where to send us had not yet been made and would depend on how the military situation developed during the coming hours.

In Southampton staff officers relieved us of all maps and stuck labels on the vehicles. We moved on and halted under some trees close to the High Street where more staff officers ordered us to dismount and remove from the vehicles all personal kit which would then be driven to the docks for loading onto ships. I decided I would be more usefully employed at the docks than waiting with the battalion in the temporary camp which had been allotted; so, leaving the rest of the platoon under Sergeant Wall, I proceeded with the drivers. The sun had come out hot after the rain and shone upon the ships as they lay along the quay.

I spent the rest of the day trying to get my carriers onto the vehicle ship. It was a lengthy and rather trying business, mainly because of continual orders and counter orders from the embarkation staff. In the middle of it all who should appear but Edward Bird of the Rifle Brigade whom I had known well at school. Edward, who was a dashing, devil-may-care sort of person, but with immense charm, immediately suggested that we should go off together and have a meal in the town. Feeling responsible for my drivers and all their kit, by this time piled high upon the quay, I declined the invitation: although I was right to do so, I was later, as things turned out, to have regrets. Tragically Edward was destined to be killed in the forthcoming Calais battle. His younger brother, Tom, my exact contemporary, survived the war with an outstanding war record, winning the DSO, MC and Bar with the Rifle Brigade in North Africa.

When our loading was nearly complete I met up with an embarkation Sergeant Major wearing 60th uniform. I immediately engaged him in conversation. He was able to tell me from which dock the battalion would be sailing: he wished us luck and said he would like to be going with us.

'I suppose you're pretty busy just now,' I remarked chattily, 'plenty of people sailing and all that.'

'Not many sailing' he replied and, lowering his voice, added 'but there'll be plenty coming home. The Regiment's going the wrong way, if you ask me.'

I did not understand, but time was marching, and with the help of a cooperative bus driver ('So you want my bus, do you? Then you shall have it.') we set out for our point of embarkation, where we found our transport, *The Royal Daffodil,* waiting for us with its gangways down. *The Archangel,* which was to carry the Rifle Brigade, must have been somewhere nearby. Our Brigadier, Claude Nicholson of the 16/5th Lancers, whom I had not seen before, and indeed had never heard of, was standing with a group of staff officers talking to *The Royal Daffodil*'s captain. A few minutes later our battalion marched onto the dock with the Colonel at its head, after a two mile tramp. No one had taken much notice of them on the way through the town, and a cricket match crowd had scarcely turned around to watch the khaki figures passing by. After all, cricket in England has always been a serous business. The kit was then carried on board and, after some delay, we all went up the gangways. There was no one to see us leave so, mercifully, no fond farewells. Silently our ship cast off and joined the other transports, *The Archangel* and the two vehicle ships, in Southampton water.

I stood on the deck amongst the men of my platoon, as we made our way gently to the open sea. The Solent was beautiful that evening with the ships at anchor and the Isle of Wight clear and silent in the slanting sun. The mouth of the Hamble, where I had once sailed in a small boat, the Portsdown forts (milestones on the road to Sussex), Bembridge with its little harbour, all brought back to me happy memories of the past and many of us would feel we would be fighting not only for the present and the future of our Country but also for

11

its heritage. Away in front of us were the other transports, while an escort of two destroyers waited in the Channel for our coming.

'Two destroyers, my foot,' it was the old familiar voice of 'Puffin' Owen, 'I expect at least the Grand Fleet and ten squadrons of Spitfires for my escort.'

We passed Netley hospital, where my sister Gwynedd was already working as a VAD, and as we reached the open sea another transport, laden with troops, passed us, heading for Southampton, followed by several more: they seemed indeed to be going the wrong way, but we cheered them nonetheless as, strangely silent, they drifted by. Darkness fell slowly till we could scarcely see the shore, and we went below to sort ourselves out. Rations were issued, and we officers had a splendid four course dinner served to us in the saloon. Before we retired for the night Jack summoned his platoon commanders – Dick, Wally, Martin and myself – as well as Sergeant Major Rawlinson and Colour Sergeant Faulkner to tell us what was happening. He succeeded in painting quite a cheerful picture. The Germans had captured or invested Boulogne with what was estimated to be a few armoured detachments. The 3rd Royal Tanks and 1st Queen Victoria's Rifles had been landed at Calais during the day and were keeping open the approaches to the town: if the approaches were still open the next day we would be landed to mop up these armoured detachments and generally restore the situation in the area of the Channel Ports. Before crossing over, however, we would be putting into Dover where the Brigadier would receive the latest information and be given final instructions. It all sounded exciting and, in cooperation with the 3rd Royal Tanks, well within our capabilities, despite our lack of artillery support.

One must not, even in retrospect, blame anyone too much for having so little idea of the true military situation at that time. The means of communication were still comparatively primitive in those days, and the speed of the German advance had caused total confusion. Yet the fact remains that what were thought to be a few armoured detachments in the Boulogne/Calais area were actually General Guderian's three panzer divisions, 2nd Panzer directed on Boulogne and 1st and 10th Panzer advancing towards Calais. Fortunately we did not know.

Despite cramped conditions below deck most of us, I think, had a good night's rest, which was just as well, for it would be quite a time before many of us would sleep so well again. But it was a short

12

night, and in the early dawn the Channel looked grey and cold with the dear old 'White Cliffs' looming closer. By about 7 a.m. we had put into Dover harbour and were drawn up along the quay. For four hours we stayed put, sitting on deck or sleeping down below. As the morning wore on and we had made no move, it seemed to many of us that we would never sail, that our venture would be finally called off; that we would go tamely back to Dorset or Fornham Park.

On shore, however, at a meeting of our Brigadier with General Brownrigg and Admiral Bertram Ramsey, a decision was being taken. Sir Douglas Brownrigg was the BEF's Adjutant General and had been given special responsibility by Lord Gort for the Channel Ports, while Admiral Ramsey was Flag Officer Dover and was shortly to be responsible for the brilliant naval evacuation from Dunkirk (Operation DYNAMO). At this meeting, a decision was made, and confirmed by the War Office, to send us immediately to Calais. Suddenly our Colonel came along the quay and stepped on board; the gangway was raised, and we began to sail. It was 11 a.m. on the morning of Thursday, 23 May.

Standing on deck as we left harbour and headed out into the Channel, I heard orders, shouted by megaphone from the nearest destroyer telling our transports to keep close together and zigzag. Jack had soon received his orders and, coming to our part of the deck, summoned his last platoon commanders' conference and (if I remember rightly) issued some sort of maps.

Weak enemy detachments, he told us, were feeling their way towards Calais from the south and had encountered elements of the Queen Victoria's Rifles and the 3rd Tanks. Apart from these two units and some anti-aircraft gunners there were no organized Allied troops in the Calais area. We and the Rifle Brigade, said Jack, would land in Calais and move to their support. Then followed detailed orders: the Company would be moving, as soon as it had disembarked, to a battalion dispersal area in the dunes, but I was to stay with the ship and report to Puffin (the Battalion second in command) to help with the unloading of our vehicles and stores. When he finished, a few questions were asked, and we dispersed to pass these orders on.

Behind us the cliffs of Dover became smaller in the distance as we continued our zigzag course. The Channel was completely deserted, and the quiet only broken by the dull thudding of guns from the direction of Boulogne. Then suddenly and unexpectedly our ship's

13

siren wailed out its warning: we were making our first contact with the enemy! Amidst intense excitement the men went streaming below, and a few seconds later the leading destroyer, just ahead of us and slightly to our left, let fly with her guns. A lone reconnaissance plane disappeared into low cloud above us as Dick and Wally swung their guns too late. There followed a crash and a column of spray, and two bombs landed close to the destroyer. Then it was over. We had seen our first shots fired in anger, and all was quiet again. Shortly afterwards a formation of British fighters roared overhead towards France. Later some of us saw what looked like the path of a torpedo pass well in front, and though the presence of a U-boat in this area was as unlikely as unpleasant, I believe that depth charges were dropped.

The coast of France was now quite distinct, with the town of Calais and its sand dunes stretching away along the shore. Soon we were drifting into the harbour, and it was possible, as *The Archangel* followed in behind us, to identify some of our Rifle Brigade friends: I saw Edward Bird, and we exchanged waves of greeting. They proved to be waves of farewell for I would never see him again. The town seemed deserted and very quiet: Rifleman Bishop, one of my cheekier ones, asked what had become 'of all the mademoiselles'.

Leaning over the rails together Puffin and I watched the companies file off and march away. When everyone had gone our unloading party brought the kit ashore and waited in the station for the vehicle ships to berth beside the quay, ours being *The Kohistan* and the Rifle Brigade's the *City of Canterbury* which had brought the QVR's to Calais on the previous day. It was pouring with rain, and the enemy made no attempt to bomb us. Puffin was in high spirits and joked about how he hoped to get 'a nice little wound, perhaps in the leg,' which would enable him to spend the rest of the war at home in comfort and to boast about it in after years.

With maddening deliberation, so it seemed, the ships manoeuvred in the harbour, and it was not until 4 p.m. that unloading could begin. It was clear, right from the start that we had many tedious hours before us. A mass of petrol cans had to be brought off first and, for the vehicles, there was only one crane, operated by a fat old Frenchman, who was clearly suffering from fatigue and lack of sleep. Our work was now being hampered by occasional enemy aircraft which flew singly over the town, usually on simple reconnaissance but occasionally dropping some bombs. We did not find it necessary to stop working during these incursions – indeed the time could not be spared – but the French stevedores insisted on taking cover each time until the 'all clear' was sounded. The first of these planes came over quite low at about 2,000 feet and dropped a bomb into the harbour nearby, wounding, so I was told, Tony Bamfylde of the Rifle Brigade, whom I had known at school. We had a fine view of this plane being shot at by anti-aircraft guns, and the black puffs of exploding shells were close to it all the time. The dock had by this time become crowded: a long hospital train, coming from the front, had drawn in with its load of dead and wounded, and the grim business of emptying its contents onto the quayside, while several naval and embarkation officers bustled about, arguing and shouting, brought us a moment's distraction. I had never before seen a dead human body and was relieved to find I was surprisingly unsqueamish. Some administrative personnel from 3rd Tanks also appeared and one of them, Duggie Moir, who had been at Sandhurst with me, suddenly greeted me with 'So you're in this party too'. He told me that a big tank battle was in progress south of the town, and he was desperately trying to get up supplies of petrol. He was referring in fact to a clash between 3rd Tanks and elements of 1st Panzer Division which was moving round Calais towards Gravelines, but this was not clear at the time. Ronnie Littledale, who had commanded our A Company in Dorset and was now on 30 Brigade Staff, also turned up and told me that the French and British armies were supposed to have counterattacked successfully and closed the gap at Douai. Had this been true (which it was not) it would have meant that all German troops who had broken through were cut off and must either fight their way back or ultimately surrender. Such a rumour, though entirely false, helped to keep our morale high.

Meanwhile B Company in the dispersal area had received orders to take up a position on the edge of the town, astride the main road leading from Calais to Boulogne. Our battalion's immediate task was to secure the outer perimeter of Calais from the coast on the west to a point on the southern edge of the town from where the Rifle Brigade would continue the line to the coast on the east side, a front of about eight miles. The QVR's and 3rd Tanks would continue to hold their forward positions for as long as possible: on withdrawing, the QVR companies would come under command of the battalion whose front they had been covering. The 2-pounder guns of 229 Anti-tank Battery RA which were effective only against light and some medium tanks were to cover the main roads. On B Company's right and reaching to the coast was C Company under command of Maurice Johnson, with Everard Radcliffe as second in command; on the left D Company, under Godfrey Cromwell and Claude Bower, while A Company under Derek Trotter was in reserve. Jack, receiving these orders in the dunes, immediately organized an advance guard under Dick, sent it off in commandeered transport and marched at the head of the company in pursuit. On their way through the streets they met large numbers of French soldiers toiling northwards: Jack Poole described them as being tired and dispirited, in no state to fight. Later, he was to write in his autobiography *Undiscovered Ends,* 'Excepting the personnel of the Calais Forts, the French troops in my vicinity were in their best "Nous sommes trahis" mood and, having thrown away their arms and dissociated themselves from active participation in the battle, were busily engaged in looting what liquor they could find.' As soon as the position allocated was reached Jack organized the defences and sent out patrols under Dick and Wally.

Back at the docks I knew nothing of these moves, and the unloading dragged slowly on. Already we were behind schedule, and Puffin became short tempered as time went slipping by: I saw him seize a bottle of wine from a rifleman's lips and dash it to the ground. As each vehicle came off the boat it was taken by a driver and guided by a dispatch rider to the rendezvous of the company concerned: when a sufficient number had assembled then another DR took them forward. Just as darkness was falling I went with one of the B Company batches and on the way was surprised to see large numbers of French soldiers lolling and smoking in the doorways. We passed a squadron of our tanks heading towards the centre of the town which looked large and comfortingly formidable in the fading light.

I found Jack in the back room of a building which looked like a pub, and he told me to swallow some food while the going was good.

'There's some sort of German force, with artillery, coming up the road towards us,' he told me, 'so we'll probably get shelled tonight.'

I ate some excellent tongue with bread and butter, had a cup of tea and then went to find my platoon: it was in reserve behind a high bank, everyone obviously in the best of spirits, with Sergeant Wall very much in control. For my return journey I borrowed a motor-bike and took with me Rifleman Martyn, one of my own DRs. As we recrossed the canal in darkness now complete, the quiet was

16

suddenly shattered by a succession of what sounded to me like the most appalling crashes in the dock area, and the whine and 'swoosh' of shells became audible overhead: the first bombardment had begun. We had no idea whether we ought to take cover or not; never before having been under fire I did not know 'the form' on such occasions. Anyhow, we pushed on until we reached the barrier of the dock guard, where we learned from a sergeant that shells were falling on the *Gare maritime*, and Captain Sir David Hawley, our Transport Officer's voice from the darkness told us to come in behind a wall until 'the party' was over. This we did with relief and alacrity, but already the bombardment was dying away, and very soon we were able to proceed. It was quite an experience, really, and as far as I was concerned, the war had very definitely begun.

3

THE DEFENCE OF BASTION 9

Throughout the night we worked away, often operating the crane ourselves and manhandling the seemingly endless stream of petrol cans. Puffin drove us on relentlessly, allowing no pause for rest, determined that the battalion should have all its vehicles, ammunition and petrol when the battle began. We were luckier than the Rifle Brigade whose ship took on board a number of wounded and others at Calais and sailed back to England before unloading was complete.

Soon after dawn on Friday, 24 May I reported to Jack with the last of our vehicles and learnt that the enemy were drawing closer. Wally had been out with a carrier patrol from my platoon and reported small parties of German infantry advancing up the road toward the village of Coquelles some three miles from us. Now Dick was about to go forward with another of my sections, the one commanded by Corporal Gorringe, to renew the contact. I wanted to go in Dick's place, but Jack did not wish to do the briefing and orders all over again and said he had another task for me. I felt the day had started badly and, tired from the long hours of unloading, I was now frustrated by missing two of my own platoon patrols.

I watched them go off down the road, Dick in the first of the three carriers, and was then immediately involved in a most unfortunate incident. One of my section commanders accidentally discharged his rifle while pulling it out of his carrier and blew a nasty hole right through the middle of his hand. He was in great pain, and as I had to collect the dock guard I took him back with me to an aid post of the 3rd Tanks. I have never seen him again but know that somehow he got safely home.

Near the docks I found a familiar face under a Tank Corps beret;

18

Toby Everard's. He had been my first Senior Underofficer at Sandhurst, and we exchanged friendly greetings.

The docks themselves, when I got there, were in a real mess: there had been more shelling, or possibly bombing, debris lay everywhere, and several buildings were blazing furiously. It was all rather dramatic and exciting. One of the ships, probably the Rifle Brigade's *City of Canterbury*, was preparing to leave, and no doubt her Captain was only too keen to get moving: wounded men were hobbling, or being carried on stretchers, up the gangway. In the midst of this desolate scene I was accosted by an elderly-looking major who was about to go on board, probably one of the BEF administrative people quite legitimately being evacuated: 'Come on, young feller', he said, 'you'd better get away while the going is good: there's only one safe place just now, and that's England. This may be your last chance.'

Having collected the dock guard, I returned to B Company where Jack met me.

'The enemy is only thought to be a weak column', he assured me, 'trying to fight its way back to the German lines, though with a few guns which they have probably captured from the French, so we jolly well ought to be able to stop them.' This 'weak column' was in fact Major General Schaal's 10th Panzer Division, backed by the guns of General Guderian's XIXth Panzer Corps and with 1st Panzer Division, which had inflicted the casualties on 3rd Tanks the previous day, working round Calais towards Gravelines.

Jack then gave me my task, which was to defend a high semi-circular fortification, marked on the map as Bastion 9, but which has always remained in my memory as 'The Redoubt': it had concrete blocks along it at intervals, with plenty of cover from scrubby bushes as well as from the blocks themselves. Available to me was one section of 7 Platoon, two sections of 6 Platoon and some company headquarters people, while my Scout Platoon, less one section, was to be in company reserve though under me. 8 Platoon (Martin Willan) was away out of sight on our left, between the Redoubt and D Company's sector. Wally, with his 7 Platoon less one section, was holding a covering position way out to our front, while Dick had one of my sections on the patrol and one of his 6 Platoon sections on the right of the road. The general layout was as shown in the diagram.

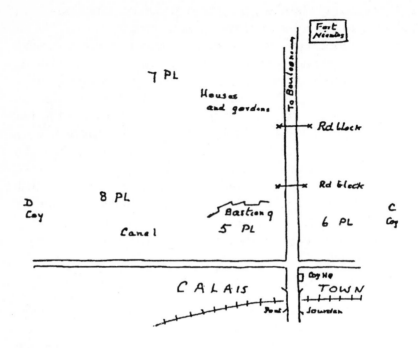

Digging was fairly easy, and if we had had some mines and wire, some artillery to provide defensive fire and a weapon with some chance of destroying a German medium tank, then the Redoubt could have become a formidable strongpoint. It lay immediately on the left of the main road to the village of Coquelles and beyond it to Boulogne and overlooked all approaches from that direction, while the built-up area of the town started 100 yards behind.

Company Headquarters were in buildings near the Pont Jourdan railway bridge. C Company was on our right with its flank on the sea, and A Company was in reserve.

The Rifle Brigade held the outer perimeter from our D Company's left flank to the sea on the east side of town. In Brigade reserve were the 3rd Tanks and QVRs less their own B Company: the latter was deployed with our C Company and included a detachment at Fort Nieulay just to our front. Although this is a purely personal account and not a history of the battle, I have given this brief description of the Brigade's deployment in order to provide some necessary background setting.

A motley collection of people was streaming up the road ahead of

20

the advancing Germans, hoping to find refuge and security in Calais. One old lady, hopelessly lost and confused, reminded Jack of his mother. As well as these refugees, there were some exhausted French troops and a few British anti-aircraft and searchlight people, many eagerly volunteering to help us. One young gunner officer told me that seventy-five per cent of his battery had been killed when German tanks overran their position; and that he and his party had been chased by infantry all the way from Boulogne. Their willingness to assist us was in stark contrast to the attitude of the French troops passing through.

The first hour or so of daylight has always been the best for me, and this promised to be a beautiful day – weatherwise at least – and as we set about improving our positions my spirits rose. Here we were at last, taking a proper part in the war with every prospect of the action and excitement we had craved while in Dorset and Essex. After all, I had so much wanted to be a soldier, ever since those OTC days and here was the reality at last. My NCOs and Riflemen caught my good humour and soon cockney jokes were flying around. There was a sublime confidence that we were about to give the Germans, coming along the road towards us, a very bloody nose.

We were, however, deployed on a wide front. On our right there was only C Company and two QVR platoons between us and the sea which was over 2,500 yards away. The gap between me and Martin Willan on my left was nearly 600 yards which precluded any closely interlocking fire plan and meant that one of my scout sections had to be constantly on patrol between us. This section was commanded by Corporal Byrne who had been our Company Clerk when I joined the Regiment and promoted into my Platoon only a few months before Calais. His father had been a well-known Regimental Quartermaster Sergeant, and his younger brother was to become Regimental Sergeant Major of our 1st Battalion after the war. At 6 a.m. Mike Sinclair's Scout Platoon from A Company was sent up to cover the area between B and D Companies. I saw Mike as he came up to check our positions: always methodical he was carrying a huge map-board scrupulously marked up in chinagraph with the latest battle situation. His story and mine would become closely interwoven before the war would end.

The sounds of battle developed as the Germans drew near, and occasional shells began to fall among us. We made difficult targets among our ancient battlements, and no one was hit, though a few

21

landed unpleasantly close to me as I moved about. I remember now and then dropping to one knee as their whistling approached – the maximum concession I could make, with so many heads turned towards me, to my instinct for self-preservation.

At 7 a.m. Henry brought round some rations and gloomily remarked that nothing had been heard of Dick's patrol. Shortly afterwards a solitary scout carrier was seen coming slowing down the main road towards us: it pulled in near Company Headquarters and stopped. Out of it jumped 'old' Bateman (aged about thirty-five and the most elderly member of my platoon) calling urgently for help. In front of the carrier, slumped behind his Boys rifle, sat Lance Corporal Smith, dead. Beside him, exhausted and in pain, was the driver, Wilson, with a huge jagged wound in one leg. Blood was everywhere, and the armoured plating on the front of the vehicle was twisted and mangled. Bateman reported that the patrol, advancing down the main road, had suddenly come under fire: they had tried to outflank the enemy by manoeuvring the vehicles, but the two leading carriers, commanded by Dick and Corporal Gorringe, had been put out of action and, he thought, their crews all killed. He himself had opened fire with his Bren gun: then his carrier was also hit, but they had somehow managed to get back.

It no longer seemed quite such a lovely morning. I was extremely fond of every single member of my platoon: we had come quite a long way together, and each one killed would be a personal loss for me. It was still early in the day, and the battle had scarcely begun. I had already lost eight dead, wounded, missing or injured out of a total of forty. But one just had to get on with everything: there would be time for sorrow later on.

Meanwhile Corporal Byrne's section, patrolling on the left, had been in action against German motorcyclists and infantry: one carrier had been hit by small-arms fire (I saw the bullet marks later) but no one had been hurt, and they had forced the Germans to retire. Martin's 8 Platoon had also been in action.

Sometime around 9.30 a.m. Dick returned on foot. He reported that the crews of his and Gorringe's carriers had been either killed or badly wounded: Gorringe and Bishop, he was sure, were dead. He himself had jumped from his carrier when it had been put out of action and found cover beside the road, whence he had shot one German with his pistol. He had then managed to crawl back slowly along a ditch and eventually reach Fort Nieulay where some QVRs and French troops were still in control. He had a nasty flesh wound in his leg and a neat bullet hole through his tin hat; yet he steadfastly refused to go back for medical treatment at the Aid Post, fearing he might miss the coming fight.

Pressure against B Company's front developed slowly throughout that long morning. We were under constant, though sometimes spasmodic shell fire, many falling within the Bastion and all around Company Headquarters. The sound of explosions and the rattle of small-arms fire – the latter mainly to our left and out in front suggesting Wally's and Martin's boys were under direct attack – became almost continuous. Our vehicles, dispersed in the street behind us, began to get badly knocked about. Luckily no casualties were suffered in my sector, though a bullet chipped some concrete one inch from Rifleman Mather's nose as he peered round one of the blocks. I had just sat down beside him when it happened, but he was quite unperturbed, merely saying 'Cor! Look at that'. I kept thinking to myself that this was war, the real thing which we had waited for, trained for, read about and thought about, but so far it all seemed fairly straightforward, except for the loss of my patrol. Jack came walking up to our position and warned me that the Germans were expected to use tanks, and he was trying to enlist some support from the RAF, Royal Navy and possibly from the shore batteries. There were two destroyers in the Channel which might provide some defensive fire, and 3rd Tanks could probably help.

At 11 a.m., quite suddenly, German infantry started to pour out of a wood, about a mile away to our left front, and to advance towards D Company: there must have been at least two companies of them coming on. Suddenly shells, presumably from the French shore batteries, began to burst among them, and most of the Germans fled ignominiously back into the woods. It was an exhilarating sight and most exciting, but the attack was soon resumed, the enemy this time making better use of hedgerows and dead ground, though they were eventually held. I heard later that 8 Platoon as well as D Company had been involved and that fighting had been intense, with casualties on both sides.

Now the Germans turned their attention onto our sector as well, and as we came under increasing shell fire we could see, on the high ground to our front, continual flashes which suggested that guns had been moved forward. We were able to pinpoint some of these positions and report them back: eventually a few of our naval

Swordfish flew over and dropped some bombs. Fortunately the German Air Force was not at this stage much in evidence, though I did at one moment see one of our planes, a Lysander I think, come spinning to the ground with one wing shot away. The French gunners produced no further fire, and I heard later that they had run out of ammunition and spiked all their guns. Meanwhile Fort Nieulay and Wally's positions were being pounded, while German Infantry tried to work their way forward: but Wally and his two sections replied vigorously, their Bren guns inflicting extremely heavy casualties, and the attack bogged down. But now a new menace loomed as German tanks suddenly appeared on the high ground. It was about noon.

I watched fascinated, and I am sure the eyes of us all were on them, while what seemed to be a squadron of medium tanks slowly deployed into two long lines. Through my field glasses they certainly looked powerful and full of menace: they scarcely seemed to move, but the distant growling of their engines and clanking of their tracks told us they were coming on. I wondered how we would stop them if they just kept rolling forward, which was probably what they intended to do. In fact they eventually descended into dead ground where we could not see them, bypassed Fort Nieulay and supported an infantry advance against Wally's two sections south of the road and against the gap between us and C Company on our right: here enemy infantry succeeded in getting into a cemetery but were quickly driven out.

The German tanks, however, had remained out of sight and were in fact held up by an obstacle of some kind, probably a stream or sunken road. This gave Jack time to arrange our support by three light tanks of 3 RTR under command of Second Lieutenant Gregg. In later years he was to become something of a RTR character and be known as 'Gunner' Gregg, but now he was a real morale booster, bursting with enthusiasm and spoiling for a fight. I asked him whether the Redoubt would be of any use as an obstacle to the tanks and whether our Boys rifles would be effective, at least at close range. I well remember his reply, 'None whatever,' he said. 'They'll laugh at this bank, and your Boys rifles wouldn't blow a track off at point-blank range. Our only hope is to bluff them, make them think we have a big force here. By Jove, what a sight if they come at us.' And he went off to position his tanks, as happy as a king.

Now the Germans, with their tanks and infantry closely co-operating together, advanced against us. 8 Platoon (Martin Willan's) was severely pressed, but, after a prolonged and at times rather desperate fight, repulsed the enemy and destroyed two of his light tanks, but only after two counter-attacks had restored their original positions. Meanwhile Wally Finlayson and his two sections were forced to abandon their forward posts and came back to join us in the Redoubt. This cleared the way for the enemy to come forward into the houses and gardens immediately facing us, and a lot of bullets started whizzing past our ears or chipping the concrete blocks. Whenever a target appeared we engaged it with Bren-gun fire, but we were careful not to blaze off too much ammunition, as the resupply situation was uncertain. Section commanders kept a strict control on the use of weapons and, with the Redoubt providing good cover, I was able to move around continually.

It was at this stage that I began to lose all account of time and became aware only of the need for all of us to keep our heads: at all costs we had to dissuade the enemy from launching at us his tanks which eventually edged their way slowly forward. One poked its nose down the main road and put a shot from its big gun into the road block nearest to it. Jack had managed to get hold of some gunners with two 2-pounder anti-tank guns which now opened fire on this leading enemy tank. Whether they missed or their projectile just bounced off the target I do not know, but with two shots the tank smashed certainly one of the guns and possibly both. The tank then proceeded to destroy our two improvised road blocks with gunfire. I watched the nearest one jumping in agonized jerks and finally fall to pieces. Yet the tank came no closer, being content to take up a concealed position whence it could send a stream of tracer bullets down the road. By this time other tanks were appearing in front of us, manoeuvring among the houses and gardens and keeping us busy with their machine guns. We replied with some intense firing, as we were now getting good targets, and were expending a lot of ammunition (which worried me a bit, as I am a hoarder by nature!) while Gregg's tanks darted here and there, using their mobility to good effect. Our resistance must have impressed the enemy – the noise was certainly terrific – and he made no attempt to advance further.

We were hitting the tanks hard with our Boys rifles and the machine guns of our own tanks, but the penetrating power of the armour-piercing bullets was limited. I thought to myself that we were sunning ourselves in Fornham Park only three days ago: it seemed a world away! We were also able to deploy our two 3-inch mortars, having at last been issued with some ammunition for them, and their fire, under Dick's direction, was most effective. So far we had miraculously sustained no casualties in the Redoubt, though elsewhere the Company had been less fortunate.

Because the main pressure was on B Company at this juncture, the Colonel sent us up some reinforcements in the form of a search-light troop, Royal Artillery, employed as infantry under their own officer, Airey Neave. Jack positioned them just behind the Pont Jourdan. Neave was to achieve considerable fame later as a successful Colditz escaper, as 'Saturday' of M19, a leading Conservative politician and finally as an IRA victim. Writing after the war in his book *The Flames of Calais*, he described his meeting with Jack:

> Fatigue, thirst and the need to do the right thing made it difficult to think clearly as I reached the railway embankment. A figure, standing below me on the tracks, beckoned me to climb down. It was Major Poole . . . 'I'm afraid they may break through,' he said. I was very surprised at the anxiety in his voice. 'Get your people in the houses on either side of the bridge and fire from the windows. You must fight like bloody hell.'

Neave was soon in the thick of it with us. He continues:

> Tank shells and machine gun bullets came thick and fast . . . ricochets off the walls and flying glass . . . the wall had ragged gaps where mortar bombs had flung bricks into the street . . . heat from the burning buildings led to an intolerable thirst.

Then he was hit and removed in an improvised ambulance, but his men remained with us.

We certainly appeared to have persuaded the Germans that we were too strong for them to make any further advance in our sector; but the noise and excitement went on until about 8 p.m. when the battle seemed to subside. In fact the Germans merely switched the pressure northwards against our C Company without much success. Our Regimental Annals (Volume VI) were later to record:

> The Germans were not happy about the situation. The 10th

Panzer Division War Diary states, 'Enemy resistance from scarcely perceptible positions was however so strong that it was only possible to achieve slight local success,' and, in its evening sitrep to Corps, reported that one third of its equipment, vehicles and personnel and a good half of its tanks were casualties, and the troops were tired out.

I think it was with some justification that the thought uppermost in our minds at the time was 'Well done us.' Alas, in the latter stages of the battle I had lost another member of my platoon; Rifleman Arnold, killed instantly by a bullet. He had been a very nice young rifleman and I remember him vividly, even after all these years, playing a minor part in our Stalbridge amateur dramatics.

The light was now just beginning to take on that evening glow, and an ominous silence reigned over our sector. There was time metaphorically to mop our brows and be satisfied that we had endured a good many hours of shelling and 'strafing' and brought the enemy attack to a standstill some 300 yards from the Redoubt. Yet we could scarcely believe that the enemy would not try again at any moment, and spasmodic bursts of fire, mainly aimed down the main road, broke the silence and reminded us of his proximity. Then, quite suddenly with a roar, five or six of our Swordfish planes from the Navy flew over our heads and dropped several loads of bombs on some target to our front, probably tanks withdrawing to rest and refuel, and a great cloud of dust and smoke rose up before us. This was followed by the sound of heavy firing away to our left, and then silence again.

Most of our transport had been destroyed by the shelling, and none of our wireless sets was working properly, most of them having also been destroyed. We were thus out of touch with Battalion Headquarters and the Companies on our flanks. Jack therefore sent Henry Scott back to find out what was going on. Daylight began to fade, and no sound or movement could be heard or seen in front of us, except for an occasional line of tracer bullets fired down the road. It was quite eerie. Henry eventually returned with disquieting news: the Companies either side of us had, he reported, evacuated their positions and withdrawn towards the docks, and only our own B Company remained on the outer perimeter. This in fact was not quite true for, while D Company had been pulled back, as its position had become untenable, C Company's withdrawal was purely tactical and limited: such is the fog of war. Jack was sufficiently perturbed to send Henry straight off to check on our flank companies, while he himself set off too for Battalion Headquarters: his anxieties were not allayed when he met a QVR officer who told him that Brigade Headquarters was deserted and, he believed, an attempt to re-embark was being made.

Thus I was left in charge of B Company. It was almost dusk: time dragged on and nothing happened, so I started to tour the Company area and was told by Colour Sergeant Faulkner that Jack was just around the corner talking to a French officer. Together we set off and found a French motorized company halted in the street and were told that 'le commandant Anglais' had gone off with their commander 'to make investigations'. I have never seen such vehicles as those French ones: they must have been relics of the first war and all roaring with their throttles out for, as one of their drivers explained to me, if the engines stopped it was doubtful whether they would ever start again!

It all seemed very unsatisfactory. Jack and Henry had both disappeared, and for all I knew everyone was withdrawing to the docks except B Company of which I seemed to be in command: I strode back to the Redoubt where Wally informed me that the men were becoming restless. There was no information, no meal, not even a cup of tea: it was getting dark, and the Germans might and could rush us at any moment. We were just discussing how we could best adjust our positions for the night when Jack came walking back, though he had failed to make contact with anyone. He, Wally and I sat down, lit cigarettes and held a council-of-war, as a result of which Jack decided that the Company was now too exposed and would therefore withdraw into the town and re-establish contact with the other companies.

And so it was that we began to prepare the withdrawal from our sector of the outer perimeter which we had defended so successfully all day. I believe Jack should have left me and my platoon out there to cover the Company while it reorganized further back, but I only had five scout carriers left and he probably thought this inadequate.

It had been a long day, and the part played by B Company was to be summarized in *The Annals of The King's Royal Rifle Corps* as follows:

Determined attacks, supported by artillery and led by tanks, had resulted in fierce fighting in B Company's sector, which continued all the afternoon till about 2000 hours, when the enemy withdrew. Several enemy tanks were destroyed, and German losses were estimated at sixty. When anti-tank ammunition was exhausted, B Company's advanced posts were evacuated, but the main line was held most gallantly, with the guns of a French post giving valuable support.

The Annals concluded;

Casualties were difficult to estimate. C Company reported fifty-seven; B and D must have had nearly as many.

4

DEATH MOANS AND SINGS

'The thundering line of battle stands,
And in the air death moans and sings'
                              Into Battle by Julian Grenfell.

B Company's withdrawal would scarcely rank as a tactical master-piece, but at least it was uncomplicated: it was probably fortunate that the Germans seemed to have had enough for one day and chose not to interfere. All our wheeled transport, except possibly in Martin Willan's 8 Platoon, had been destroyed or else hopelessly damaged, but I still had five scout carriers and my wireless set intact. I was therefore given the role of rearguard which was appropriate for a scout platoon and one for which we had been trained.

Jack led the remains of company headquarters, 6 and 7 Platoons back into town on foot, with 8 Platoon conforming on our flank. I still had about twenty-five men and with them remained pre-cariously perched on the Redoubt, feeling isolated and exposed but determined we should give a good account of ourselves if the Germans tried to come on. Eventually the time came for us to retire, and, at first, all went well. An enemy plane circling overhead, however, looked ominous, and sure enough, a few moments later, there was a loud explosion behind me (presumably a bomb) and my rear carrier was severely damaged and had to be abandoned. We pulled up, sorted out that little bit of trouble and proceeded on our way, hoping that Jack and the rest were still somewhere in front. We had not got very far when we became muddled up with A and D Company vehicles emerging from a side street, and in the mêlée which followed we were more or less carried along for about 100 yards. Near a crossroads the whole mass ground mercifully to a halt. My driver managed to pull in beside the kerb, and I was able to collect my own people together.

Men and vehicles were everywhere, and I had no idea where Jack with the main body of B Company had got to. To complicate matters further, the Colonel now appeared and ordered me, in my secondary role as Battalion gas officer, which I confess I had forgotten about, to come with him and inspect two riflemen who were claiming to be suffering from mustard gas. They were standing on the pavement nearby, their faces covered with bleachpaste, and wearing goggles: although at this stage one was ready to believe almost anything, a close inspection proved their fears to be groundless; their burns, which were not very serious, being almost certainly caused by a shell bursting close to them.

Back with my platoon I found two of our A Company officers, Norman Philips and Alan Wigan. Alan, a supplementary reserve officer who had joined us soon after the outbreak of war, I only knew slightly, but everyone knew and loved Norman who had been commissioned from Sandhurst in 1936. They were both very cheerful people, and it was good to see them. They had had quite a battle away to our left, and their Company had suffered, they thought, about sixty casualties; the Company commander, Derek Trotter, and the second in command Charles Stanton had both been wounded, though not seriously. I also saw our Technical Adjutant, Charlie Madden, who was rushing off somewhere on a motor cycle. None of these could give me any news of Jack, but at last someone appeared who had seen him, and I was able to find him in one of the streets nearby. If he was tired, as we all were, he did not show it, and, as always, his presence was a tonic.

'There are a lot of rumours flying around,' he said, 'that we are about to re-embark. I want everyone to understand that this is quite out of the question, and I'd like to know where this idea has started. We have come here to defend Calais,' he declared, 'and that's precisely what we are going to do.' This was splendid stuff, and I do not believe that anyone in Jack's Company had any illusions from then on that we were going to do anything except fight it out. 'The Company,' Jack continued, 'will spend the night in empty houses and take up new positions at dawn.'

Although at this stage it all seemed to be rather a muddle, Jack assured us platoon commanders that all was under control: most of us were too weary to care very much anyway, and I found it a great struggle to prevent my desire to sleep from swamping all other considerations. Platoons were assembled and checked and, in my own, the ranks seemed pretty thin. Among those missing was my faithful batman Smith, though he turned up later, and his loss seemed to me at that moment irreparable. We found a suitable house, broke into it, for it was locked, and turned the wretched occupant, a middle-aged, bespectacled man, out into the night. I tried to apologize to him in my execrable French and explain that these were our orders, but he must have hated us. My carriers were used as road blocks and guards posted to cover them. Finally we all turned in, sprawling about the house with our weapons loaded beside us.

Not everyone was resting, however, as would soon become apparent. The Brigadier had in fact decided, during the afternoon, when our battle was at its height, that the outer perimeter would have to be abandoned. Euan Miller, our Colonel, had been given several platoons of the Queen Victoria's Rifles and one from the Rifle Brigade to form a strong point behind the inner canal line, while patrols of the 3rd Tanks were sent out to dispute any enemy advance. We were now within the strongpoint with the prospect of some rest and sleep. At 4 a.m., however, I was woken and told to report at once to the Colonel. I arrived at Battalion Headquarters, just as Mike Sinclair (A Company's scout platoon commander) was leaving, to find the Colonel standing on the pavement. He told me that I was to take one of my sections and patrol out to Bastion 9 and, if possible, to reoccupy it, call up the rest of my platoon and hold an outpost position astride the Coquelles road. Mike Sinclair, he said, was about to leave and would be similarly deployed on my left.

It was not long before we were on the move, but as we approached the Pont Jacquard I was met by Mike with two carriers coming back with the warning, 'Be careful when you've crossed the canal as there are Germans quite near, and I have had my own carrier shot from under me'.

It was lucky for me that he had been sent out first, for as he moved slowly down one of the streets just beyond the bridge he had seen two Germans hastily disappear round a corner: the next moment, a ball of fire, as he described it to me later, had crashed into the front of his carrier, passing between him and the driver, tearing apart the frontal armour and smashing into the engine at their back. The carriers behind him moved immediately to cover while he ordered his own crew to bale out. The Germans then opened up on them with machine-gun fire. Mike's dispatch rider, with great presence of mind, instead of trying to turn round and thus present an easy target, drove flat out straight towards the enemy, swung rapidly into a side street and made his way back to the bridge by a circular route. Meanwhile Mike's driver and wireless operator ran back up the street under heavy fire, no doubt achieving an astonishing burst of speed, and reached the corner safely. Mike himself was less agile: as he leapt out of his carrier, he got hung up on the side of the vehicle by his revolver lanyard and for several moments dangled helplessly before he could wrench himself free, an instance of comedy which might easily have ended in tragedy. Fortunately for Mike and his men the enemy were firing high (they had probably forgotten to lower their sights) for as he ran back Mike could hear the shattering of windows above his head.

During this drama I, in my leading carrier, was approaching the bridge. I pulled up momentarily to receive Mike's warning and then moved on again. On reaching the bridge I was surprised to see Puffin Owen (the Battalion second in command) standing on it as if enjoying the morning air.

'Come here,' he said, 'where are you off to!'

I told him. He thought for a moment, 'I don't think there is any point in your going on. We now know that the enemy is in the town and quite close. Funnily enough I drove all round at first light and never saw any, but they've probably just turned up. Go back to the Colonel and tell him what I've said.'

My lucky star was evidently still in operation, for if Puffin had not been there at the moment I reached the bridge my three carriers would have driven on into a lot of trouble. As we went back I turned and saw old Puffin still standing on the bridge as if he had no care in all the world: the camel stick, which was such a familiar reminder of our days together in Aldershot, Tidworth, Stalbridge and Bocking, stood out clearly from beneath his arm. I would never see him again.

The Colonel listened to my report and sent me back to B Company, which spent the next two hours breaking into houses, thoroughly searching all buildings and occupying defensive positions, shown diagrammatically on page 35. We were now on the left flank of the battalion, with D Company on our right and the Rifle Brigade on our left. The latter actually held positions beyond the canal to our front, but were forced back that afternoon, so that we were thereafter in the front line.

My platoon was given the task of preventing the enemy crossing the canal and the bridge leading to La Place Norvège and protecting the approaches to our Company Headquarters. My carriers were removed and used as road blocks. During this time there were continual bursts of rifle and machine-gun fire, which kept us on our toes and jangled our nerves: though the presence of 'Fifth Columnists' and snipers was rumoured and suspected, it was impossible to tell whence the shots were coming and for whom they were intended. We continued to remove all civilians from the area and, amazingly, few of them complained. Goodness knows where they went, but I suppose someone had been made responsible for them: one attractive young mademoiselle seemed to think it all rather funny: she was very pretty, and I have often wondered what became of her.

We made our positions in the houses and cellars as strong as possible, but there was not a great deal we could do. We had no engineers to help us, no explosives, no mines, no sandbags, no wire and no artillery support: in fact our situation was probably quite hopeless, but certainly at platoon level we were not too worried; our morale was good and optimism prevailed. Rumours, of course, were plentiful: the main BEF battle was going well, we heard, and the front had been restored, while the enemy in front of us were completely cut off and trying desperately to regain their own lines! Someone also had a story that the British 42nd Division, 'commanded by an expert gunner and reinforced by additional artillery units' (amazing how such stories usually include picturesque and often absurd details) was marching to our aid and would arrive at any moment: indeed three of 3rd Tanks' cruisers trundling past were greeted with cheers in the mistaken belief that they were the 42nd Division's cavalry regiment sent on ahead of the main body.

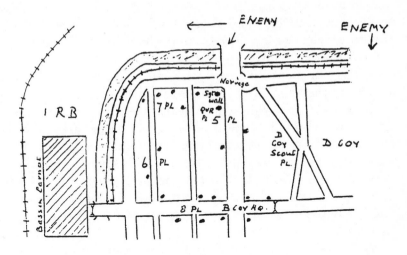

B company's positions

Meanwhile we were all frantically busy, barricading ourselves into houses, removing all glass from windows, siting weapons, posting sentries and generally preparing for action. Rations, tea and cigarettes were brought up and distributed, which gave me an excuse to walk around. I discovered that Battalion Headquarters were not far behind us and was astounded to find that Sergeant Dalton, still in charge of the officers' mess, had put up a long table under some trees, covered it with a beautiful white tablecloth and was busily serving huge helpings of omelette: that it was so unexpected and seemed so out of place did not prevent me from accepting his invitation to partake of the feast, and I am glad I did; five years would pass before I'd have so good a breakfast again. But I had to eat fast for the enemy bombardment was just starting, and the first shells of the morning were beginning to fall: I returned therefore to my little headquarters which I had set up with Sergeant Wall as a strongpoint in a house in La Place Norvège overlooking the canal bridge.

The shelling, however, was only spasmodic in our area at this time, certainly not heavy though unpleasant if one was caught in the open. I was walking along a street with Henry, delivering rations, when some shells or mortar bombs began to fall near and around us. Two lorries stood, damaged and abandoned just ahead of us, and we ran like hares and crouched down in the gutter beside them: showers of bricks and debris flew in all directions, and the noise seemed to tear us apart. It was over in a few seconds, and we had hardly emerged, Henry remarking, 'Lord, what a frightful din, most upsetting,' when we saw ahead of us the body of a civilian lying face-down in the road, and making little kicks like a wounded rabbit. We rushed to him and, with the help of some riflemen, carried him into a house and laid him on a bed: he had a ghastly gaping wound across his back and was obviously in considerable pain. To our astonish-ment he drawled out, 'thank you, boys,' and Henry asked if he was an American. 'Yeah,' he answered, 'and a goner too,' then a fresh wave of pain swept over him . . . 'For Gaad's sake give me a bullet, boys, and let me go quick.' I wish we had, for although he was given morphia and removed to medical attention, I doubt he could have lived. I wonder, even today, who our poor American might have been.

At midday we had an amusing and unexpected diversion: German planes, probably Fieseler Storchs (the equivalent of our Lysanders) suddenly flew low over our positions dropping leaflets. They were heavily engaged by our Bren guns, and I heard later that one had been brought down. The leaflet read as follows:

La ville de Calais est sommée de se rendre immédiatement. La garnison de la ville quittera la ville sans armes, les mains levées, dans le delai d'une heure, sur la route de Coquelles, dans la direction de Coquelles. A toute résistance continuée sera repondu par de nouveaux lancements de bombes et par un bombardement avec le plus lourde artillerie. Le general cdt le corps d'armee.

This was a real good laugh and did wonders for our morale, partly because the idea that we would all throw down our weapons and start streaming along the Coquelles road seemed so hilariously ridiculous, and partly because the leaflets promised us a whole hour without being shot at, so we used the time greatly to our advantage; improving our positions, issuing and distributing ammunition, resting, eating (though rations were already getting short) and doing what we could to clean ourselves up.

At the same time the Germans (we heard later) sent the mayor of Calais with an interpreter to persuade our Brigadier to surrender; but Claude Nicholson told them that if they wanted Calais they would have to fight for it, and the two Frenchmen were locked up in the post office where they remained until the battle ended.

'André Gerschell, the mayor, was respected and courageous,' wrote Airey Neave later. 'His dilemma in seeking to halt the battle was that of many a civic functionary in war. He knew that, if the British held on, the old part of Calais would be destroyed, but he had no reason to sympathize with the Germans. He was Jewish and had most bravely remained at his post in the Hotel de Ville when others had fled. Some months afterwards he was arrested by the Gestapo and died in a concentration camp.'

The Germans tried again, this time sending a German officer, accompanied by a French officer and a Belgium soldier, but their request was politely though firmly refused by the Brigadier.

At 1 p.m. we were ready for the bombardment which started punctually: it was the severest 'strafing' we had yet endured, but in our area it might have been worse. We watched the shells bursting all round, the bridge in front of our position being a popular target. When the assault came in it fell on C and D Companies to our right and on the Rifle Brigade to our left, and I heard later that some savage fighting developed, including the use of hand grenades and bayonets. It was probably at this stage that the Rifle Brigade company beyond our bridge was withdrawn, leaving us, and particularly my platoon, very much in the front line. After a time the shelling in our area subsided but remained enough to make movement in the open fairly risky. Martin Willan was conspicuously gallant: he still had a truck and drove about, continually under fire, evacuating wounded, bringing up ammunition and generally making himself useful.

As the afternoon wore on the shelling round us became more violent again, and there was an added menace: accurate mortar fire, directed from the tall tower of the Hotel de Ville, which overlooked most of the old town, increased the misery, while the enemy were even able to sweep some of the streets with machine-gun fire. I pointed this out to Henry, who was about to cross the street near one of my positions.

'You'd better move quick,' I said.

'Oh Lord,' he cried, 'they'll shoot me up the bottom, what a dreadful thing,' and they nearly did, for bullets kicked up the dust only a few inches from his tail as he slid into a cellar opening. I was on my way at the time to see Jack who gave me the latest orders from the Colonel, 'Present positions will be defended at all costs to the last round and the last man'.

One had received that order so often on training, particularly in the OTC, and it had always sounded amusing and pompous: now it seemed appropriate to the general atmosphere of rubble-strewn streets and burning buildings. The whole area had become badly knocked about, there was a lot of smoke, and sparks were flying in all directions. An ammunition truck, which had just arrived at Company Headquarters, caught fire and sent off bursts like a battalion of machine guns. The situation in other sectors was unknown to us but in fact was much worse than in ours, and further false rumours were flying around: Calais would be relieved tomorrow; Canadian troops had landed; the Germans had broken through. Significantly nothing more was heard about possible re-embarkation, and most of us were entirely resigned to a fight to the bitter end. Now we heard that Battalion Headquarters was surrounded and must be rescued immediately. Jack sent me, with part of my platoon, and with Richard Warre in his scout carrier to provide mobile support, to clear things up. This, I thought, would be my big moment: I gave out the orders, we fixed bayonets (called 'swords' in the 60th and Rifle Brigade) and I led the men at the double up the road, dodging the sparks from the buildings and stumbling over scattered pieces of debris. My wonderful batman, Smith, thought that this should be his big moment too, and would keep getting in the way, barging in front of me, determined to shield me from harm and generally spoiling the effect! Alas, we were heading not for glory but for comic anti-climax, as round the corner, accompanied by Alick Williams (the Adjutant) and Martin Gilliat (the Signals Officer) came the Colonel. They stopped and watched with amazement our war-like advance which, under their gaze, ground to a halt.

'What on earth are you doing?' asked the Colonel.

'We've come to rescue you.' I answered lamely.

'That's good,' he replied, 'we are just sending up a party to rein-force you!' Then it all ended in smiles.

It was soon dark. The town was blazing furiously, and there was fairly continual sniping, either from 'fifth columnists' (who had become the fashionable military bogeys of the 1940 campaign) or, more probably in my opinion, brave German soldiers who had infiltrated our lines. Whoever they were they kept us dodging about when we tried to move around, anyway until it was quite dark. At around 10 p.m. I reported to Jack in the cellar at the rear of his Headquarters for any further instructions he might have and was told to visit Richard Warre's post, which linked us to D Company: I was to find out why they were keeping up such heavy fire. I discovered that Richard had collapsed into a deep sleep, utterly worn out by his tremendous efforts of the last two days: his performance had been superb, both during the heavy fighting of Friday when D Company took the brunt of the earlier German assault and throughout this Saturday when he had done great work with his carrier, often under fire, covering our people who had to move about. Now fatigue had overtaken him, though under the constant and devoted care of his splendid Corporal Birt: neither would survive the battle. Now his platoon were blazing away over the canal, claiming they could see enemy tanks so I sent Birt to stop them. A few moments later a shot rang out from down the street behind me. Our Company Sergeant Major Rawlinson, himself by now dead tired, had failed to answer a sentry's challenge outside Company Headquarters and had been shot through both cheeks, which Jack later described, 'at Calais the tempo was entirely different (from the First War's trenches) and few of us knew from one moment to the next whether houses were occupied by friend or enemy. In the wild confusion of close quarter battle my CSM was accidentally shot in the face by a rifleman who thereupon went completely berserk and had to be restrained by a clout on the head with a riflebutt.'

Rawlinson was carried off but survived to be awarded the Military Medal for his splendid services up to that moment. Later on Jack, and at the end I too, much needed such a stout hearted man beside us.

Poor Jack was having an awful evening, for no sooner had the CSM been taken away than two French women insisted on climbing over the barricade formed by my carriers and were shot in the legs: as they were removed to medical attention their screams and yells echoed hideously through the night.

Jack took me round on a tour of inspection while Henry snatched a little sleep. First we visited Dick and then Wally on the left flank, Jack sending the former with Sergeant King to bring in a 2-pounder gun which had been abandoned near the canal. At one moment we took cover behind some smashed vehicles when what sounded like a whistling bomb came screaming over our heads and eventually exploded quite near us with a tremendous crash. Then we completed our tour, taking in my platoon and Richard Warre's and also the

QVR platoon which had come up to reinforce us. The high hopes with which we had all arrived in Calais had been superseded by a grim determination to resist and stick it out.

During this tour Jack told me there had been savage fighting for the canal bridges on our right, where A and D Companies had just managed to hold firm: on one of the bridges the enemy had got across but been driven back. He also gave me news I found quite devastating, that Puffin had been killed.

At last, around 2 or 3 a.m., I got back to Sergeant Wall's post. Wall had been splendid all day and had everything under control: he had distributed such ammunition that was still available, but food and water were running out. For the time being there was nothing more for me to do. I could not know, as I dropped gratefully off to sleep, how enormous the catastrophe and how painful the calamities the coming day would bring upon us all.

5

CRACK OF DOOM

Calais could justifiably be called a soldier's battle. For most of us it was the house or the crossroads or the street which mattered: what was happening beyond our immediate vicinity was of little concern. All that Saturday we in B Company had been hammered by shot and shell but not actually attacked: this was our good fortune, for the companies on our right had had a rough time holding the canal bridges, while the Rifle Brigade on our left had been under great pressure all day and their CO, Chan Hoskyns, mortally wounded.

My last orders to Sergeant Wall before I slept was to make sure I was woken well before dawn: I was angry and momentarily alarmed, therefore, to find broad daylight when I eventually opened my eyes. Wall had tried to wake me but apparently I rolled over and muttered, 'For God's sake go away,' and he had therefore let me sleep on!

The old town of Calais, in strange contrast to the previous day, was absolutely quiet as we breakfasted, very sparingly, off our remaining supplies of biscuits and bully beef. No early morning tea that day! Anyway, water was now unobtainable. The peace and quiet did not last long: suddenly, with a stupendous roar, the shelling opened up, and the whole place seemed to shake as with the wrath of giants. As the sun rose the bombardment became more intense, and the Company began to suffer casualties: Martin Willan was killed, and a rifleman who ran to aid him was killed also.

One of our worst handicaps was the lack of any wireless communications, for all our sets were now destroyed or damaged beyond repair. Crouching in our makeshift cover we felt very out of touch, so that officers and senior NCOs had to keep moving round despite movement having now become a thoroughly dangerous undertaking.

After a time I felt the need to find out what was happening, so with Smith I made my way back towards Company Headquarters and met Dick Scott near the crossroads. His face was grim as he shouted to me across the street and above the din, 'Henry has been hit and is dying. See if you can give Jack a hand while I try to bring up a truck,' and off he went, regardless of the danger all around.

'Oh no!' I thought. 'Dear God, not Henry.' But it was true enough. As I slid down the opening into the headquarters cellar Jack was bending over a prostrate figure. We brought him up from that cellar on a large blanket and laid him down in the front passage, ready for Dick's truck.

'Leave my tin hat on,' he said, as his batman tried to remove it and make him more comfortable. He never spoke again. Dick then arrived with a truck – goodness knows how he'd found one – and backed it against the door but the enemy were watching and, as I stood in the doorway, I saw the canopy ripped by bullets right in front of me. Jack ordered Dick to come into the house, which at that moment seemed to become a priority target for enemy mortars, with bombs landing on the roof and all around. The Germans were astonishingly quick and accurate with their mortars. At first we all lay down on the floor to avoid flying splinters of wood and brick: then seeing that Henry was now dead and at peace amid the chaos all around him, Jack ordered us to dash for the next house and led us out across the garden.

He was just clambering over the wall into the next garden when disaster nearly struck: a mortar bomb landed right among us: we were very lucky not to have all been killed. Jack disappeared over the wall with great rapidity while the rest of us dived for cover: I was not quick enough, however, to avoid losing a tiny bit of my right shoulder blade and getting a neat tear in my battledress blouse. We picked ourselves up, found to our astonishment that we were still alive and followed Jack like greased lightning to arrive panting in the cellar of the 'front' house. I was scarcely aware at the time of any injury and it was not until later in the day that some-one noticed the blood.

I have often wondered to what extent we felt fear during the battle and I am sure we all had quite a lot of bad moments. Fortunately for officers and senior NCOs they are either busy or resting and anyway have the job of setting a good example, and this helps greatly. The Germans kept most of us very busy in Calais anyway, and this helped too.

42

Now it was time for Dick and me to rejoin our platoons. The street leading to the bridge being under small-arms fire, either from across the canal or from the tower of the Hotel de Ville, I was glad to reach Sergeant Wall unscathed. I think my batman, Smith, got back there too. We seemed under control around the Place de Norvège, but away on both flanks there was the sound of heavy firing and the constant crackle of small arms. The continual bombardment was wreaking the inevitable havoc and, referring to this in his official report for the *Regimental Chronicle*, our Adjutant, Alick Williams was later to write, 'Our defensive positions in the inner town were reduced to a shambles and set in flames'.

Even so the riflemen remained cheerful enough, though each post was feeling increasingly isolated, despite such visits from platoon commanders as were still possible.

As long as the inner canal bridges remained standing our battalion position was vulnerable to the superior enemy strength, and a serious attempt to blow them up was now, at this late stage in the battle, to be made. Some naval engineers were landed, together with a company of Royal Marines under Captain Darby Courtice. During one of my rounds I met Wally Finlayson bringing some engineers along to look at our bridge, and the three of us were caught by shells suddenly bursting all around my headquarters: we lay flat down in the yard behind it and were pinned down there for a short time, one shell or mortar bomb hitting the roof of the house next door and showering us with debris. One of our destroyers in the Channel attempted to fire back, but its spotter plane was blinded by the smoke from all the burning buildings, and air above us continued for some minutes to seem alive with the whirr of shells. It was not nice at all.

The Navy did, I believe, succeed in partly, though ineffectively, damaging some of the bridges, or maybe only one, but ours remained intact. In any case no enemy had yet approached it, and around 9 or 10 a.m., I felt it was time to do a round of visits and find out from Jack what was going on. The enemy still had the crossroads by company headquarters in view and I thought I was shot at as I slid into the cellar. A determined effort had in fact been made to search the area for snipers but none was found. No sooner had I arrived than the dive-bombing began. The Stukas appeared in large numbers, and for two hours circled around above the Citadel and C Company's area to our right and the Rifle Brigade positions by the Gare Maritime and in the sand dunes to our left. Although a few bombs fell near us, our company sector was mainly spared, and we could watch from the cellar as the Stukas, one after the other, came hurtling down with sirens screaming. Airey Neave (*The Flames of Calais*) wrote, 'No-one who experienced the attack on the morning of the 26th is ever likely to forget it. A hundred aircraft attacked the Citadel and the old town in waves. They dived in threes, with a prolonged scream, dropping one high-explosive and three or four incendiary bombs.'

Each of this series of attacks lasted twenty-five minutes. The first effects on the defence were paralyzing but, as others had experienced with Stukas, the damage was moral rather than physical, but not entirely so, for Neave continued, 'The air attack hit the 60th in Bastion II and round the Citadel especially hard. The French at Bastion II lost three officers and many men killed on a single raid. The Stukas came and went, leaving Calais Nord a furnace, and then German infantry attacked again.'

While all this was going on Jack and I sat together in his cellar discussing the situation. Jack was absolutely calm, totally unruffled and a real tonic for all with whom he was in contact. We could see the Stukas above the docks, and I thought what wonderful targets they would have been if an occasional Spitfire or Hurricane could have appeared, though no doubt the Stukas had Messerschmitt protection. Jack was very relaxed and light-hearted, and I was much amused when he suddenly turned serious and said, 'It's too bad, you know: this is the second bloody war I've fought in, and I haven't advanced yet,' a remark which I have remembered and cherished with great pleasure. It was at this moment that he told me a War Office signal had just been received by Brigade Headquarters. Jack commented on this signal when he wrote in his book, 'On the third day's fighting a signal from London reached my company, the eyes of the Empire are on you.' I remembered the similarly worded telegram sent by the War Office years before, when I was on the long winter campaign in North Russia. One did not have to be unduly cynical to realize that the end must be near indeed.

As the Stuka attack died away our contemplation was quickly disrupted, for down the street came running and clattering some fifteen men, headed by Richard Warre (the D Company Scout Platoon Commander) and his Corporal Birt. They flooded into the house and cellar, Richard reporting that our forward positions had been shelled out and the enemy had forced the line of the canal.

With the influx of this party our company headquarters was crowded out and in total confusion, and Jack decided he must 'clear the air'. He therefore told me to take everyone not required at head-quarters back to the next line of defence and, looking out of the cellar with me, indicated the way I was to go. Gathering my party together, with Corporal Birt behind me, then about ten others with Richard Warre bringing up the rear, I stepped out into the street: as I did so something exploded right in front of me and, partly by an instinctive desire for cover, Birt and I somersaulted back into the house carrying several people with us and landing in a heap on the floor! Our second attempt to leave was more successful, though I never saw Birt again, and later he was killed. Throughout the battle he had been a splendid example to all around him. Desolation now reigned in the streets, debris scattered everywhere, houses mostly in ruins, the air thick with smoke and dust, machine guns chattering away and shells exploding. I was able to collect a small party together but found I had little idea what I was really supposed to be doing. We made our way back until we reached the swing bridge leading to the Gare Maritime: it was guarded by a section of the Rifle Brigade. In the station, on one of the platforms, I met up with Major Alex Allan now in command of the Rifle Brigade, who told me that the 60th had started to withdraw and that I should remain with him until my company arrived.

It was much quieter here. The Stukas had gone, only a few shells were coming over and everything seemed under control. I had lost Richard Warre, and the little party I had brought with me was absorbed into the local defensive positions. The enemy were said to be advancing in the sand dunes to our left, while on the extreme right, beyond the Citadel, where C Company was struggling to hold its line, a tremendous bombardment was in progress, black smoke and dust towering into the sky. There was no sign of any 60th with-drawal going on, so I picked up a rifle and some ammunition and, feeling very alone and rather vulnerable, I walked forward again into the town, into the smoke and dust and flames, not at all sure what I was going to find.

I found a fighting patrol. Fortunately it was one of ours, cautiously moving along a street and I asked its rear scout who was in charge. I received the answer, 'Mr Scott, Sir.' I hurried up to Dick and he gripped my hand.

'Thank God you're alive,' he said. I was equally glad to find him still in one piece, for we were great friends.

Meanwhile Jack had been sorting the Company out and re-adjusting some of the positions, and I found him in a house close to the bridge. No enemy had crossed the canal, at least in our company sector, and we seemed to be holding our own; but with the withdrawal of D Company's Scout Platoon our link with D Company on our right had gone. For the first time I thought Jack looked strained and anxious: Airey Neave had noticed a similar look about him on the Friday, but to me up to this moment he had seemed cheerful and confident. Now he told me that our casualties were mounting and that Richard Warre had been shot and killed outside our company headquarters; also that he had deployed a QVR platoon, under Second Lieutenant Banbury, behind Sergeant Wall's post which was now under direct fire from the enemy beyond the canal. I suspect that I must have looked tired, for Jack insisted I sat down, eat a biscuit and drink some wine he had found, before letting me get back to my platoon.

'Keep in touch, old boy,' he said to me, 'Make sure I know what's happening.'

The men of my platoon were still incredibly cheerful, especially those who could see the enemy. Now and then some good targets presented themselves. The best appeared while I was doing a turn behind Wall's Bren gun; a party of Germans and some transport moved slowly towards us and I put a whole magazine of twenty-eight shots among them. All movement stopped. I suddenly felt wild with exhilaration.

Time was passing and, after walking or rather dodging round my little area and calling on the QVR platoon, I made my way back to Company Headquarters. I wasted no time and moved rapidly: even so, as I slid into the cellar of the 'front house.' I fancied I'd been shot at, and Jack told me later he had himself been under fire at that spot. There were several people in the cellar under a Corporal Walker or Corporal Spanner (I think) but Jack, they told me, had crossed the garden and set up his headquarters once more in the 'rear house' cellar. Mortar bombs were bursting around us again. Then I saw Dick who was crossing the street towards us and smiling cheerfully. He shouted that he had news for Jack.

'Run quickly,' I shouted back, 'You're under fire.' He ran towards the cellar opening, and I grabbed him to pull him in. The bullet went right through his head as I held him. He did not die at once, but he never regained consciousness, lying still and peaceful till he had gone. For a moment I was overcome with anguish, but the battle had to go on. I set off across the back garden to find Jack, while the bombardment rose to a new height of frenzy, and black smoke raised its columns in the summer air.

It was just as well that we were ignorant of events beyond our sector, for they were moving rapidly towards the final crisis. It was now afternoon, and in fact some of the battalion positions had been driven in: a general withdrawal back from the canal had begun on our right, while on our left the Rifle Brigade were also beginning to give ground, with the enemy now directly threatening the docks and Gare Maritime. B Company was thus in danger from both flanks, and the end was not far off. Of this Jack and I were blissfully unaware, perhaps because Dick had been unable to deliver his message: we had restored and strengthened our positions, were still holding the canal and seemed, we thought, to be doing quite well. Wally Finlayson was now commanding 6 and 7 Platoons on the left; Colour Sergeant Faulkner controlled the centre around Company headquarters with Sergeant Balchin commanding 8 Platoon; and Sergeant Wall, with Banbury and his QVRs still dominating La Place Norvège and the canal bridge. This situation was not however to last much longer.

I found Jack in his cellar and told him of Dick. We talked for a moment, and then Banbury appeared bringing bad news. The docks had been captured and German infantry and tanks had been seen and heard round our right flank. B Company, he reported, was now encircled. Banbury then quite properly dashed back to his platoon and Jack decided he must go himself to Battalion Headquarters and report the situation to the Colonel. I was to stay and command the company until he returned. When I argued that Jack should not go himself but rather send me (not that I was all that keen to go, as the noise outside was quite deafening) he simply said, 'I know, old boy, but it's got to be done and I'm the chap to do it'.

Meanwhile (as I heard later) Wally received a message that Jack had been killed, and that he was to report at once to Battalion Headquarters. He got into a truck, therefore, and started off, leaving his Sergeant Bristow in command of his two platoons. His driver claimed to know the way, but they got lost and came upon a troop from Headquarters Company which, under Captain Duncanson, was desperately trying to withstand the enemy's final effort. I was now, therefore, the only officer left in B Company.

When Jack found the Colonel, he was told that the Rifle Brigade had been overwhelmed, the Citadel with the Brigadier and his Advance Headquarters captured and Battalion Headquarters under direct threat. The Colonel had therefore decided that further resistance was pointless and was sending out a message to all companies, 'Every man for himself: break up into small parties, hide up and try to get away through enemy lines.' Jack was determined that B Company should receive this order at all costs and not, as previously ordered, fight to the last round and last man. He therefore set off at once but was captured on the way.

Back at Company Headquarters we knew nothing of all this drama, so that the sudden appearance of enemy infantry on our right flank and rear, though confirming Banbury's recent news, came as an unpleasant surprise, to say the least. The Headquarters was quite indefensible against an attack from this direction, and I could only conclude that 8 Platoon's positions on that side of us had been overwhelmed or driven back. I therefore rushed our little party across to the cellar of the next house which was on the street leading to our canal bridge and had been used as an alternative Company Headquarters, intending to withdraw them up the street to join my 5 Platoon in La Place Norvège. One of the corporals (Corporal Walker, I think, who was an excellent man) suggested we should stay put as we were already surrounded and the street outside under enemy control. Although it was good advice, I still thought we would do better joining up with 5 Platoon if we could. I merely shouted, 'Come on,' and climbed out into the street. It was the exact spot where Dick Scott had been killed.

As I emerged into the open it was soon apparent how right the corporal had been, as there were enemy at both ends of the street. Those of my party who started to follow me either scattered or ducked back into the cellar. They were absolutely right to do so, but it was too late for me to turn back. I ran flat out for Sergeant Wall's position, coming under fire at point-blank range from an enemy machine-gun post at the nearest corner of the square. I cannot imagine how they missed; they must have been startled by my unexpected appearance. Anyhow I managed to reach cover behind the house which had been badly knocked about and appeared to be deserted.

With Germans just across the street on the other side of the house and in the square, I was pretty well pinned down. Cut off from my Headquarter's party, and having failed to contact 5 Platoon and Banbury's QVRs, I managed eventually to extricate myself, though

48

with some difficulty, being fired at as I climbed over a garden fence. I now hoped to make contact with 7 Platoon along the canal on the left, and perhaps 6 Platoon too, and see if they could help and prevent any further enemy advance into B Company's position. I could not, amid all the excitement, remember their exact positions and, while standing near the canal and looking about, I came under fire from across the canal and was hit. I must have been an easy target.

One bullet went through my right arm and another hit me in the side. People do not often describe what it feels like to be shot, so I can record that it felt as if I had been clouted in the ribs with a sledge-hammer. Later I could remember dropping my rifle, but it took me a second or two to realize what had actually happened. I staggered a few steps towards a burnt-out truck, hoping to find cover behind it, but I was hit again, this time in the head. I was conscious of starting to fall and then must have passed out.

When I regained my senses, which may have been a few minutes or an hour later, I found the slightest movement agonizing, the pain coming mainly from across my back. My tin hat was still under my head and half full of blood. I had no idea one could bleed so profusely, and there was quite a lot of blood all round me. 'I've had it,' was my first thought, and it all seemed quite natural that this should be so. I had that same day seen Henry dying, Dick killed and others too. At least I was not in any great pain, and for some time I just lay there, in the gutter as it were, waiting peacefully for the end to come. My only regrets were that we had lost the battle and that my mother would grieve for me. After a bit I remembered about my field dressing and tried rather inefficiently to tie it round my head, but the movement was too painful. I continued to wait. Presumably I was suffering from shock, loss of blood and the bang on the head.

The battle had died down, was indeed more or less over, but there were occasional bursts of firing and I thought I heard someone yelling, '60th-60th', but it could have been my imagination. Not knowing that the 'last man' order had been rescinded, I wondered if I were the only officer still alive. Some shells suddenly landed quite near, fired maybe by our destroyers in the Channel. I could see the Germans moving about beyond the canal, and then an enemy section came straight towards me, but they took no notice of me and passed by. They returned a few minutes later with a British soldier, his hands above his head. Poor devil, I thought, how ignominious, and closed my eyes.

Gradually it became dark and began to rain, the first rain since our move from Fornham to Southampton. When was that? Tuesday or Wednesday? So much had happened in between.

Time passed, and the realization slowing came to me that I was not, after all, going to die. The thought brought neither pleasure nor relief. Most of my friends had probably been killed and I did not want to be a prisoner. I had been more than ready to go. On reflection I imagine that my present condition had blunted my natural instinct for survival; my will to live had deserted me. But life apparently had to go on, and I began to take a more positive view of my predicament. Why lie there, getting soaked to the skin? Could I move? Where should I move to? Was there any cover? I began to look around and take stock.

There was a small hut or shelter a few yards away. Very gradually and extremely painfully I began to move, sliding inch by inch along the ground towards the hut which began to look very inviting. Getting over the ledge into it was horrible but I made it. Almost at once I fell asleep, or perhaps again passed out.

Later, I was suddenly awake. It was dark. Someone with crunchy boots was approaching. A German soldier came in with a torch, scavenging no doubt. The beam of his torch waved around, then, as it fell on me, he suddenly jumped back, whipped out his bayonet from its scabbard and held it menacingly above me, his torch searching my face. 'Perhaps, after all, this is it', I thought. He bent down.

'*Verwundet?*' (You are wounded?)

'*Ja,*' I replied, '*Verwundet.*' At once this splendid fellow put away his bayonet, looked very carefully at my wounds, replaced my field dressing with his own which he tied round my head.

'*Hilfe kommt,*' (help will come) he said and departed.

I have often wondered who he was and whether he survived the war. I shall never forget his kindness and humanity, and he kept his promise as eventually they came and, just as morning had broken, found me. The unbelievable had happened, and I realized with a sudden feeling of shock and dismay that I was now a prisoner of war.

6

A PLACE WHERE NONE CAN THRIVE

The school library at Copthorne, where my greatest friend was Jack Anderson who was to win the Victoria Cross and a DSO, was full of books about the recently finished First World War. Among them had been several by ex-prisoners of war, like A.J. Evans' *The Escaping Club* and *The Road to Endor* by E.H. Jones. I can remember others too. Furthermore my housemaster at Winchester, 'The Jacker,' had been a prisoner, as had Jack Poole, and both had talked, though not very much, about their experiences. Back in Dorset I had attended a lecture on how to cope if captured. Yet despite all this, never in my wildest dreams had I ever contemplated, even for a moment, such a fate befalling me: now, incredibly it had.

The two young Germans who had come to collect me were not at all sure what to do, and the language problem did not help. Something obviously had to happen, and I was able to indicate that, if lifted very slowly and carefully onto my feet, I might be able to walk. And so it was that, with one soldier helping me and the other walking behind me we set off, making very slow – and for me very painful – progress into a large square. We came to a ruined house, and my captors indicated that I was to climb through the window, the doorway being blocked. I could not possibly climb through any window, so I was carefully lifted over the ledge by the German soldiers. The house was in fact a German medical aid post, and I was received by a pleasant looking doctor who spoke English. Sitting on a bench, filthy with dirt and sweat, were two of my own platoon riflemen. Both had flesh wounds, and we compared injuries, saying how glad we were to find each other alive. I do not remember asking them for any details of my platoon's fate which shows, I think, that I must have been suffering from the effects of my head-wound and general bewilderment at our predicament. The doctor examined our wounds and applied fresh bandages, saying we would be taken to hospital. Things seemed to be looking up a bit.

We made our painful exit through the window and assembled in the road outside. Several other Riflemen joined us, some of whom I knew, others being from the Rifle Brigade or QVRs, and guarded by two German soldiers we were led slowly off to a big church. We spoke but little, merely asking each other how we were and inquiring for news of others. I was immensely relieved to hear that Jack Poole had not been killed as he had been seen marching away in a column of prisoners. The attitude of the Riflemen was one of feeling that they had done their best against heavy odds and if they were prisoners then 'C'est la guerre' or, as we were to hear so often later on, 'Krieg ist Krieg'.

Finally, having covered 200 yards at snail's pace and, as far as I was concerned, feeling very groggy, we reached a large church, which had been damaged during the battle, and were marched in. Here we got our first real introduction to the nastier side of war. For it was full of wounded, mostly French. I remember wondering where all the French soldiers had come from. The church was divided into three sectors, one for those only very lightly wounded, another for average cases and the third for severe. In the latter section the poor devils were all on stretchers laid out in rows, groaning and crying out. There was no medical attention, no sanitary arrangements and no issue of food or drink. Some French women came in with bottles of water and a little food and, despite the smell and horror of the place, these gallant people did what they could. Amongst the English I found several old friends from the battalion, some from my own platoon. They all bore various wounds. We were delighted to see each other and inquired after each other's adventures and mishaps, though I do not seem to have found out very much and was probably in no mood to take things in.

Throughout the whole of that long day we just sat about. I myself felt that the whole situation was unreal. Only a few days ago we had been in England under comparatively peaceful conditions, yet here we were in a ruined church, filthy dirty, wounded, unshaven and prisoners: around us people were groaning with pain. And, worst of all, we were in enemy hands. As for the situation, what we knew of it, it hardly bore thinking of. The Channel ports had been lost; those Channel ports to retain which we had fought so desperately and with such appalling losses during the Great War. And what of the BEF, somewhere on the Belgian frontier? How could it escape destruction with a victorious enemy round its flank and in its rear? Yet, with all this clear before them my little batch of Riflemen remained in good spirits. No word or suggestion of grievance was evident, and their behaviour and discipline remained beyond reproach. One of them I remember particularly: he was a battalion stretcher bearer and, although nastily wounded in the hand or arm, never ceased to try and help us, begging or stealing food or tins of milk, adjusting bandages and seeing if everyone's wounds were as comfortable as possible.

That night we lay down where we could, and in the morning some of us were lucky enough to have our wounds dressed by two French nurses who were allowed into the church. The morning dragged slowly on.

About midday all British walking wounded were singled out and taken off. We went in threes very slowly through the streets to a small hospital, which was being run by British doctors and padres and some French nurses. Some of us found it difficult to walk at all, and we had to help each other along. The Germans left the place completely alone and only came once a day to collect a numerical report. It was very overcrowded and in our ward at least thirty men were lying on the floor. There were no seriously wounded cases in this ward, but some were suffering from smashed knees, head wounds and nasty flesh wounds. The doctor in charge, from the Royal Marines, had a look at me and ordered me straight to bed, where I was washed. The beds had no sheets but coverlets instead and I felt really comfortable and luxurious. One officer gave me a toothbrush and another a slab of French chocolate, and I in turn produced some Players cigarettes I had been given, which had not been seen in the ward for two days.

Among the officers and soldiers in the ward were Riflemen, Gunners, Tank Corps, Marines and so on. They were in good spirits and in none of them could I detect any slackening of discipline or loss of morale. They accepted their position as one to which their duty had brought them, and there were consequently no grounds for complaint or self pity. Indeed an extraordinary and wonderful spirit of optimism was evident, some saying that the BEF would retake Calais in a few days, others that the Germans in this area belonged to units which had broken through and, finding themselves cut off, were attempting to cut their way back to their own lines, so that the wounded would be left behind and could wait quietly for the entry of French and British troops. Another reported that the whole Anglo-French army had been driven southwards, but that strong reinforcements had come up and that the tide of battle was once again surging north. I was ready to believe all these stories: I would soon be in England again, for France could not be so easily conquered, not France which had fought so gallantly in the previous war.

After a reasonably comfortable night I was woken up with a cup of weak coffee and a small piece of bread. My wounds were dressed and I was able to shave. A British padre appeared. He brought me the wretched news that Norman Philips, one of our A Company subalterns, had been brought wounded into the hospital and had just died. He also presented me with a special POW post card, stating, 'I am a prisoner of war: I am well/unwell,' which he asked me to complete and sign and promised to send it home as soon as possible. That postcard took six weeks to reach my mother and, as will now be related, was the first news she had that I was still alive.

War is particularly ghastly for wives and parents. My mother had only guessed that it was we who had been rushed to Calais, but her suspicions were not confirmed until she heard the report of Churchill's speech to the House of Commons on 4 June, in which he said:

> The Rifle Brigade, the 60th Rifles and the Queen Victoria's Rifles, with a battalion of British tanks and 1,000 Frenchmen, in all about 4,000 strong, defended Calais to the last (cheers). The British Brigadier was given an hour to surrender. He spurned the offer (cheers) and four days of intense street fighting passed before the silence reigned over Calais which marked the end of a memorable resistance. Only thirty survivors were brought off by the Navy and we do not know the fate of their comrades.

My mother found that last sentence particularly chilling. For some time she heard no news of me. Then our adjutant, Alick Williams, after many adventures, turned up at home. He had escaped from the line of marching prisoners and, together with the Brigade Major of our Calais Brigade, Captain Talbot of the Royal West Kents, and the Brigade Signals Officer, Lieutenant Millett, reached the coast near Berck, south of Le Touquet. There, after much searching they found a party of French soldiers trying to repair the engine of a motor boat and eventually crossed the Channel with them, to be picked up by a British destroyer off Folkestone. At home, Alick had passed round the many anxious families such news as he could. He contacted my mother; he had apparently heard that I had been reported killed and told her in a tactful letter that, while he had nothing definite to report, what he had heard was 'not very encouraging'. The weeks went by and she eventually advertised. I still retain the cutting which I found amongst her papers when she died in 1973, which read:

DAVIES-SCOURFIELD.
Sec. Lieut. EGB DAVIES-SCOURFIELD, 60th
Rifles, last seen wounded on May 26th at Calais.
Any information gratefully received by his
mother, Mrs. Davies-Scourfield, Annington House,
Steyning, Sussex.

Some weeks later she was returning in her car from shopping in Steyning when, breasting the hill up to Annington, she was amazed to see our family nanny, Nanny Bridge, who lived with her, hat askew and purple in the face, running along the road towards her, waving in her hand my postcard sent by the padre in Calais. Thrusting it through the window of the car, she collapsed across the bonnet speechless, breathless and totally exhausted.

Sometime during the morning the Germans cleared the lighter cases out to make room for more serious ones. Before I left I heard that Gerry Duncanson, brother of Robin, had just died from his wounds. Gerry was in the Rifle Brigade, while Robin commanded our Headquarters Company.

'You are to leave with this party for another hospital,' said the doctor. Reluctantly I put on my filthy clothes, said goodbye to those who were remaining, and joined the party in the street outside. We walked through the streets at a very mournful pace, stared at by German soldiers and the inhabitants of the town. We stopped for some time outside a large hospital, and a QVR officer told me that two of my friends were just inside. Our guards did not seem to mind what we did, so in I went. Here I found Charlie Madden and Alan Wigan, sitting on mattresses and propping themselves up against a large pillar. They were both wounded in the leg, but extremely cheerful. They told me that several officers, including the Colonel, were still alive but had been made prisoner. I often wonder now what would have happened if I had sat down with them and stayed. I should almost certainly have received good treatment for my wounds and eventually been sent with these two to the Spangenburg camp. Perhaps it was as well that I did not. Anyhow I do not believe that I had the choice.

Our column moved slowly on. I walked with RSM Chapman and CSM Austin, both of the QVRs. Chapman was wounded in the leg. We seemed to go a very long way. We were in the old town now, back amongst the sights of battle – broken windows, ruined houses, bomb craters, rubble. We came to the canal. We reached the Citadel, crossed the drawbridge and found ourselves in a large square with some shattered buildings all round, which had once been married quarters. In this square were hundreds of French, Dutch and Belgian prisoners. There seemed nothing to do, so we sat down. It was very hot and we were very dirty. I had no shirt (it had been cut away when my wounds had been dressed) my battle dress was filthy and clotted with blood. None of us British had any hats: CSM Austin's had been taken away during the walk by a German who required a war trophy. We had been photographed too by German soldiers, but for some reason I had covered my face.

We continued to wait. Finally some Germans tried to sort us out. They used a French sergeant, who spoke English and German, as their interpreter. He was obsequious to the Germans and impertinent to us. Austin informed him very plainly that we were taking no orders from him. The French, in contrast to us, were well clothed and with a certain amount of belongings.

Before evening many of the prisoners had been marched away. The remainder of us were taken to the Citadel and installed in some married quarters. The whole area had suffered badly from the recent shelling and was full of English soldiers. We made ourselves as comfortable as we could in these rather forlorn surroundings. There were in our little British party three or four officers besides myself: we were allocated the use of a flat and told that we need not attend roll calls. Our warrant officers and sergeants were put in the flat next door.

I was already making a few notes, which transformed into a diary when I reached a permanent camp. My first entry reads:

Sunday, 2 June: We have now been prisoners in Calais for one week. We are being unexpectedly well-treated and fed. Our community is large and consists mainly of French. Our little party of Brits includes Ray Snowdon (QVR), Lieutenant Commander Buckleigh (shot down in his Swordfish over Calais), Nicholson (RA), Moulder (RE), Ashford (60th) and two others besides myself. . . The food is quite adequate, though cigarettes are hard to come by. For the time-being we have few complaints.

The Germans, though correct towards us, were very trying. They attempted to sow discord between us and the French by being specially friendly to the latter and making us wait for meals until all the French had been served. Regrettably I must record that the French played along with their captors only too willingly. Our first 'brush' with the Germans was rather amusing, when one of their officers, who had been unobtrusive and inoffensive, appeared with a more senior and less attractive specimen of the German officer corps – he may have been SS. Two of us were summoned before him and Ray, who spoke good German, came with me. We were then warned in far from friendly or courteous terms that 'if the British continue to fire at German pilots descending by parachute, for every German so killed *Feldmarschall* Goering (he had not yet been made Reichmarschall) had decreed that fifty British prisoners would be shot'. We listened in silence and made no comment, which seemed to infuriate our informer, who said with heavy sarcasm, 'You have heard, no doubt, of our *Feldmarschall* Goering?' To which my companion replied, 'Goering? Goering? No I don't think I've heard of anyone called that.'

Then, turning to me, he asked in full English if I had heard of this Goering. Playing up, I shook my head and said, 'No never.' Both Germans, realizing we were 'taking the micky', went purple in the face and stormed off.

On Monday, 3 June, someone dressed my wounds, which were still rather painful. We were then put into lorries and driven off towards Boulogne. I saw the Redoubt, which we had defended only ten days before, and the White Cliffs of Dover which were clearly and tantalizingly visible from the hilltop above Coquelles. We spent that night rather uncomfortably in an open field surrounded by sentries and barbed wire, somewhere near Cambrai and Le Cateau. I noticed several British cemeteries, memorials to those desperate first war battles to keep the Germans at bay. Now the roads were jammed with German columns of tanks, self-propelled guns, half-tracks and trucks of various kinds. We were witnessing the victorious German Army sweeping south towards Paris and beyond.

At about 6 p.m. the following day we reached another transit camp in a little place called Cotillon. When we arrived, there were large numbers of prisoners being marched away, mostly French, but I saw no officers with them. What I did see was a real live doctor, a French officer who gave me a careful examination. When he came to my arm he shook his head and said: 'It's badly infected. I shall have to get the poison out which will hurt, but only for a moment.'

He then seized my arm in both his hands and gave it an almighty twist, as though squeezing out a cloth. Poison shot out of my arm from both ends of the wound in a great squirt. He said I had been very lucky, as the head wound had been very close to my eye and the exit wound in my back within a hairbreadth of my spinal column. He told me to sleep in the Infirmary and he would try to get me into hospital next day. The Infirmary turned out to be an old farm shed which smelt horribly, though I did receive a plate of soup for supper which I devoured ravenously.

All next day I was left in the transit camp but never got to hospital. It was very hot, and I developed a severe tummy upset, despite which I began to undergo real pangs of hunger, like nothing I had ever known before. I knew no one in the camp but talked with some of our soldiers who told me they were being made to move ammunition around, even stacking it at gun positions. I therefore demanded to see the Commandant and was taken before a Lieutenant Colonel and made my protest, which he would 'take note of'. Obviously my complaint got no further. I 'mucked in' with two very nice Regimental Sergeant Majors (my diary gives their names as Mr Mercer of the Military Police and Mr Chilton of the Pioneer Corps) and at their suggestion I slept the next night in an old wrecked car near the edge of the field. The following evening we set off again.

This time I was in a truck with fifteen French soldiers and five British Tommies, all, like me, wounded. After only fifteen miles we stopped and spent the night lying on the pavement in a small town on which, as we lay there, the RAF came along and dropped some bombs, though luckily not near us. We were off at crack of dawn, but it soon became almost unbearably hot. We British had no food or drink at all, and the French, who seemed well equipped with bread, margarine and potted meat, offered us nothing. Fortunately we were momentarily held up near some German troops, and a friendly English-speaking officer came over, discovered our predicament and produced, just for us British, some welcome prunes and rice. I dislike prunes normally, but those particular ones tasted just marvellous.

We were driven on through the lovely Belgian Ardennes, at 3 p.m. crossing the German frontier, which had been moved west to enclose the Belgian province of Malmedy. I must admit my heart sank when we crossed the frontier; from every window were hanging Nazi flags. Here for some unknown reason we were searched and questioned and, further on, spent the night at a transit camp where we were treated quite well and actually fed on bread and soup. Next day, we were paraded with a host of French and Moroccan soldiers and trailed slowly off to the station. Here I received my first dose of the cattle truck (forty hommes, eight chevaux) but only for an hour. We got out at a place called Ponsfeld, where I was patched up at a medical centre and then herded with everyone else into a huge marquee where we slept on the straw. It was a hateful place.

Saturday, 8 June: Very hot this marquee became at midday and, amidst all the dust from the straw, I got asthma and hay fever. I was very glad when evening came. A black day.

Sunday, however, was better as we left by train in the afternoon. As the only officer in this huge crowd of French and British, I was allowed in a third class carriage among German civilians, though of course with a guard. No one took much notice of me but, while still in the station waiting to depart, some tiresome fellow, probably a local Nazi, who was standing on the platform, kept thrusting his head through the window and subjecting my fellow passengers to an harangue, I heard him keep saying, *'Der Führer hat gesagt – Jawohl – Bestimmt – der Führer hat gesagt.'* I got fed up with this and was thankful I could not understand what the Führer was supposed to have said.

We slept that night in the train, getting out next day at Limburg and trailing off once again to a hutted camp. I was immediately taken to a medical centre where my wounds were examined and dressed, and someone told me in English that I was being taken by truck to an officers' camp. Soon afterwards I was driven off with a section of German soldiers. The latter were in great spirits, full of news about the German victories in France and chaffing me about the war being as good as over. It was all surprisingly good natured, and the atmosphere seemed friendly and relaxed – very different from the ghastly Ponsfeld place. One of the soldiers could speak French and acted as interpreter for me, but my own French was too bad for him to be of much help.

At about 1 p.m. we reached Mainz and drove under an archway into what appeared to be a military barracks. This turned out to be the final transit camp where all officers were assembled before dispatch to properly established camps in Germany. I was taken off and given food at tables and chairs in the pleasant shade of some trees. There were about 100 officers sitting there, mostly French but quite a few British: I did not recognize any. This was the best meal I ever remember the Germans producing for their prisoners – a bowl of thick, barley soup with potatoes, a whole loaf of bread and margarine. For some reason, however, I was not hungry, gave half my soup and potatoes to a large woolly dog which was walking about and was about to dump my bread and margarine when a horrified British officer came over and stopped me.

'That bread and margarine is ration for a whole week, you know,' he told me, bringing me down to earth with a severe bump. That this small loaf was my bread ration for the next seven days was certainly very bad news.

I stood up, a strange sight, dirty, unshaved, my arm in a sling, my body bulging with bandages round my middle, my head swathed in what must have looked like a great white turban, though obviously less conscious of my appearance than those beholding me.

It was at this moment that I suddenly saw Jack and Wally. I could not believe my eyes. I just stood there and looked at them. They were twenty yards away and staring at me.

'Good Lord, Jack, that's Gris,' said Wally.

'No, old boy,' replied Jack, 'It can't be, and you shouldn't say things like that. We both know he was killed. It looks a bit like him, that's all.'

At last I found my voice.

'Jack,' I called, 'Wally. It's me, it's Gris,' and they rushed over to where I stood.

I was two nights at Mainz which proved to be a time of reunion: a number of my friends from Calais were there and more came in next day. It was also a time of news gathering: I learned that our battalion had had nine officers killed. As well as Puffin, the two Scotts, Martin Willan, Richard Warre and Norman Philips, we had lost Charles Stanton, second in command of A Company, Claude Bower, second in command of D Company, and our REME officer, while the Rifle Brigade casualties included their CO Chan Hoskyns, Arthur ('Boy') Hamilton-Russell, whose mother lived near Steyning and was a great friend of my mother, Edward Bird (a grievous blow to me), Gerry Duncanson, whose brother Robin of our battalion survived and David Sladen, one of my Sandhurst friends and contemporaries. The number of NCOs and Riflemen killed we could not even estimate, and it was not until much later that I heard to my infinite sorrow that Sergeant Wall had been killed.

At least there was some joy in learning of those still alive and meeting up with some of them, and Jack introduced me to our Brigadier, Claude Nicholson, who told me that we had all done well at Calais and that he had been congratulated by the War Office for holding out as long as we had. All this did something to outweigh the appalling news, such as we could get, from the front that the Germans seemed to be everywhere victorious and were rolling on deep into France. The German officers and guards at Mainz could hardly contain themselves and were constantly looking at one of us and saying, ' For you the war is over,' a phrase I found just as irritating as 'Der Führer hat gesagt.' But it was all very depressing, and one French General hanged himself at Mainz while I was there. I saw someone rush out asking who had a knife with which to cut him down.

That evening I had my official interrogation which turned out to be purely routine. I remembered from the lecture I had once attended, that one must only give one's name, rank and number, and the only extra information they asked for was about our Brigade of which, in any case, I knew nothing.

From Mainz we were moved to a permanent camp at Laufen, on the Bavarian-Austrian border (it was no longer a frontier) not far from Salzburg. For most of us, after so much journeying and for the majority so much weary marching, the idea of a permanent camp held some attraction. Jack Poole, with his previous experience of imprisonment, did his best to disabuse us, warning that it would be 'no picnic,' and how right he was. To start with it was a lousy journey, lasting from Wednesday morning until Friday morning: there were forty-two of us in our cattle truck, which meant we were jammed very tight and which I found excruciating, particularly where my wounded back was concerned. The Germans could not have cared less. We had a little bread, sausage and margarine for the journey; what we did for washing and the calls of nature I cannot remember, but I do remember that we had to take turns in lying down.

Laufen, the village, contained what had once apparently been the ancient palace of Salzburg's Archbishop, and this was to be our prison. Despite the attractive countryside around it, the lovely River Salzbach which flowed by it and the breathtaking view of the Alps which it provided, Laufen was in fact a vile place. An extract from my diary reads:

> **Saturday, 15 June:** Today we got finally settled into our new surroundings and conditions of life. Tony, Charlie, Wally, Pat, Francis and myself were put into a room with 117 people. The box beds were in three tiers and jammed together. There were a few tables and stools, but not nearly enough, and we had to climb up onto our beds to eat – agony for me as the wound in my back is still open and the muscles round it shot away. Food is as follows: 7 am, one cup of black 'ersatz' (artificial) coffee: 11 am, one mug of watery soup with one, sometimes two seed potatoes, the latter often bright green and stinking of rot: 5 pm, same as 11 am. About twice a week we get a tiny piece of sausage, a small pat of margarine, some cheese on Sundays and a loaf of rye bread issued once a week to last the seven days.

Our little group actually consisted of seven; Tony Rolt, Charlie Weld-Forester and David Fellowes were Rifle Brigade, while Wally Finlayson, Pat Sherrard, Francis Williams and I were 60th. We made up a small mess grouped round a table, and the friendship between us was one of my very few happy memories of that time.

> **Sunday, 16 June:** We had a church service with communion held in the garage. I must admit that during the communion I

was thinking of the sausages we used to have at home for Sunday breakfast! I am feeling pretty weak, have lost masses of weight and am always desperately hungry. We have written our first letter home.

Laufen was the principal camp for all the British Army officers captured in France, except for a few who were sent to a smaller camp not far away at a place called Titmonig. We were among the earlier arrivals. A huge contingent of officers from the 51st Highland Division, captured at St Valery on the Somme, arrived a few days later. With them came their commander, General Victor Fortune, and his three brigadiers. They included several of my former fellow-cadets at Sandhurst.

We all loathed Laufen. Jack Poole wrote in his book:

> Looking back on those first three months of captivity I place them rock bottom of the many dark periods of my life: it was the dead-end level of existence. Lack of food, lack of literature and lack of any kind of privacy combined to make life's burden quite intolerable. There is probably no more demoralizing experience in life than near-starvation; character may suffer more than health.
>
> From the very beginning the Germans showed little interest in our welfare. Rations were pitifully meagre, and even the ubiquitous potato was eagerly devoured, often in a decaying condition.

It would be wrong and thoroughly misleading to conceal or minimize the inexcusably bad treatment we suffered at German hands during the early part of the war. They were winning and did not give a rap for anybody else. Later on, especially as the fortunes of war began to shift, our treatment improved, but meanwhile we had to grin and bear it. At this time, for example, it was no use quoting the Geneva Convention because the Germans announced they did not recognize it as the Weimar Government had in fact signed it but the Nazis did not recognize Weimar either! Later, when lots of Germans had been taken prisoner, they decided that they recognized the Convention after all.

To make matters worse, there were no parcels coming through which meant not only near-starvation rations but very few cigarettes: one needs to remember that most young people in those days were habitual smokers. We were actually issued with eight cigarettes every four days, and we used to endure agonies of indecision, trying to decide whether to smoke all eight straight away, or two each day or none until the fourth day and smoke all, and so on. One had the same problem over one's loaf of bread, issued once per week to last seven days. It is regrettable to record that bread-stealing was by no means unknown, and literally 'to lose one's loaf' on the first or second day of issue could be a near-tragedy, and it therefore had to be carefully safeguarded; it was not even safe in one's bed at night unless tied to one's arm or leg!

Thanks mainly to the rotten potatoes, many people were soon suffering from violent tummy troubles, sometimes referred to as 'colitis' or more usually 'enteritis'. Long queues formed at all the rather limited number of lavatories, some of the queuers being unable to hold out until their turn, so the whole place quickly became highly insanitary. The very worst cases, which I remember included Jack Poole, were isolated, and issued with white bread, but I hung out in great pain and inconvenience until eventually cured by being given a large dose of castor oil. The Germans, growing uneasy at our rapidly deteriorating health, began to provide us all, on payment with the ridiculous camp money, with a daily mug of separated milk: often it arrived sour and lumpy but if tied up in an old sock and hung from the side of one's bed turned eventually into something vaguely akin to cottage cheese! We were of necessity becoming quite 'inventive'. For example, the chap who had the bed below mine carved himself a pipe out of the bed-post and then smoked straw from his bedding – the ghastly and very peculiar stench remains with me to this day.

It was occasionally possible to buy some quite revolting Polish pipe tobacco in the canteen. One of the Royal Marine officers discovered it could be increased in quantity, if not in quality, by carefully blending it with dried droppings from the horses which pulled the vegetable carts. Finding a frustrated major (majors seemed very elderly to us subalterns) walking about continually sucking an empty pipe, he told him he had managed to barter some rather better quality tobacco from one of the guards, and would the major like to swap it for a week's margarine ration? The major decided he would. Thereafter the Royal Marine, having concluded his deal satisfactorily, deemed it wiser to avoid the major but was eventually sought out a few days later and cornered: he waited for the fury to be unleashed.

'I say,' said the major, 'I've been looking for you. I wanted to ask if you could possibly get me some more of that excellent tobacco!'

The lovely snow-covered Alps frequently drew people to the windows to admire their beauty or gaze longingly at the freedom they represented and, sometimes, in the case of those with artistic leanings, to draw or paint them. The Germans issued an order, however, that to lean out of windows was forbidden. Not long afterwards, a young officer was painting the view from a window in the top storey when a sentry in one of the towers spotted him and started shouting at him to move back. We, down in the exercise area could hear him, but the artist up top could not and continued to paint. After several warnings and all of us shouting to the painter to get back and to the sentry not to fire, we saw the German kneel, take careful aim and shoot. General Fortune immediately demanded an audience with the Commandant, made the most vigorous protest, demanded that sentries' orders be changed and warned him that he would be held personally responsible for this young officer's death. I believe that the Commandant did not survive the war to face the consequences, but such an incident is indicative of the relationship between captor and captive at that early stage in the war when the Germans were convinced that total victory was within their grasp. The miserable summer dragged on. A typical diary entry read:

Sunday, 21 July: An uneventful week except for Jack, Tony, Charlie, Wally and Francis all going down with enteritis and being taken away into isolation.

Nevertheless our conditions did improve. During August a small but very welcome dribble of Red Cross supplies began to come through from England, and one or two people who had connections abroad received small parcels. I wrote to Mrs Krebs at The Hotel Krebs, Interlaken, where my mother had taken me, my sister Margaret and old Nanny Bridge in the summer of 1934, and received a super little parcel of chocolate and biscuits and a very nice letter. I also received, through some regimental initiative, a parcel from an Englishman named (I think) Wharton Tiger, who was working in Yugoslavia, several small parcels from a Mrs Stilwell in Portugal and one from Mrs Milton in the United States. It is impossible to exaggerate the value of, and the pleasure and indeed excitement from, these truly wonderful gifts. Even so we remained seriously undernourished and desperately hungry.

In July we received some information, from where I cannot recall, about the Calais casualties. My platoon had had eight killed, twenty-nine captured and five wounded and evacuated during the battle. Of the prisoners quite a few were thought to have been wounded. Eight killed was not as bad as I had expected, but still a grievous loss of such good chaps. The Battalion had lost nine officers and over 100 other ranks killed. I had to wait until the end of October, however, for my first letter from home and learn, to my great relief, that my batman, Smith, had survived and was a prisoner.

The need, duty and desire to escape was never far from the minds of some of us. Quite early on one of my closer Sandhurst friends, Ralph Pilcher, who had been captured with the Welsh Guards at Boulogne, approached me and suggested we might team up. At the time, however none of my wounds had healed and still required (and were receiving) constant medical treatment and this, added to the lack of proper food, had left me in very poor physical shape.

Early September saw the first successful break-out when Pat Reid (of *Colditz Story* fame) and a party totalling six, got away through a tunnel but, after several days of freedom, they were caught and brought back. No one was sure at the time what the Germans would do to prisoners who escaped and were recaptured. In fact they were sentenced by the Commandant to periods of solitary confinement of up to twenty-eight days or more, but before the sentence had been completed were sent to another camp, a place called Colditz.

As the war dragged on the news remained thoroughly depressing. I remember seeing a notice displayed somewhere, possibly in the newspapers, of a map of England with a huge German bomb exploding in the middle of it. At least no invasion of England had taken place but, while remaining almost unreasonably optimistic about the final outcome; we realized that the German bombing must be severe. What few of us could accept was that our final victory would be postponed for several years, because such a thought at that time would have been unbearable. Each year the war, somehow, just had to be over by Christmas.

Not long after a bleak, meagre and thoroughly depressing Christmas I became involved with escaping. It was high time, for I was by now reasonably fit (though hungry as ever) and extremely frustrated. A tunnel was being planned with three teams to work it, and Ronnie Littledale asked Mike Sinclair and me to form one with him. I knew Ronnie very well. He had commanded one of our companies at Tidworth and I had ridden his charger in the regimental point-to-point. When war came he was commanding A Company and continued to do so until joining Claude Nicholson's staff at the beginning of 1940, where he remained until captured with us at Calais. He was a bachelor, athletic and a strong Christian. Sinclair, who has appeared several times already in this narrative, was tough mentally and physically and absolutely determined to escape and fight again or perish in the attempt.

This tunnel started in a small music room leading off the main reading or recreation room. This latter was very large, like a big hall, and even had a gallery. It was the only comfortable place in the camp but always very crowded. The mouth of the tunnel had been constructed by a sapper and brilliantly camouflaged. When our team was on construction duty Ronnie and Mike went down the tunnel to dig while I stayed above ground with my eye glued to a peep hole. Whenever Germans approached, which meant their crossing a small yard, I received a hand signal from the gallery opposite. On receipt of this signal my task was to pull out the wire from its wall plug, thus plunging Ronnie and Mike into immediate darkness. They then would pull the wire into the tunnel while I replaced the cover over the tunnel and then sat down and strum or play scales on the piano. Unfortunately the Germans learnt in some way or other about the tunnel, for on our third day of duty they came rushing along, three of them and one Alsatian. I received the warning and just had time to take the necessary action and be sitting at the piano when the Germans burst into the music room, ordered me to stand up with my hands above my head, then went straight to the tunnel and removed the lid. At this point I was marched off with a pistol in my back, to the amazement and concern of most of the prisoners in the recreation room, and escorted thus to the Commandant's office. While waiting in the passage outside, I was joined by Mike, similarly escorted and covered in dust and dirt from the tunnel. After some considerable delay we were both marched in, told by the Commandant that we were very stupid and, refusing to answer any questions, sentenced to forty-two days' *streng arrest*. Ronnie stayed quietly in the tunnel and was never found.

'*Streng arrest*', not invented for us but in general use within the

German armed forces, meant solitary confinement in a cell block somewhere outside the camp. One was allowed no books, no writing materials, no cigarettes or tobacco and no cards and for three days out of every four one was given bread and water only and slept on bare boards (on the fourth day one got a mattress and two meals of soup). This, we discovered later, was entirely contrary to the Geneva Convention, and my solitary confinements later in the war were pleasant by comparison. We did however have a daily walk in the camp, though under strict guard, and our friends, while not allowed contact with us, used to hide little parcels of biscuits and other goodies in the snow which now lay everywhere, and we usually managed to pick them up.

To have absolutely nothing to do day after day except to pace one's cell or sit and think or merely sit sounds rather grim, but at least I could fall back on my huge store of poetry learned at school which always gave me the greatest pleasure to recite. It is not entirely strange, therefore, that I look back on my '*streng arrest*' time with less distaste than the rest of my time in Laufen. I can only imagine that I found the peace and quiet of my lonely cell a welcome change from the dreadful overcrowding which remains one of my many unhappy memories of a place which had so little to commend it.

Before our sentence was completed we were told we would be going to a new camp and that quite a lot of others from Laufen would be going too. We were therefore released back into the castle to get ready for our journey.

Laufen was undoubtedly a beautiful place, as I was reminded many years later when I returned with my wife to have a look. The Bavarian countryside, the river and the mountains were wonderful. Yet I and doubtless those who were there with me, have been left with the most hateful memories of it all. The hunger and the sickness were unforgettable and the humiliation of being shut up, losing one's freedom, were with us all the time. This is hardly surprising, I suppose. To quote an old anonymous inscription in Edinburgh's tollbooth:

> *A prison is a house of care,*
> *A place where none can thrive:*
> *A touchstone true to try a friend,*
> *A grave for one alive.*

7

ESCAPE FROM POSEN

After those months in Laufen it was indescribably exciting and exhilarating to be once more on the move. We travelled by train. This time we were spared the cattle trucks and instead were locked into normal carriages. Our destination, we were told, was Posen, to a special camp called Fort VIII.

Posen, or Poznan to give it its Polish name, lies halfway between Berlin and Warsaw and well within the frontier of Poland as designated by the Versailles Treaty.

Ronnie, Mike and I kept together during the journey and spent much of our time trying to make a hole in the carriage floor through which to escape. Constantly interrupted by the appearance of guards in the corridor, we found the task too difficult, and no one during this long journey managed to get away.

From the station at Posen we were marched off by a lot of noisy, shouting and thoroughly offensive German guards and police, some of whom were mounted on horses. We had brought with us from Laufen as many of our carefully accumulated possessions as we could possibly carry. I had all mine done up in a huge bundle in a sleeping bag – two Jaeger blankets sewn together, which had come in my first clothing parcel from home – and it made a heavy load. Thus burdened and still being in very poor physical condition, I soon dropped to the back of the column and for three quarters of an hour staggered along as best I could, constantly cursed and shouted at and, occasionally, half-ridden down by a mounted policeman. All this has remained with me as one of the least pleasant memories of my long imprisonment (though by no means the worst), and by the time we reached Fort VIII I was utterly exhausted.

Our new prison camp reminded me of these old forts on Portsdown hill which I had so often passed on my way between my home in Sussex and my school in Winchester. Fort VIII was part of the old defences of Posen, was turfed over and approached by a bridge across a wide moat and then a huge black hole leading into the interior. Here we were halted and kept hanging about for some time. A photograph showing me in a crowd later got into the British press (presumably sent home by a prisoner). My mother was able to identify me in the foreground, just right of centre, talking to Mike Sinclair hatless with his back to the camera (see plate section).

We were then addressed, through an interpreter, by our new Commandant who explained that we had been brought to Fort VIII because of the maltreatment of German officers in Canada. Apparently the Swedes, who were Germany's Protecting Power in the same way as the Swiss were ours, had produced a report, part of which was now read out to us, about conditions at Fort Henry in Canada. The German officer prisoners there were alleged to be suffering unpleasant restrictions which included sub-standard accommodation, inadequate exercise facilities, no proper eating utensils and were locked into their rooms at night with just one latrine bucket, often for thirty or more officers. Furthermore the Canadian guards carried (Oh! Horror!) rubber truncheons! Therefore, the Commandant explained, the German Government had decided that a similar number of British officers would be subjected to exactly the same conditions. Fort VIII had been chosen for this purpose but was not to be thought of as a reprisal camp ('We Germans do not take reprisals against defenseless prisoners') but as an 'equality camp' and would be thus maintained until the situation in Canada improved.

Although this was hardly an auspicious start to life in our new camp we found it was infinitely preferable to Laufen. The worst thing we suffered was from the fleas which infested all our blankets in enormous numbers. Whether they were intended to be part of the 'equality' I do not know, but most of us got badly bitten. Strangely enough there were some whom the fleas found particularly delicious and some whom they found distasteful. I was about average, perhaps good in parts like the curate's egg, but the worst cases were completely covered from head to foot in bites. We used to have a competition to see who could produce the most dead fleas at bedtime, catching them from one's own blankets or clothes by use

70

of a wet piece of soap. A particularly enthusiastic flea hunter accounted one evening for a record bag of 150. Despite the fleas, the nocturnal latrine bucket, eating with our fingers and the underground existence, we were delighted with the change of scene and our morale, aided by the splendidly cheerful example set by General Victor Fortune, rose accordingly.

On one occasion I was sitting on the loo in our very basic and substandard lavatory when the General went into the next compartment. After a short time he suddenly said, 'I say, you next door, do you think there are as many flies in your pan as there are in mine?'

The Germans themselves represented another improvement. They were less excitable than those at Laufen, perhaps because they were northern rather than southern Germans, and altogether more friendly. The Commandant even had a sense of humour, a rare commodity among Germans. One night some of my friends were caught attempting to escape across the moat (or maybe it was just a reconnaissance, I cannot remember) and we were all immediately paraded in the corridor to be counted and told how pointless it was to try and escape. There was however no shouting or shoving by any of the guards, and when the Commandant appeared and we were called to attention he said in English, 'Gentlemen, the ghost-train he has passed'.

This may not sound terribly funny but it was one of the very few German attempts at humour that I have ever encountered. *Hauptmann* Priem at Colditz was to produce some others. *Hauptmann* Eggers, Colditz Security Officer, author of *Colditz – The German Story* and editor of the fascinating *Colditz Recaptured*, wrote of Priem, 'On the whole we found him a jolly good fellow', and so did the British who described him as 'the only German officer with a natural sense of humour'.

But I digress and jump ahead, so back to Posen.

After three weeks, when we had more or less sorted ourselves out and begun to settle down, Mike and I were suddenly summoned before the Commandant, informed we still had ten days of our Laufen sentence to complete and locked up, together this time, in a turret!

Although we were allowed no exercise, we did not have to endure the hard boards and bread and water treatment. Instead we had a rat problem. There was an usually large one sitting on one of the beds when we arrived! Naturally we made a great fuss, especially when we discovered that the wainscot was riddled with rat-holes, and were eventually provided with some tin, nails and a hammer. Although the rats continued to make much noise at night, rushing around, squeaking and gnawing at the boarding, our improvised defences held out.

Each evening Mike and I were allowed to go down the passage, accompanied by an armed sentry, to wash in some basin which had a cold tap. As I have already indicated, the Posen guards were on the whole quite reasonable, and we used to spin out this washing time as much as possible, conscientiously stripping down and washing ourselves thoroughly all over. This procedure caused our guards utter astonishment, even some concern, and one told us with great solemnity that it was dangerous to wash too often, particularly one's feet. Our incarceration, though it had its drawbacks, passed quickly and pleasantly enough.

The war was hotting up again. The sinking of HMS *Hood*, which plunged us into gloom, was balanced shortly afterwards by our sinking of the *Bismarck*. Further there was all the excitement over Rudolf Hess absconding to Scotland, the German invasion of the Balkans and their conquest of Yugoslavia and Greece.

Then a strange thing happened. A German officer, from the Luftwaffe I think, escaped from Canada and eventually got back to Germany, probably the only one to do so. He was sent to visit Fort VIII to see whether the conditions he and his comrades had suffered in Canada had been faithfully and accurately reproduced. I cannot vouch for the details of this story, but we understood that, after looking carefully round, he had complimented the Commandant. 'Very like Fort Henry,' he said. He then asked how long the British officers were kept under these conditions and was appalled when told we would be kept there until such time as things improved in Canada. He then explained that no German officer was in Fort Henry for more than forty-eight hours, as it was purely a transit camp, and that conditions in the permanent Canadian camps were very good. To do them justice I must say that the Germans behaved very well over this. We were paraded before the Commandant who apologized for what had clearly been a misunderstanding and told that, while it would take some time before we could be moved, our conditions would be immediately improved and the roof permanently open to us during the daylight hours. I give our Posen gaolers credit where credit is due, but I doubt whether they were quite so pleasant as my memory suggests. As the years pass one tends to remember only good things and forget the bad, like 'school days being the best days of one's life' which of course is untrue. Our Commandant here was however decent enough to us. As for our Luftwaffe benefactor, I was sorry to hear he was later killed in Russia.

It must have been early in May when Ronnie, Mike and I at last evolved a plan for escape which seemed to have some prospect of success. It had the advantage of comparative simplicity. Rubbish from the kitchen was collected by British orderlies throughout the day, each load being packed into a small handcart. When enough refuse had been collected to fill the cart, the following routine was followed: two of the orderlies carried the cart over the moat to the main gate and shouted to the guard commander; the gate was then unlocked and the orderlies, under the supervision of one armed guard, proceeded to a large pit about eight yards from the camp and emptied the rubbish into it. They then returned to camp.

This procedure offered obvious possibilities. It was Mike, however, who worked out all the details and made the plan: it was Mike, too, who obtained an introduction, through a young Polish boy who worked daily in the camp as an assistant to the German electrician, to the Polish Resistance organization in Posen. I learnt years later that he was one of the Klichowski brothers.

Once the plans had been made, preparations to put them into effect were thorough and intense, including constant rehearsal and practice. One of the problems concerned the handcart itself which proved to be just too small for our purpose: a new and slightly larger one had therefore to be constructed, large enough for one of us to be concealed within it and small enough to look like the original. Then we had to prepare suitable civilian-type clothing, mainly from blankets or any odd scraps of material that might be available, some food to take with us, German money (difficult at that time to obtain) and other essentials like a razor, compass and a map. All arrangements were eventually made with the help of several other people, and the escape launched on 28 May 1941, almost exactly one year since our capture.

There is no doubt that escaping is a desperately exciting pastime, and my two escapes, unsuccessful though both eventually proved, were the most nerve-racking things I have ever done; more exciting than the fighting at Calais, and more exciting even than my first point-to-point ride. Pat Reid sums it up very graphically in his prologue to *The Colditz Story*, 'I can think of no sport that is the peer of escape, where freedom, life and loved ones are the prize of victory, and death the possible though by no means inevitable price of failure.'

Mike was the first to go. His task was to contact the Poles at a certain address in the town and arrange for Ronnie and me to be met at 4 p.m. close to the tram terminus. At 11 a.m. we watched from the roof of the Fort and with our hearts in our mouths saw the hand-cart tipped into the pit. We had selected a time when a suitably lazy sentry was on duty (discovered by constant observations over a prolonged period), and as was expected, this sentry did not bother to go right upto the pit but stood watching from the path ten yards away. The two British orderlies did a marvelous job, emptying the contents of the handcart, which included Mike, without arousing suspicion. Mike waited in the pit until the 'all clear' signal had been given from the fort's roof, which was visible to him, then clambered out and walked off into the town. He was wearing khaki trousers dyed blue, a short mackintosh coat (a modified army rain-coat) and a home-made Polish civilian cap. It was a great moment.

At midday the Commandant ordered a parade of the British order-lies for 3 p.m. This meant that Ronnie and I must leave earlier than intended. As soon as Ronnie had been signalled away out of the pit I climbed into the handcart, was covered up with rubbish and carried out. It all seemed to happen too quickly for me to have any last minute nerves, although I was naturally keyed up to the limit. I was emptied out satisfactorily with my 'all clear' signal given by Peter Douglas (who escaped later by our method to reach Sweden and home) and away I went.

Our enforced early start, which Mike could not have known about, meant that one hour had somehow to be filled in before Ronnie and I could meet at the rendezvous. I therefore walked aimlessly about in neighbouring streets, feeling very conspicuous in my home-made clothing. I was sure that anyone noticing me would know at once that I was a British officer escaping. At the same time I was filled with exhilaration at being free, no longer in the power of my captors whom I had so completely outwitted. I knew of course that my road to absolute freedom, now stretching so enticingly before me, would be long and hard; how long and hard it was to be I fortunately had no idea.

At 4 p.m. I went to the rendezvous, where I could see that Ronnie had already arrived. He was standing by a tree, shooting out little nervous glances in all directions. As I came near he gave me a quick look and hastily crossed the road. I followed, but he darted round a tree and dived back to the opposite pavement. Disconcerted, I eventually caught up with him.

'Oh,' he exclaimed in obvious relief. 'It's you, is it?'

'Who on earth did you think I was?' I replied.

'Well,' he said. 'You look a bit different in those clothes, and you've shaved off your moustache. I thought you were some inquisitive Pole trying to come and chat with me.'

We had arranged through Mike that whoever came to collect us would take off his hat and scratch his head as a recognition signal, and we would then do the same.

By 4.15 (H-hour plus 15) noone had come up to us scratching his head, although we had scratched ours furiously at several likely customers. One man gave us a very disapproving look; he probably thought we needed a bath! Mike had told us that if no one had come by 4.30 we must assume he had been caught. In which case we would abandon the idea of contacting any local Poles and put into operation our alternative plan to hide up on a goods train which we knew was scheduled to leave for Stuttgart at 9 p.m. It is intriguing to speculate how this might have worked out.

4.30 p.m. came and went. We decided to wait a further fifteen minutes before giving Mike up for lost, and ten minutes later we saw coming towards us the young Polish electrician. He took off his cap and scratched his head. The die was cast.

With him we walked into the centre of the town and came to a block of flats, into one of which we were ushered and found Mike talking to two women. A magnificent tea, with white bread and butter, jam and cakes, was produced. It seemed like magic. Later, another boy, brother of our contact, appeared and we were led away separately. My guide took me by tram. These consisted of two coaches, the first being reserved exclusively for Germans ('*Nur für Deutsche*'). Finally we walked into a small yard and knocked at a door leading to a basement. The door was opened by a middle-aged man, and a whispered conversation followed. Then the man, speaking in German, asked me to come in and said he would be honoured if I would stay the night in his house.

It all seemed quite unreal. This was our first escape, and if we had known more about the business we would have realized that all we

75

needed were identity, documents and money: instead we allowed ourselves to accept offers of concealment and transport to the east and active assistance along each stage of our journey. I would soon discover that the promises made by all these splendid Poles were born of an intense desire, rather than any actual ability, to provide decisive help.

The basement flat consisted of two small rooms, as well as a lavatory and a kitchen. The family, made up of the man, his wife and three children were extremely welcoming, though the woman was understandably nervous at having me there, and were eager to hear what I thought about the war and how long it might last.

For two or three nights I was moved to different flats. I noticed that the town seemed full of Germans in uniform. I was told that before the war the Poles made up eighty per cent of the town's population but that now, after mass arrests and deportations, they were only fifteen per cent. All this part of Western Poland had been annexed into the German '*Reich*,' whereas the centre of the country, including Warsaw and Cracow, had become a sort of German colony known as The General Government, surrounded not by a frontier but by a strictly controlled customs border. Eastern Poland had been seized and annexed by Russia. The deportation conditions had been appalling, many of the Poles in the Posen area, including women and children, being moved at a moment's notice, sometimes on foot, sometimes in open trucks, sometimes in crowded cattle wagons. Arrived at their destination somewhere in the General Government, they had to fend for themselves, find shelter, work, food. Inevitably thousands died.

Eventually I was taken to a large flat, where I found Ronnie. Our hostess was a woman about thirty-five with a small daughter. Ronnie told me that Mike was in touch with certain Poles who could give us clothes, identity papers and addresses further to the east. In other words we would be passed 'down the line'.

Next day we were visited by a large, elderly and rather distinguished looking man who, we learned, would be referred to as 'The Doctor.' He shook us warmly by the hand.

'You are English officers?' he spoke in English. 'You wish to reach a neutral country?' We nodded vigorously. 'Then it is lucky I have come. I can help you.'

We thanked him profusely and explained we wished to go to Russia. 'I will arrange everything for the journey. I shall be back later with Lieutenant Sinclair. We shall discuss what needs to be done.'

He returned in the evening with Mike, the boy, two other Poles, and a bottle of brandy. He seemed very excited and was thoroughly enjoying the drama. He evolved the following plan. The three of us were to remain hidden in a small box room at the back of the flat, where the woman would bring us food and generally look after us. We were never to leave the flat, night or day, as a German woman in the next flat used the adjacent kitchen. Meanwhile civilian clothes and identity papers would be obtained and means of changing our appearance provided. As soon as possible we would be handed on to friends of the Doctor in Lodz. A car would be provided for the journey. Arrangements for the rest of the journey would be made in Lodz. A fair-haired young Pole, known to us as Nicholas, was hoping to reach England and would accompany us.

We were ten days in that crowded little room where only one of us could stand up at a time. Occasionally the Doctor came to see us with the latest news; the British had occupied Syria; there was tension on the Russo-German frontier; Hitler, Brauchitsch and their staff had passed through Posen heading east. He also told us that three more officers, who had escaped from Fort VIII after us, were being looked after in the town. These were Kit Silverwood Cope, Ken Sutherland and Peter Winton. There was in fact a fourth officer in that party, John Crawford. One day Nicholas arrived with a barber who bleached my hair and eyebrows to a strange golden copper colour, darkened Mike's ginger hair and turned Ronnie's grey. Another time the Doctor burst in, highly excited, to say he had just attempted to blow up a goods train, but the explosives had gone off too soon.

On the ninth day the Doctor visited us again. He told us to be ready at nine the next morning. We were then to watch out of the window and would see him standing on the other side of the street. When he removed his hat we were to go down at intervals of half a minute, then turn right and get into a low red car which would be waiting at the first corner. Nicholas would already be in it. The driver was half German and must on no account discover who we really were. He had been told we were Germans travelling to Lodz on business. Nicholas would keep the driver busy with conversation: if the driver tried to speak to us, then only Mike was to reply.

It sounded a bit tricky to me, but all went according to plan. At 9.15 on the following morning we were speeding along in open country.

It was a strange journey. Ronnie, Mike and I sat woodenly silent in the back of the car. Mike was able to allay any suspicions the driver might have had by explaining that Ronnie and I were suffering from the bombing in Hamburg and were in a highly nervous state, though he must have thought us a strange pair.

When we reached the outskirts of Lodz, which had now reverted to its German name of Litzmannstadt, we left the car and proceeded by tram. The journey had taken about four hours. The tram now took us through the ghetto, a sector of the town completely surrounded by a high barbed-wire fence. All streets running through it had wire along the gutters so that the Jews could not leave the pavements. Those wishing to cross the road had to use wooden bridges which had been erected at intervals. The pavements were so crowded that movement must have been difficult, but the shops seemed almost empty of goods. Many of the Jews wore normal Western-style dress, but some had long oriental robes, tall Jewish hats and plenty of beards and curly side-whiskers. All wore, by German command, the yellow Star of David. The whole scene, with the wire and overcrowding, left an unpleasant taste in the mouth and thoughts of 'man's inhumanity to man'.

In those days most British people had only the vaguest idea of the German treatment of the Jews during the Nazi era, but I was surprised to encounter a considerable degree of anti-semitism among the Poles. All the time I spent in Poland I never heard much sympathy expressed for the Jews, although a number actually adopted Jewish children smuggled out of the ghettos, bringing them up of course as good Catholics!

I was later to hear of one particular case in Warsaw and was interested to read after the war a book about this same child, written by the mother and called (I believe) *Three Came Back*. Amazingly both parents survived the Warsaw ghetto uprising (not to be confused with the Polish Underground Army's battle for Warsaw in August 1944) and several years separated in different concentration camps. Eventually, at the end of the war, the parents found each other, then located their child, and all three emigrated to the States where the child became a successful New York publisher or lawyer.

Having reached a big square in the centre of the town we left the tram and proceeded on foot. After our ten cramped days in the little room I felt unsteady on my feet and shaky at the knees. Nicholas took us to the address supplied by the Doctor which was owned by an elderly man named Mr Wolf who lived there with his young nephew. They had been expecting us, and both seemed pleased to see us; showing not the slightest anxiety at the prospect of harbouring three British prisoners of war. The flat was large and bare; its drainage system was out of order and the food plain but adequate.

Nicholas went out and returned with two young ladies from the local resistance movement who brought us playing cards, English books and some magazines. They talked glibly about identity cards but were disappointingly vague about ways and means of crossing over into the General Government. On the following day we were joined by a friend of Nicholas, a tough looking sailor with plenty of commonsense, energy and resource who spoke excellent German. Each day he and Nicholas disappeared into the town while we three stayed indoors reading, playing cards and doing PT exercises in order to get a little less unfit. Mr Wolf and his nephew went off to work early in the morning so we three were mostly on our own and had plenty of time to discuss our situation and the options open to us. As far as our destination was concerned we agreed that the Russian frontier, which since the war had been advanced westward to the River Bug, offered the best prospects, and in any case we were more or less committed to it. Sweden, Turkey and Switzerland remained possible alternatives, despite complications of distance, additional frontiers and (in Sweden's case) the sea. Also there would be problems over obtaining the necessary information which, in the case of Russia, could probably be provided by the local Poles. We also considered whether we were right or wise to continue relying on help from the Poles, particularly in view of the risks to them involved. At that moment however their assistance appeared to be working rather well and to offer a real chance of success.

After a few days Nicholas and 'The Sailor' succeeded in making arrangements for us to cross the border with the help of some local smugglers. Once in the General Government we would trek eastwards, getting what help we could on the way, especially information and food.

We had been ten days in Lodz when we started off on the next part of our journey. Leaving Ronnie and Mike in the flat for the time being, Nicholas took me to the north-east outskirts of the town by tram. Here a small, youngish woman was waiting outside a café and, having introduced us, Nicholas went back. I and my new-found friend and guide loitered about until dusk and then got into a pony cart with about six other people – I had reached the stage when nothing could surprise me. My guide, who spoke German, told me I was to be her nephew from Posen, and that our excuse for talking together in German would be my desire to learn the language as quickly as possible! I thought this a rotten reason but could not think of anything better, and there was little time to discuss other possibilities.

The pony cart took the road towards the east and the border which lay five miles ahead. Fifteen minutes later we picked up a man who, unfortunately for me, turned out to be a friend of my guide. He was very talkative and, after a few minutes, addressed me in Polish. I made no reply. The woman explained that I would speak only in German. He addressed me in German. I did not understand and made some idiotic reply. The woman tapped her head significantly. Immediately all eyes were upon me. No one spoke for about five minutes. I was highly embarrassed and sat grimly in my seat as the pony jogged steadily on. Obviously I had to play my part, so I assumed what I hoped was a suitably dotty expression with my mouth half open and my head cocked slightly to one side! Even now, over sixty years later, I still feel embarrassed when I recall my journey in the pony cart and, if there was an amusing, almost farcical side to it all, I cannot forget the danger which my presence posed for the companions of my travels. I was a threat to the lives of all who helped me, and this remained for me a hideous anxiety which I could not immediately shed and with which I had to live and come to terms.

As we went trotting along in our cart, twilight changed to darkness. We passed several Germans in uniform, but they took no notice of us. One by one our fellow travellers got off, until only the driver, the woman and I were left. Eventually we turned into a small country lane, passing through a large wood with some beautiful ponds shining in the moonlight. Frogs, which seemed to abound in Poland, were croaking loudly. At the end of the wood we reached the outskirts of a village, and opposite the first cottage we got out. The woman bade our driver goodbye.

In the cottage I was received warmly by the occupants and we shared their food. We spent the night there. I was disappointed at not pushing on and crossing the border under the cover of darkness, but I was in their hands. I bedded down on the couch with one of the men, their being no apparent alternative, but creepy-crawly things quickly made themselves noticeable, so I spent the night on the hard brick floor. Fleas devoured me hungrily but they were preferable to creepy-crawlies which in fact were bed-bugs or lice. Lice carried typhus which was prevalent in eastern Europe during the war and maybe always has been.

We were off again at first light, walking two miles to another village which, like so many in Poland, stretched a considerable distance on both sides of the road. We entered one of the first houses, receiving another warm welcome, and were given a much needed breakfast of eggs, bread and milk. Ronnie, with 'The Sailor' and two very fat women, came in, and we all ate together.

During this repast various reports kept coming in about the movement of border patrols and the position of guards. Then an 'all clear' was given and the woman and I set off up the village, leaving the others behind in the house. I was wearing a grey tweed suit and a blue homberg hat so that I looked all right but was ill at ease: this was not my idea of how a border should be crossed. Suddenly the woman breathed a deep sigh of relief:

'*Gott sei dank*,' she murmured.

'Why?' I asked in German.

'Did you not see that German policeman standing under the tree?'

I had seen nothing, but at that moment we saw another policeman, or perhaps he was a border guard, cycling down the path (for it was scarcely a road) straight towards us. This was a bad moment, but the woman remained completely calm.

'Leave this to me,' she said. 'Look as stupid as you can and say nothing.'

So once again I had to become a lunatic! I put on a real loony expression as the German dismounted from his bike and told us to stop.

'Halt! Where are you going?'

'My cousin and I have three days' holiday, and we are visiting Frau 'X' at the end of the village. My cousin is not very well.' (Here I grin sheepishly and try to look absolutely daft.)

'What have you got with you?'

'I will show you.' She opened her bag. 'We are bringing some supplies for Frau 'X'.'

'You have too much food with you: too much sugar and too much jam.'

81

'Oh, that's not much for three days. By the way don't I know your face? Perhaps you have been to my little café – I have plenty of vodka there.'

'Certainly I have never seen you before nor been to your café.' Then, his expression softening, 'But I would like to come.'

'Then you shall come: come on Monday if you like,' and she gave him some address.

'Goodbye then for the present,' he said, 'but remember, on no account stray over the border.' He then leapt onto his bicycle and pedalled off. I was so relieved I wanted to break into song.

We proceeded for several hundred yards and then turned into yet another cottage. The owner's wife was German but she considered herself Polish. I was put under her orders, and my brave and competent guide said goodbye and departed, returning to Lodz for Nicholas and Mike.

Throughout this trip I never had any idea of the plans. This, I would discover, was usually the case when being helped by Poles. If one questioned them they merely countered with such phrases as, 'You will soon see,' 'everything will be all right' and 'all has been thought out'. This was partly due to the Polish love of mystery and intrigue but also to the need for maximum security so that, if we were caught and tortured, we would not give too much away.

After sitting for three hours in this cottage, wondering what the next step would be, I was told by my hostess, who came suddenly and hurriedly into the room, to bring my things immediately into the garden. Standing behind a bush she thrust some Polish money into my hand. The border, she said, was now clear of patrols and lay along the railway line at the end of the road. Her daughter, with 'The Sailor', would lead the way and, when I saw Ronnie, I was to join him. We were to keep fifty yards behind the others. She wished me luck.

Ronnie soon came walking up the road, and I joined him as instructed. We walked along, feeling thoroughly conspicuous in the broad daylight. We reached the railway safely, crossed quickly over and breathed freely once again. The border was behind us and we were no longer in Germany. It was 21 June; Midsummer's Day.

1. Training at Stalbridge shortly before we embarked for Calais.

2. Rifleman Smith, who was my batman during the Calais battle and also became a POW.

3. The Gare Maritime where we disembarked after our crossing in *The Royal Daffodil*, whose sister ship *The Royal Sovereign* is shown here.

4. A Matilda tank covers an orderly withdrawal of the BEF towards the coast.

5. Calais – a tragic scene of carnage.

6. Two improvised barricades, Pont Faidherbe in the foreground, and Rue de Bruxelles, top right, which B Company of the 60th manned. I was wounded in this area.

7. A graphic view of the quay in front of the Gare Maritime after the battle.

8. A German light tank carrying British wounded passes a group of POWs under guard.

9. POWs arriving at Posen. Remarkably my mother recognised me (circled) from this photograph.

10. Colditz Castle. My 'home' for much of the war.

11. The British contingent at Colditz. Spot me if you can!

12. Not my favourite photograph!

13. Flight Lieutenant Jack Best after re-capture.

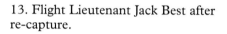

OFLAG VII CH 530

14. Lieutenant Colonel Prawitt, the Colditz Camp Commandant.

15. Hauptmann Hans Püpcke, Colditz Camp Officer 1941-45, was the German whom we POWs liked best.

16. Colonel Reinhold Eggers, the Security Officer at Colditz, who became a friend after the War.

17. A group of British prisoners. Mike Sinclair and I seated to the right.

18. Michael Alexander, a 'Prominente' prisoner.

20. Colonel Willie Tod, the splendid Senior British Officer.

19. Charlie Hopetoun was also a 'Prominente' prisoner.

21. Giles Romilly who, being Churchill's nephew, was a 'Prominente'.

22. Fellow Wykehamist and brother officer, Lieutenant Michael Sinclair who was shot and killed attempting to escape.

23. The German guard he so brilliantly impersonated, *Stabsfeldwebel* Rothenberger known as 'Franz Josef'.

Ausweis Nr. 301 Ausgestellt am 1.7.43.

Kommandantur
Oflag IV C Colditz

Dieser Ausweis berechtigt zum Betreten des deutschen
Teiles des Oflag IV C Colditz

Oberfeldwebel
Dienstgrad   Eigenhändige Unterschrift des Inhabers

Rothenberger   A. B.
Name

Fritz
Vorname   Hauptmann und Adjutant

24. Michael's forged pass.

25. Liberation Day 12 April 1945. An American tank crossing the Colditz
bridge.

26. Diana and I, 24 November 1945.

27. A portrait taken in 1945.

Dr. Reinhold Eggers
7765 Bodman / Bodensee 2. 12. 1973.
Haus Edeltraud

Dear Brigadier Davies-Scourfield,

it is with the utmost pleasure that I express my gratitude for your kindness to write an article for „Colditz Recaptured". It is unique because it deals with the rare event that a P.W. stayed for weeks in midst a hostile country – and his camp authorities even had not noticed his absence! My personal „cigar" from Prawitt had a particularly bitter taste by his threat to punish me for having made false reports! I was much relieved when I had you back, and am still more relieved for counting you among my friends.

Reinhold Eggers

28. Reinhold Egger's letter to me, 1973.

29. Karol Whitehead, who so courageously sheltered me in Warsaw, photographed by me in 1991.

30. Visiting the Klichowskis at their home in Lublin, 1991.

31. A Colditz reunion with Julius Green, myself and Peter Parker standing together. Behind (left to right) Phil Pardoe, Mickey Burn, not recognised and Pat Reid.

8

ON THE BANKS OF
THE VISTULA

We were now in the General Government of Poland, probably the most ruthlessly oppressed area of German-occupied Europe. We had taken another, but only a very small step towards our freedom. There would still be a long way to go.

Ronnie and I continued to follow our two guides for a further 400 or 500 yards, during which time we buried our identity papers as they were not valid in the General Government. Then we came to a pub and were shown into a small room at the back where there were two beds. We gave some of our food to the proprietor, and she prepared it for us. I slept till evening in a sitting position and soon after supper I was again asleep.

Next morning, 'The Sailor' went into the local town to contact friends and make temporary arrangements for Ronnie and me until Mike and Nicholas should join us. He returned at midday having failed to make any contacts and as our room in the pub was no longer available, we began to wonder where we should spend the night. Eventually we found a suitable barn.

We met up with Mike and Nicholas in the morning. They had crossed the border, accompanied by my woman guide, without incident. Now we were all set to rendezvous in a small café. Accordingly we set out in strange procession with Nicholas and 'The Sailor' first, then the woman and finally, each at intervals of fifty yards, Ronnie, Mike and I. In the café we ate some of our provisions while the others, at a different table, discussed future plans. There were a number of people about and we felt very conspicuous. We pretended to be talking quietly together. Every now and then Ronnie, in the interests of reality, let out a loud Tak, which he pronounced incorrectly as Tark, which he had learnt was the Polish for 'Yes', and, as his rendering sounded like the squawk of a raven, this gave me the giggles.

It was in this café that our friends learnt of the German invasion of Russia. This would now make things awkward for us, and I am afraid that the news of Russia now being on our side was not greeted by us with the enthusiasm it deserved as crossing the frontier would now present far greater problems than we had anticipated. 'The Sailor', however, (what would we have done without him?) said he knew of people in Tomaszow who could help us, and the woman agreed to go on ahead of us by train and arrange accommodation in a village near the town. This meant for us a twenty-five mile walk.

While we were still in the café two German airmen came in and ordered drinks. At first they took no notice of our party but later became friendly and inquisitive. 'The Sailor' engaged them in conversation and, in answer to the query, explained that we were Poles looking for work. Why were we three so silent? Because we were tired and had not had much to eat.

At last we set off. Throughout the morning and afternoon we trekked across flat, open, rather dull country, using small roads and lanes which were mostly dust tracks. At first we were cautious, with Ronnie, Mike and me keeping well behind, but later we relaxed the precaution and all walked together. As on previous days it was extremely hot. After losing our way several times we found our village about 5 p.m. and were met by a young man who had been briefly introduced to us in the café and now took us to a small cottage owned by a reasonably prosperous peasant family. We were extremely tired and thirsty and were greeted with a marvellous welcome and a splendid meal. Friends from other cottages came in to see us, and we were made to feel like heroes.

After the meal our splendid woman guide (I never knew her name) said goodbye and set off back to Lodz. Our profuse thanks and good wishes, which were all we could give her, seemed totally inadequate for everything she had done and the risks she had run for us. We washed under a pump and bedded down on hay in a barn at the back of the cottage. There the three of us stayed all next day while Nicholas and 'The Sailor' went into Tomaszow. They returned in the evening, gloomy and depressed. They showed us a German-language newspaper which confirmed the invasion of Russia and claimed that the Russian armies were already in full retreat. I particularly remember the huge headline:

'*Abrechnung mit dem roten Pack*' ('Settlement with the red rabble') with the sub-heading underneath it:

'*Vom Nordcap bis zum Schwarzen Meer*' ('From Northcape to the Black Sea').

'That means that the Finns and Roumanians are in it too,' said Ronnie. Meanwhile no one had been found in Tomaszow to help us, and the local police were said to be already making inquiries about our arrival in the district.

Sitting on a bank beneath some fruit trees in the evening sunlight, we held a council of war. 'The Sailor', who had been our mainstay since leaving Posen, had now lost heart and said that as it was no longer possible to reach Russia, he intended to go back. Nicholas, on the other hand, suggested we should go on to Warsaw, where he had friends and in a large thickly populated city we would be able to hide quite safely until some fresh plan could be made. Finally, it was agreed that Nicholas should go by train to Warsaw and arrange for us to be collected from an address in Chmielna Street which he gave us. We three would set out on foot before dawn and aim to arrive on the third day. 'The Sailor' could return to Posen alone.

Our peasant hosts supplied us liberally with bread, for they told us that food in Warsaw would be scarce.

Punctually at 3 a.m. we were off. It was cold, and the stars were shining brightly. As we made our way through the village all the dogs began to bark. Ronnie said this reminded him of Evans' escape through Bavaria in the First War (he probably said 'the last war) told in his book *The Escaping Club* when he described barking dogs as a special menace. Reaching the main road we saw a signpost which said 'Warsaw 104 Km'. The road continued very straight through agricultural land, switch-backing as it went. To begin with we were moving due east, and presently, as it grew lighter, the sun peeped up over the horizon straight ahead.

We walked steadily on through rather dull sort of country, occasionally getting water from wells beside the road. It was developing into another very hot day, and thirst always seemed a problem. Twice we asked cottagers for water, Mike saying '*woda prosze*' ('Water, please') which was one of the few Polish phrases we had so far learnt, and no one seemed surprised or inquisitive about us. Even the German soldiers, who were continually passing us in trucks, and the police, whom we occasionally saw in the villages, took no notice of us. We spent the first night in the depths of a large wood, but dense clouds of huge hungry and determined mosquitoes prevented any sleep. It was a dark and gloomy wood and, remembering my 'Saki' whose stories I have always loved, I could not help wondering whether there might be wolves around, but Ronnie was adamant that there were none in Poland west of the Vistula.

It was a wretched night, but at least it was not cold, and when dawn eventually came we moved to the edge of the wood and looked down on the main road below us. A long column of horsed cavalry were moving along it towards Warsaw, and for an hour we watched them pass. When the last of them had disappeared we took the road ourselves.

According to the signpost we had covered forty-five kilometres the previous day, and this time we were to do forty. Once again it became very hot, and we were tiring, but we kept plodding. The road remained tediously straight in a north-easterly direction, though the country itself was now rolling and therefore a bit more interesting. At one cottage, where we asked for water, a large dog was set on us, and Mike was bitten in the leg. Otherwise we encountered nothing but friendliness. This time we had some difficulty in finding a suitable place for the night, as the country was so open, and eventually we had to walk some two miles back to a wood which we had passed. Then, probably because we were tired, we had a tremendous argument about water. Ronnie wanted to drink before eating: he said his mouth was far too dry to swallow any food. I said we should eat first, because we would be at our most thirsty after food. Mike said he was not prepared to go and ask for water twice. So we ate first and then went to a cottage, but Ronnie made an awful fuss and chewed his bread very slowly and in dead silence. When we finally got settled into the wood the mosquitoes attacked again, and this time so viciously that Mike, himself by now bad-tempered, insisted we move into the open. So off we trudged again and found a small hollow in the middle of some heathland and lay down. The mosquitoes soon discovered our new lair, and again we had no sleep. I put my thick tweed jacket right over my head but they bit me through it nevertheless. Although Ronnie and I were able to lie down and so at least get some rest, Mike who was ginger haired and red skinned (while Ronnie and I were both dark) suffered greatly and stood miserably all night, waving his arms violently about. I smile at the memory, but it was not much fun at the time.

We were now only twenty-five kilometres from Warsaw. As usual we moved off soon after dawn and, before long, had reached the outer suburbs. Frogs, I remember, were croaking everywhere and, as we walked and walked and walked, the suburbs seemed endless. I have always been a good walker, and I fared better than Ronnie and much better than Mike whose weary steps got slower and slower. It was quite evident we were entering a great city; in the distance tower and tower stood up against the morning sky. On we went: we did not dare to stop, as so many people were walking about. We were tired and thirsty, and my two companions became rather short-tempered. I on the other hand remained quite cheerful and, though not normally a great optimist, began to feel that all was going rather well and that our arrival in Warsaw was another step, this time a big and successful one, on our road to freedom. My experiences as a prisoner of war already seemed far behind.

We had discussed how best we could find Chmielna Street in the middle of this concrete jungle and decided we should take a horse and cab (a 'droszka') which was the equivalent in Warsaw to a taxi and, as soon as we had got well into the town, this is what we did.We found our droszka without difficulty, gave the cabby our destination as 'this end of Chmielna Street', and breathed sighs of relief when he seemed to understand Mike's German and find the instructions entirely adequate and normal. Had we but known it we could almost certainly have announced, 'We are three British officers on the run, please take us to Chmielna Street,' and he would have been delighted to help us on our way, but we were being very cautious and rightly so. We had been warned that, while no Pole would dream of giving us away, there were in Poland plenty of 'Volksdeutsche' (Poles of German origin) who could not be trusted at all.

Thus we rumbled into Poland's capital, thankful to be sitting and resting our weary legs and feet. Indeed it was rather fun, jogging along and seeing the sights. Ruins from the 1939 siege and bombing were very much in evidence, and we noticed German anti-aircraft posts on some of the higher buildings, mounted no doubt against possible Russian air attacks. We wondered how the battles were going on the new eastern front. Soon we were passing the main railway station and turning into Chmielna Street at last.

We got off, paid the cabby and walked up the street to examine the number which Nicholas had given us. We had been told it was a sweet shop but in fact it turned out to be a small café: unfortunately, as it was only 7 a.m., we had two hours to wait before it opened and, not knowing about street checks and having no identity papers, we felt somewhat vulnerable. However, there was nothing for it but to walk about the streets until 9 a.m. when we returned promptly to our rendezvous, by this time once again tired and thirsty.

It may seem strange that we should have been dogged by thirst and weariness, but I imagine we were paying the penalty for our year of deprivation. A photograph taken by the Germans at Laufen makes me look almost like the victim of a concentration camp (see plate section), and even now we were by no means all that fit. As for the thirst, the days had been extremely hot and our clothes were thick and heavy.

Anyhow, we decided that Mike, being the linguist, should go in the café and find out the form, while Ronnie and I paraded up and down outside. We wondered what we should do if the contact failed us and Ronnie, obviously worried, became extremely crotchety and kept muttering, 'What on earth is Mike doing?' 'Why doesn't he come out?' 'What's going on?' and such like. Thus we staggered up and down, at one moment gazing longingly into a shop window at several basketfuls of cherries. There were lots of people bustling about, but no one seemed to notice us.

At last Mike emerged.

'I think it's all right,' he said, 'but I've still got some explaining to do: there are two women in there, and they are a bit suspicious. You had better stay out there while I talk with them further.' Ronnie and I exchanged despairing glances: we really felt we had to sit down.

Finally, after what seemed like an age, Mike reappeared. 'We can come in,' he said, 'but we weren't expected till this afternoon, and they are trying to get in touch with Nicholas. If they can't contact him we'll just have to walk about till he comes: they won't let us wait in the café indefinitely.'

'I won't walk about any more for anybody,' said Ronnie. We entered the shop.

There was a counter on the right and three small tables on the left, unoccupied. We sat down at the one furthest from the door and Mike ordered a large bottle of raspberry cordial. There was a woman behind the counter, and while she was fetching our cordial Mike whispered, 'This one doesn't know who we are; it's her assistant who was expecting us and who is now trying to contact Nicholas.' The woman brought our drink and began talking German.

'Who are your friends?' she asked, 'and what language do they speak?' Mike replied, 'They are Slovaks and only know a few words of German.'

It was only later that we learnt how similar are most Slav languages, and it would have been safer to say we were Hungarians or Scandinavians. The woman did not seem very satisfied with Mike's explanation but nevertheless asked no more questions. We drank our cordial greedily and, using some filthy tobacco which Mike had obtained somewhere, rolled some cigarettes. It was wonderful to be sitting in a chair.

The café remained empty for some time, and then a man and woman both about thirty-five years of age, came in. They spoke to the woman behind the counter, and the other woman appeared from the back premises and joined in the conversation. Presently the newcomers came over to us.

'Do not be afraid,' said the man in German, and I noticed he had some gold teeth. 'We are friends of Nicholas and were expecting you this afternoon. You are to come back with us now to our flat.'

We left the shop, walked through the streets for some minutes and then boarded a tram; the man with gold teeth paying our fares. The ride took about ten minutes; then we got off and entered a ground floor flat. I noticed many uniformed Germans in the street. The flat was quite spacious and accommodated not only 'Goldtooth' and his wife but also his mother and two sisters.

We had a wonderful reception. We were given a much needed bath (the first real one we had had for over a year) and an excellent meal. We were then shown into a room with two sofas, given an enormous jug of fresh fruit juice and told to have a good sleep. Our shirts, underclothes and socks were removed for washing and mending and new ones provided. We slept soundly till the evening, Ronnie and I on one couch and Mike on the other. At 7 p.m. we were woken to have an excellent supper, after which we talked with our hosts in German. They told us we should find it very difficult to leave Poland, as Hungary and all the Balkan states were now hostile territory, and the front in Russia was already moving east. We would be comparatively safe in Warsaw, they said, for a large city was the best possible hiding place. We asked what they suggested we should do, as we did not wish to stay in Warsaw, however safe and comfortable, but rather to push on and reach neutral territory with the least possible delay. 'Goldtooth' replied that he was getting in touch with an organization which helped escaped British prisoners, and its people would know how to advise us.

It was at this point that I began to realize what a difficult position we were in. From now on, however much we might want to get on, and however much risk we might ourselves feel willing to take in order to proceed towards our objective, we now had to think very carefully about all those Poles who had helped us and would be helping us in the future: our recapture might jeopardize their safety, particularly if we were tortured for information about them. It behoved us therefore to listen carefully to their advice and ensure we did nothing to endanger them unnecessarily. In a sense, because of our obligation to all our new-found friends, we would no longer be completely free agents.

We slept like logs the whole night, except for a few moments when the air-raid sirens went. Nicholas arrived after breakfast, which consisted of ersatz coffee and unlimited bread and jam, and he told us that a fat old lady would arrive during the morning and take us away.

Sure enough, around midday, the old lady arrived, accompanied by a younger woman. The former, whom we came to know as 'Mrs M' spoke perfect English but with a noticeable foreign accent.

Mrs M was in fact British to the core. She had originally been governess to a branch of the Austrian royal family and married a Polish civil servant called Markowski. After the First War they had left Austria and settled in Warsaw, where she taught English to influential families. When Germany invaded Poland she decided to stay in the country ('A British woman does not like to run away', she told me) and was consequently held and questioned by the Germans for several days, before being released as a harmless old lady. But she was far from being harmless and quickly formed an effective organization for helping escaped British prisoners of war.

With Mrs M and her companion we took another journey by tram, having said a fond farewell to the family whom I shall always remember for their great kindness and courage. Now we entered a kind of office and through to a small room at the back where Mrs M lived with her husband. Mr M to whom we were now introduced, was older than his wife and, though kind and friendly, rather a pathetic figure, whom his wife treated with ill-disguised contempt. However, she called him 'Daddy' with a rather grudging show of affection.

The little room to which Mrs M took us was really her head-quarters. 'Daddy' looked after it and lived there, but she usually slept elsewhere. After an excellent lunch, prepared by 'Daddy', we held a council of war. Mrs M said the situation was difficult and we might have to be patient. Things had been easier when Hungary had been neutral, and she had managed to help several prisoners to get there. Among them had been one of our battalion riflemen, by name of Hosington, who eventually reached Egypt to join our 1st Battalion and was awarded the DCM. She also had helped some go to Russia, but the situation on the Eastern Front now ruled that option out, and Hungary's entry into the war made a southwards journey difficult: but she had a lot of Polish connections and was confident some scheme could be devised. In the meantime we could stay, she said, with her Polish friends, changing our 'billets' every few days for reasons of security.

While we were talking a very smart woman came in and brought with her a British corporal who had recently escaped from a working party. He was added to Mrs M's list: she was already looking after about five 'Tommies' as she always called them. After these two had gone a man of about fifty came in and introduced himself as Mr Olszewski: we came to know him as 'Puffy' on account of his promi-nent cheeks. He had been Reuters' correspondent in Warsaw – or maybe it was Associated Press – was a great friend of Mrs M and had formed with her this self-appointed organization to help escaping British prisoners of war. He spoke perfect English and was one of the most charming and delightful people I have ever met: just as Mrs M was to become a mother to us while we were in Warsaw, so 'Puffy' was as a father, and I shall never forget all that he so bravely did for us. Thus began our strange sojourn in Poland's capital, temporary guests of those many brave and generous people who willingly accepted all the risks involved to help us on our way, so that we could continue the fight against the Germans. Quite by chance at my prep school concert, at the end of my last term I sang a solo, the first verse being 'In Poland stands an inn, in Poland stands an inn, in Poland stands a Polish inn and there the people all go in, for nothing all their food they win, they do not pay a pin.' Appropriate and in my case prophetic.

Strangely enough life became for us at this time comparatively uneventful. Mrs M and Puffy provided reasonably smart clothing and other necessities for us, and we were billeted separately in different houses and flats. Conditions naturally varied, but food was entirely adequate, sometimes very good, sometimes rather basic. After five or six days with one family someone would call for us and take us elsewhere. I stayed in large flats, small flats, villas, detached houses and so on. The people were charming, friendly and, despite the danger of sheltering us, delighted to have us, or so they made us feel. Most people we met spoke either French, German or English, so that conversation was not difficult. I found the Polish language almost impossible, but my German became, with plenty of practice, rather good. Sometimes we were taken out to cafes and restaurants, but for the most part we stayed indoors reading and playing patience – the latter a favourite Polish pastime.

On the surface much of life in Warsaw seemed fairly normal. Germans were everywhere, of course. Police, soldiers, airmen and contingents of SS could be seen on every street, but they appeared to interfere little with Polish life except for anything suspected of being against German interests. Most of the visible and normal policing was carried out by the 'Polish' police: these men, who wore the ordinary Polish police uniform, consisted mainly of ethnic Germans (the hated 'Volksdeutsche'), Ukrainians and White Russians, but there were some Poles too; these latter performed valuable work as spies for the 'Resistance,' finding out and passing on information on police intentions, issuing warnings and taking messages in and out of prisons. One day, for example, a Polish policeman called on Mrs M and advised her to move some Tommies to another district, as they had been too long in one place and too many people knew about them.

Although there was at this time no open resistance, apart from an occasional piece of sabotage and at least one political assassination, people were continually being arrested for subversive activity. If they were lucky they were shot, although they might first have been interrogated under torture: if they were unlucky they would be preserved for some foul concentration camp, probably Auschwitz. This grisly place, not far from Cracow, had not yet achieved its international reputation for horror, and at this time no one really knew exactly what went on there. I met quite a number of people who had relatives there, and I was told that when an inmate died or was killed the family was sent a parcel containing his or her shoes, the only intimation they received. Just occasionally a prisoner would be released, sometimes through bribery at high level on the part of well-placed friends, but they seldom spoke of their experience.

Mass arrests in the street were not uncommon, though I personally never saw one, mainly because the Resistance usually received tip-offs and passed them on to us. Reasons for such round-ups were various – reprisal, pure terrorism, labour requirements and so on – and the method simple: lorries full of police and troops would suddenly appear from different directions and cordon off the selected area. Everyone in that area would then be rounded up and whoever they wanted would be carted off, sometimes the young men, sometimes young girls, sometimes the whole lot. Only those who could produce papers, proving that they worked in some way for the Germans, would be spared. One heard continual tales of German inhumanity in their handling of the Poles, like mothers being forcibly parted from their children, men savagely beaten and many others. At all events no Pole could ever feel safe or secure or able to rely on any law to protect him from the whims of his conquerors.

The food situation in Warsaw was surprisingly satisfactory for those who had cash. Food shops and restaurants were well supplied. For the poor, however, (and there were plenty of them around) these were hungry days. The official rations, which could be bought at a reasonable price, were totally inadequate, and the Germans excused this state of affairs by explaining that Poles required less to eat than Germans. I was later to hear the same theory expounded, but then it concerned horses rather than humans, as I shall recount in due course. Consequently the streets were full of pathetic-looking beggars. Money, however, could buy almost anything, and there was plenty to be bought – eggs, meat, fresh vegetables, fruit of most kinds (including strawberries, raspberries and cherries), white bread and sugar. Chocolate, milk, tea and coffee, on the other hand, were virtually unobtainable.

The ghetto was situated near the centre of the city, surrounded by a high wall and guarded by detachments of police. It was appallingly overcrowded and the sanitary arrangements were ghastly. Large numbers of the Jews were continually being moved to other parts of Poland, many no doubt to the gas chambers of Auschwitz or Treblinka, while many other were murdered by the SS inside the

93

ghetto itself. I lived for a few days near the ghetto and could hear the rattles of machine guns in the night. I was also told many horror stories about what went on behind the ghetto wall. Movement in and out, unless specially authorized, was absolutely forbidden. One could go through by tram but any attempt to board or leave the tram during transit was prevented by the use or threat of firearms. I went through once in this way and noticed with interest that Jewish police in uniform and appointed by the Germans, were on the beat, while the German police patrolled in pairs. Every Jew was compelled to wear the Star of David.

For the Poles the possession of a wireless set, whether in working order or not, was strictly forbidden under threat of death or concentration camp, yet they were well supplied with news. Legal news consisted of street loudspeakers, an official Polish language newspaper and the usual German papers. At the same time there was considerable traffic in 'illegal news' as many Poles had hidden wireless sets, and they and their friends would listen regularly to BBC broadcasts and then pass on the news by word of mouth. There were several secret newspapers, too, which printed the BBC news and sold many hundreds of copies daily. I was later to work on one of these newspapers. Soon after our arrival, Mrs M took Mike and me to listen at a friend's flat, and I shall never forget my excitement at hearing again, after so long, the chimes of Big Ben: they sent out, somehow, a message of encouragement and hope and proof that 'home' really did exist.

The morale of the Poles, rich and poor alike, was, considering the circumstances, amazingly high. Collaboration with the Germans was practically unheard of among the Poles. That was left to the *Volksdeutsche*, Ukrainians and White Russians. All classes were united in a determination that resistance to the Germans, either active or passive, must continue, and that they owed this not only to their own national future but also to their ally, England: no persecution, however cruel and intense, could shake their resolve, and their hatred of the Germans was fanatical. One and all looked for salvation, not to the Russians whom they distrusted and feared as a traditional foe, but to the British and Churchill as their particular friend. Caught geographically between two national enemies the Poles were too proud and haughty to play off one against the other, preferring to believe in the ultimate triumph of their cause and the eventual rebirth of a Poland more powerful and prosperous than before.

Since our arrival life had been comfortable and comparatively secure, and the friendship and hospitality showered on us by the Poles were wonderful indeed. Yet it was in many respects a lonely and boring existence and I hardly ever saw Mike or Ronnie, and much of my time at first was spent in sitting, reading and thinking. Gradually some normality returned. For example I remember going for walks and occasionally to church or the cinema. I believe my admiration in later life of the Roman Catholic Church, though without danger of desertion from my own, began here, for I shunned Protestant churches which tended to be full of Germans. In the big Catholic churches (and I remember especially The Church of the Three Crosses) it was easier to get lost in the crowd. Too much skulking in people's houses or flats could attract the attention of inquisitive house porters, and it was safer to walk about and lead as natural a life as possible. Germans in any case seldom spoke to me in the street and, if they did, I knew enough German now to answer quite fluently and arouse no suspicions.

Mrs M and Puffy had in fact been making great efforts to evolve a reasonable plan for our further travels. They had useful contacts with a number of underground organizations, both official and unofficial, but for some time no progress was made. The alternatives were Sweden, via a Baltic port and neutral ship; Turkey via the Balkans; Switzerland via Germany; or Yugoslav guerrillas; and Russia. I preferred the idea of Sweden, but for some reason our Polish friends strongly discouraged it, perhaps because the Resistance used that route and did not want it compromised. All routes in fact had drawbacks, particularly as good identity documents and travel permits were difficult to come by. We did make contact with a Polish major who sent word to Mrs M that he could take us through the German lines in Russia. Mrs M arranged for him to come and discuss the project with us, but he sent a friend instead. This chap, however, would answer no questions about the major, nor would he discuss the plan at all, and of the mysterious major we heard nothing more.

It may reasonably be wondered at this stage why, having received food, clothing and money, we did not set off on our own and try our luck at getting somewhere. After all, we had not much to lose. If we were caught there was a good chance we would merely be sent back to a prison camp from where we could probably escape again. The longer we stayed in Warsaw, the greater would be our relatives' suspense and the danger to our Polish friends. Furthermore, if we were recaught after a prolonged period (and it was already beginning to be long) the chance of being tortured to disclose our helpers, and the likelihood of us succumbing to intolerable pressure and spilling the beans, would increase. Why did we hesitate? Our chief reason was that the Poles had already done and risked so much for us, and we had made such efforts to get so far, that we felt it would be stupid in the extreme to waste all this to go off into the blue without proper plans and preparation and with little chance of success, when by waiting just a little longer some really good plans might be laid. In fact, with hindsight, I think we were wrong, but it was certainly the advice of all our Polish friends that there was no hurry. They said something could certainly be fixed if only we were patient. They stressed that good personal documents, which had not been obtained for us, were in any case essential before we moved on. Another factor was the strange and unfamiliar circumstances in which we found ourselves and the atmosphere of intrigue, resistance and espionage. We came to believe that some wonderful scheme would eventually be worked out which would speed us effectively on our way home, if only we could wait a little longer.

Life in Warsaw that summer should really have been quite enjoyable. After all we had the best of food and shelter; we made numerous friends; and Mrs M and Puffy looked after us as though we were their children. We were always impatient, however, to continue our journey and we were becoming increasingly anxious about the dangers to which our presence exposed our Polish friends and made us wonder whether it was all worthwhile. For example, supposing the police had happened to search a house or flat where I was staying, and I had been discovered, then the whole family, children included, would have been arrested and either executed or sent to some horror camp. First, though, they would be interrogated to find out how it had come about that I was with them. Under torture some of them might well break down, then names would be divulged, further arrests made, more torture applied, information extracted, until many of those who had had anything to do with us would have been carted off by the Gestapo and never heard of again. This was a heavy burden of responsibility for anyone to bear, and the months we spent in Warsaw were consequently months of considerable strain and anxiety. To be honest, we had got ourselves into an extremely tricky situation.

One day, in the middle of August I received a message bidding me to come to a certain address in order to discuss a proposal for the next stage of our journey. The address given was that of a well-to-do young couple whose large flat was where Mike and I had spent our first five days. It also served as a kind of second home for Mrs M. On my arrival I had a short discussion with Mrs M, Ronnie and Mike and heard about the plan. A woman, well known to Mrs M and Puffy, had made arrangements for four Polish officers to go to Budapest en route for Turkey and a Polish organization in Hungary would be arranging the next stage of their journey. They would go by train to Cracow where a guide would meet them and take them through the mountains into Slovakia. There they would be met by a car and be driven south to the vicinity of the Hungarian frontier. They would be taken across by a guide and then would have to make their way by train to Budapest, where friends would meet them. They had room in their party for an additional passenger and had originally agreed to take one British officer with them. Puffy had pressed them strongly to take the three of us. Eventually a compromise had been reached; they would take two British officers, and one of the Poles would stand down and go the following month in a second party which could include another British officer. Ronnie, being the most senior of us would obviously go, and I knew he would like to have Mike with him as interpreter, so I, the most junior of us, readily though regretfully agreed to wait behind.

Mrs M then told us that the woman organizer would be arriving any moment, bringing with her a representative of the Underground and the Poles who were making the journey.

'While we are waiting,' said Mrs M, 'You might like to chat with some of the Tommies. There are six in the next room who have come to get identity papers.'

After we had talked together for about twenty minutes, Mrs M sent the soldiers away. These were men who had escaped off working parties and made their several ways to Warsaw, finally to come under Mrs M's care. Now they were waiting hopefully, like us, for a good opportunity to leave the country.

The party we were expecting arrived piecemeal, and soon we were all in deep discussion. Mike rightly insisted on being told every detail (a thing I found Poles hated doing) and the conference took rather a long time. It was finally decided that the first party should leave at the end of August and the second party sometime in September, depending on the guide.

A few days later four more British officers arrived from Posen. When the camp had been closed down they stayed behind in a special hide-out which they had elaborately constructed. They had then contacted 'the Doctor' in much the same way that we had, but their journey took longer to arrange. They had spent ten weeks shut up together in that little room where we had been and eventually came to Warsaw by train. They had had no walk, like we had, to get fit and regain some colour and consequently looked awful – thin, haggard and pale.

At the end of the month Ronnie and Mike departed on their long and intricate journey. I felt rather lonely after they had gone. Summer was nearly over. The Polish winter was on the way.

9

OPPORTUNITY KNOCKS
AT LAST

For the next few months I was destined to remain in Warsaw, a guest of the Polish people and beneath the shadow of their German conquerors. They looked after me at the greatest possible risk to themselves.

I was indeed a stranger whom they took in. I was naked and they clothed me, I was hungry and they gave me food, I was lonely and they brought me friendship.

Even today, nearly half a century later, having read so many accounts of 'resistance' in those countries occupied by the Germans, I still remain astounded that so many Poles, ordinary men and women, were prepared, even eager, to risk their lives, and those of their families and friends, to help and succour escaping British prisoners. To the Poles it was their patriotic duty to do so, and that, as far as they were concerned, was that. Now, looking back, I doubt whether we were justified in allowing such risks to be taken on our behalf, but at the time it all seemed part of the circumstances of war. Yet I was anxious to move on as soon as possible, as soon (that is) as a sensible plan could be made, and thus endanger these splendid people for a minimum of time.

On 3 September, the second anniversary of Britain's entry into the war, some Poles gave a dinner in honour of the British officers resident in Warsaw. Our host was supposed to remain anonymous, but I was given to understand that he was the political head of the underground resistance and one of the delegates of the Polish Government in London. He had been, I was told, a member of one of Marshal

Pilsudski's pre-war cabinets and was, allegedly, a brother of Puffy, though he looked quite different, being tall and fair.

This dinner party was a strange moment in my wartime saga. Mrs M took me to the delegate's flat. It was immediately above a German office of some kind, and we had to pass a couple of German sentries as we climbed the stairs. Present at the dinner were Kit Silverwood Cope, Kenneth Sutherland and Peter Winton (all from Posen). Crawford was apparently not present; the delegate with his wife and sister; Puffy and another resistance member; Mrs M and myself.

It was a formal dinner, happily everyone spoke English, and a good deal of vodka was drunk, including toasts to England and Mr Churchill, to Poland, General Sikorski and to us. At the end of the meal our host stood up and made a long speech about the war and the friendship between the two countries. He spoke of Poland's terrible anxiety during the delay between the German invasion and the declaration of war by Britain and France; and finally he welcomed us as 'The Representatives of the British Army in Poland' to the hospitality of Warsaw. After another long peroration by one of the other Poles there was a bit of a pause. Mrs M nudged me and said I should reply, so I rose to the occasion, aided by my Welsh blood, now liberally laced with vodka, finally ending on a high note, which ran something like this:

'I hope, and indeed I feel confident, that Poland will one day share with us the fruits of victory, just as today she bears with us the bitterness of the struggle.' What hideous irony! Yet how could I foresee that in the hour of final victory Poland, for all her loyalty, courage and endurance, would be thrown to the wolves.

After dinner we dispersed quickly in order to beat the curfew, and I was taken to live with a friend of Puffy, called Mr R. He was an active resistance worker living in a modern two-roomed flat at the top of a large building near Napoleon Square, and Warsaw's only skyscraper which had housed the offices of the Prudential Assurance Company.

Now began the most enjoyable part of my stay in Warsaw. I spent each night in an empty flat near Mr R's, but in another building, and every morning at 9 a.m. I went up to Mr R's flat for breakfast (we always had eggs) and stayed there while Mr R went out to work. I passed the time quite pleasantly, listening to the wireless (keeping the sound very quiet), reading and studying to improve my German. Late in the afternoon Mr R would return and take me out for a delayed lunch to the best black-market restaurant in town, the Frigata, for a meal. The food was excellent and very expensive, the place was always full of high-ranking German officers, and I was told that the waitresses were all countesses at least. Mr R and I spoke little on these outings (German being our only common language) and, as camouflage, I usually buried myself in a Russian-language newspaper produced for the White Russian community. But I did not deceive the countesses. One of these, meeting a friend of Mrs M at a vodka party, said to her, 'Isn't it killing, my dear? Every day one of the British officers comes to the Frigata and pretends to be a White Russian. One day, when he comes in we are going to ask the orchestra to play 'God save the King.' The following morning I received orders to eat elsewhere.

While waiting in Mr R's flat I used to make resumés of the BBC news bulletins and hand them to Puffy when he came to see me, which was most evenings. All the time I was expecting news of Ronnie's and Mike's arrival in Budapest and of my own chance of following after them. For some time, however, we heard nothing of the guide, then he was ill, and finally he declined to make another trip. Puffy then contacted a priest, who agreed to take two of us British to Budapest, and for some days hopes ran high, but he too declined at the last minute. However, we now knew that Ronnie and Mike had safely completed the first lap of their journey.

The weeks rolled by, and no further instructions came. My frustration grew and with it anxiety for all my Polish friends who sheltered me at such appalling risk. Yet if I were just to set out into the blue without proper plans and preparation I would probably be caught and my capture be followed by pressure, which could become intolerable, to disclose all sources of my help and shelter. Dark and dangerous days indeed! Nor did the war news bring any consolation. The Germans had bundled us out of Greece and Crete and overrun the Balkans, while in North Africa, General Rommel had arrived, counter-attacked and driven us right back to Egypt.

One day, as I crossed the yard on my way to breakfast with Mr R, I noticed two German Police officers standing near the entrance to the building. This barely concerned me, as one saw German policemen everywhere, and I continued upstairs and gave my usual knock on the door of the flat. Mr R almost flung the door open and I remember his face was covered with shaving soap and he gave me a signal with his hand which clearly meant 'Get away as quickly as possible.' As I turned to go, the two police officers came round the corner of the corridor. Very obviously and deliberately I bent down and studied the name on the flat door, then walked on and did the same thing outside the flat next door and finally walked quickly, but not too hurriedly, down the passage away from the policemen, disappeared down the backstairs and made my way to Mrs M to report what had occurred.

Meanwhile Mr R was having a harassing morning.

A few minutes before I was due to arrive for breakfast the hall porter had phoned to say that the two German police officers had asked about the owner of his flat and were on the way up. This thoroughly alarmed him, as he knew I might arrive at any moment, and he was therefore relieved when I got there first, even by so narrow a squeak. A few seconds after my departure there was a loud knock on his door, 'Police, open up.'

He had already stuffed his wireless into a cupboard and covered it up and had also hidden his two revolvers away in a drawer. He opened the door, half expecting the Gestapo to rush in, beat him up, turn the flat upside down and then carry him off. Instead, one of the officers saluted politely and said. 'Good morning. We wish to wait in your flat as we are expecting someone.'

He naturally thought it was me they were probably after, but this could not have been so, otherwise they would have arrested me in the passage. They spent an hour in the sitting room, within a few feet of the wireless and revolvers, while Mr R sat anxiously at his desk in the next room. Suddenly the doorbell rang and he went to answer it, only to be told (still quite politely), 'This will probably be for us; please go back to your room.' He heard the door being opened, and there followed a whispered conversation, but he could not hear what was said. Then they told him, 'I am sorry if we have inconvenienced you: there has evidently been some mistake. Good day.' This was a strange incident, and we never discovered what it was all about.

Mrs M meanwhile found me alternative accommodation, and I went to live with an elderly couple in their small but very comfortable flat. One evening I was returning there after dark from some meeting or discussion when I met in the street a young ex-officer Pole with whom I had been in contact. He told me with great excitement that he had just heard the news, the British had recaptured Benghazi and were sweeping on. We must celebrate, he said, and took me off to his flat and poured me out a vodka with some raspberry cordial added. I gulped it down in true Polish fashion, not realizing that it was the double-strength vodka known as *98 prozent* and took several moments to recover. I managed to decline a second glass as curfew time was approaching, but I must say, what with the vodka and the thought of the British victory in the desert, I went on my way with a very jaunty step.

The meeting I had come from had in fact been with Puffy, at which I had agreed he should approach London through Polish Underground Army channels, inform the Polish Government there the names of those of us in his and Mrs M's care, and ask for advice and, if possible, some instructions. Personally I never thought anything would be likely to come of it, but it was all that Puffy could think of at the time, and it seemed better than doing nothing.

A few days later a young member of the Home Army appeared in the flat, quite late in the evening, and said I was to leave at once and go with him to another address. We travelled together by tram across the city and over the Vistula to a suburb of Warsaw called Saska Kepa (pronounced Kempa). Imagine my surprise when I was greeted at the door of a flat in broad American, 'Say, welcome.' My new hosts were American Poles who had come to live in the new Poland after 1920, unwisely as it turned out, leaving the haven of the USA. The Kotyllas were a delightful couple, and I enjoyed being with them enormously. Early winter had arrived, bringing with it fine clear days with a distinct bite in the air, but entirely lacking the severity which was to come later. It was lovely to walk along by the river in the evenings and see the buildings of the city on the far bank shining in the sunlight. Warsaw could look very beautiful even in those wholly tragic days.

Before very long I was moved again. Living now here, now there, one had a very varied diet. Just occasionally it was good or better than one could wish for – eggs, tea and coffee, butter, vegetables of all sorts, white bread and plenty of meat. More usually one subsisted mainly on coarse bread, soup and potatoes. But one was never hungry, and Mrs M could always knock up a good meal from her hide-out which we called 'The Hole'. She could also provide good medical attention when necessary through contact with 'safe' doctors and dentists prepared to take the risk of attending to escaping prisoners of war. Throughout the autumn and winter there was typhus going around, and there was no vaccine available against it. Kit Silverwood Cope actually caught the disease. He was living in the flat of an elderly woman doctor and her daughter, and they nobly insisted he should stay. This was a brave and generous decision. First it was a capital offence to keep a typhus case in one's house without reporting it and secondly, it meant keeping an escaped prisoner permanently in the flat, with distinct possibility of his dying. Thirdly, there was the risk of infection. Mrs M procured the service of a good doctor for Kit, as well as a male nurse and all the necessary medicines. She even sat with him in his delirium, and it was touch and go, but he eventually pulled through. By Christmas Kit, though weak and emaciated, was up and walking about.

Anyone imagining me having a splendid time with lovely Polish girls would be disappointed. I felt any attachments or involvement of that kind might have disastrous consequences. I did however become quite fond of one very pretty girl who came, I believe, from rather a smart family. I even took her flowers when she was ill in bed! If she survived the war I am sure she will have made some lucky man a charming and attractive wife.

In November (I think it was) I had another spell with Mr R. I must have been with him for nearly three weeks before once again leaving in a hurry. One morning I went up as usual to breakfast in his flat and rang the bell. He opened the door and said, 'You must leave the building immediately and don't come back. Don't even stop to collect your things from your flat. Just go. I'll send everything along afterwards.'

I wasted no time but went. Mrs M rose as usual to the occasion and found me another billet. What had happened was this. The previous night police had raided one of the other flats in the building – it belonged to a *Volksdeutsche* – and found a lot of black market goods. They had left in the morning and told the porter that they would return and search the whole building. The porter had warned Mr R of this, adding that he thought 'his young friend' would like to be elsewhere when this happened, hence my instructions to make myself scarce. Actually the big search never took place.

Now it was real winter, and the outlook for me, as for the whole Polish nation, was looking bleak. It was at this time I was informed that a message had been received from London saying that the Polish military attaché in Berne had been instructed to assist the British in Warsaw to reach Switzerland. Shortly afterwards we had a message from the attaché saying he could provide no active help, but he sent some information about the frontier. This hardly advanced our cause, but it confirmed my own view that Switzerland was probably the best bet. Meanwhile Christmas was approaching and the winter weather made Warsaw more beautiful than ever. Snow lay thick in all the streets, and the 'droshkies' gave place to horse drawn sleighs with tinkling bells. People wore earpads against the intense cold, and picturesque fur caps began to make their appearance. Even the Vistula was frozen. To many of the Polish people the cold brought great suffering, for fuel was scarce and food becoming extremely expensive. The German authorities, in order to save electricity, would cut off the supply to whole areas at a time.

The General Government was headed by Dr Frank who was subsequently condemned to death at the Nuremberg trial and hanged. Frank ruled the residue of what had once been Poland entirely in the interests of Germany while the Polish people received no consideration whatever, and opposition of any kind was savagely repressed. One was continually hearing of new arrests, some en masse in the streets for deportation to Germany as forced labour, some individuals, often ending up in Auschwitz. The Resistance, however, was, as far as I could see, almost entirely passive; the policy being to lie low and prepare. I was able, however, to become a little less passive myself and I became responsible for all the British escapees within Mrs M's sphere of influence. This brought me into closer contact with some of the Underground Command which was beginning to take a great interest in us and actually issued me with money to distribute. This was intended as pocket money to provide cigarettes and, when necessary, to pay for our keep. One of the soldiers, I remember, used to pay his own way by buying cigarette tobacco, making it up into cigarettes and selling them in the street (often to German soldiers) at a profit. Help in getting us out of the country onto neutral territory was also promised and someone I knew as 'Colonel N' appointed two special agents to liaise with Puffy for this purpose.

There was of course great excitement when the United States came into the war, and many Poles began to believe that the end of their tribulations was in sight until early Japanese successes quickly dispelled this optimism. Nevertheless morale was given a boost a few days later, when Russian planes came over in daylight and dropped some bombs. Everyone rushed out into the streets to have a look, and, as the bombs were said to have hit the main railway station, we all made off in that direction and came to a small square just behind it. The streets here were inches thick in glass, houses were wrecked and horses lying dead. Police were everywhere. Now and then a closed ambulance would drive off, to the cheers of the Polish crowd.

'Why are they cheering?' I asked the young man who had brought me.

'They are cheering at the thought of all the dead and mutilated Germans', replied my friend.

'But haven't Poles been killed as well?' I asked again.

'Oh yes,' he said, 'but as long as some Germans have been killed it is all worthwhile.'

Now Christmas was upon us and our hosts and friends did their best to give us a good time. Puffy and his wife, who I think was French, entertained three of us to a traditional Polish Christmas Eve supper which began at 5.30 p.m. We started with vodka, in which we drank each others' healths, and ate the traditional wafer: we then passed on through the soup, two fish courses and the sauerkraut, washed down with champagne. 'Eat, drink and be merry, for tomorrow. . .' The party had to break up early because of the curfew, and off we went to our different flats. It was a bitterly cold night, and owing to the deep and frost-hardened snow one could see right down the great *Ulica Marszalkowska* (Marshall Street) with the twinkling tram lights and the last sledges hurrying home. England seemed very far away.

On Christmas morning my hosts took me to the red brick Roman Catholic Church which dominated the Radom road, and, when a woman soloist sang a hymn to the tune of 'Oh come, all ye faithful', God seemed suddenly close at hand, and I thought of the church at home and those who must be anxiously wondering what had become of me.

In contrast to the supper, lunch with Mrs M was traditionally British, with roast goose and plum pudding, though plenty of vodka too. We spent the afternoon in total repletion and then struggled bravely with tea, the main part of which was a gigantic 'tort'. Kenneth Sutherland did best of all doing full justice to Puffy's supper. He then went to the family where he was staying and ate another enormous meal lasting from midnight to 4 a.m., was called at midday Christmas Day with porridge and eggs and bacon and followed this up with Mrs M's lunch and tea! The black market was in top gear!

Immediately after Christmas I found myself a kind of job. One of the secret newspapers in circulation was organized by a man and a woman, aided by an escaped British airman. The latter was not part of Mrs M's organization and indeed had no intention of leaving Warsaw. With his technical ability, particularly in regard to wireless, he felt he could be of more use staying put. Unfortunately he did not find the Poles easy to work with, which impaired his usefulness, but he was brave and enthusiastic and was always carrying strange parcels containing high explosive, parts of wireless sets and even, on one occasion, a transmitter.

He tried to interest me in some of his far-reaching schemes, and I often wonder whether I should have joined up with him and what eventually happened to him. Instead I stuck to my goal of trying to get back home and fight again, which is what I was trained for, but I felt I was not at all cut out to be a saboteur. I did however agree to help with the newspaper and was therefore employed taking down and summarizing BBC news bulletins, for which I was given various different and frequently changing addresses, then delivering my work in the evenings to be translated, correlated and printed. Once or twice I was allowed into the little room where the printing was done. Distribution presented problems and certain people were given so many copies each day to deliver round their friends. I used to distribute about ten copies, though I did not always get rid of them all, as some people were afraid to take them. One day, as I walked past one of the big police barracks, my pockets bulging with the ten newspapers, I was horrified to see hordes of police, armed with rifles, come rushing out, breaking into small parties and disappearing rapidly in all directions. A cordon was obviously being thrown around us in preparation for a mass arrest. On no account could I be caught with all these incriminating papers on me, and I looked quickly round for a way of escape. Fortunately I kept my head and jumped onto a passing tram, hoping for the best and preparing to stuff the papers down behind the seats if it came to the worst. We trundled on towards a barrier which the police had temporarily set up. It was a bad moment, and I could see that all my fellow passengers looked strained and anxious, but our tram was waved through and carried me on to safety. It may have been merely a police practice, but whether it was so or not, I found the experience a little bit unnerving.

About this time Puffy introduced me to certain members of the

National Democratic Party, which was a right wing party and had been the principal opposition to Marshal Pilsudski. Their representatives, whom I was privileged to meet, offered to provide money and identity papers for travel, and we had long talks about the future of Poland.

One day, just as I was taking leave of the airman after delivering my news bulletin, he said he had received a message from a certain Pole, stating that two British officers had recently been captured in Bulgaria. Yes, one was a major and one of the names had been Sinclair. I immediately went round to Puffy who confirmed the news. We were all then in danger and goodness knows what pressure might be applied to Ronnie and Mike to discover who had helped them and where they had been during the recent months.

I was now in daily contact with influential members of the Underground 'Home Army'. I was sick of hanging around and needed their help and advice, but they could never make up their minds whether they wanted us British to move on or whether they would prefer us to stay and fight with them when the moment arrived. I suspected the latter. For a time I was accommodated in the same house as a Polish officer who had recently parachuted in from London, and he thought I was mad to try and leave. 'Wait until the Allies land in Europe,' he told me. 'They will land from the air all over the continent. Complete armoured divisions will come down from the sky, and you can join them when they come.'

But the longer I stayed the greater the danger to my friends, and, by the end of January, I was absolutely determined to go. By a stroke of what seemed like good fortune I suddenly heard of a likely chance.

It was a woman friend of Mrs M who had been particularly kind to us, and whom I had known ever since I first came to Warsaw, who first told me about the man I have always thought of as Mr X whose identity has remained for me a mystery ever since. She had met him at the house of a friend, and he had asked some discreet questions about British prisoners of war hiding in Warsaw. Those present had been very guarded in their replies but gathered that Mr X was able and willing to take some of us (not more than two at a time) to Switzerland. Just in case anyone was interested he lived in Cracow and left his telephone number.

Next day Mrs M and Puffy, the woman who had made the contact and I met in 'The Hole' and discussed this new proposition.

'It's rather a gamble,' said the woman. 'I don't know anything

108

about this man. He seems to be a Pole, though, and sounds genuine enough.'

Mrs M did not like the sound of it.

'If only I could see him,' she said, 'I could tell whether he was genuine.'

But that was impossible for he had already returned to Cracow.

Eventually, after much discussion, we decided to take a chance, and this was certainly what I wanted to do. Puffy later got through to Mr X by telephone, and he agreed to take two of us, to be brought by Puffy to Cracow in three days time.

The Poles were keen I should take one of the private soldiers with me, and I chose one, a Lance Corporal Weekes who had been in Warsaw longer than I and could speak Polish quite well, though he knew no German. He was an able young man and full of guts. During the few days left to us in Warsaw our papers were put in order and various arrangements made for the journey.

We left during the second week in February 1942. I spent a busy day saying goodbye to as many of my friends as possible and making wholly inadequate attempts to thank them for everything they had done. At teatime I made my way for the last time to 'The Hole' to drink a final cup of tea with Mr and Mrs M. It was desperately sad saying goodbye. Puffy then arrived to collect me. Together we walked back towards his flat, up Novy Swiat and along to the park towards Belvedere. Snow was falling gently. We stopped and drank vodka at a small bar and then moved off to the flat near the Platz Boviciela. Mr R and a friend were there with Lance Corporal Weekes. We had supper and then, after more goodbyes, Puffy, Weekes and I walked up to the park and took a tram.

These were my last moments in Warsaw, and I looked hard at all the familiar buildings. We got out of the tram by the Church of the Three Crosses, took another tram across the Vistula and on to the station in Praga. Here we met N and T, the two secret service agents who were accompanying us to Cracow.

N had a message for us from the Commander-in-Chief of the Home Army wishing us good luck.

Snow was falling fast and the train was late, arriving just after 9 p.m. Soon we were moving and heading south to triumph or disaster.

10

DANGER'S MOUTH

Keep together here, lest running thither,
We unawares run into danger's mouth.
Milton – Samson Agonistes.

The inspection of our travel and identity papers, which I always found a nerve-racking business, passed off without incident, and we reached Cracow during the following afternoon.

The town was full of Italian soldiers from the Eastern Front, all looking thoroughly miserable and most unmilitary. We also passed a group of Russian prisoners, obviously very much the worse for wear. Not many were to survive the German captivity owing to the appalling treatment and conditions to which they were subjected. I dare say German prisoners in Russia were treated no better, but I do not really know. We walked out of the station, took a tram and then, in what seemed to be in the suburbs of the town, came to a house standing apart in a little sandy street.

'That is the house,' said Puffy and rang the bell.

T had come only part of the way with us, so that we were now a group of four, waiting for the door to be opened. For me it was an anxious moment; what would he be like and what would he be able to do for us? So much was at stake. At last, after what seemed to be a lengthy pause, a window above us opened, and the face of a middle-aged man appeared with, above it, a shock of vivid red hair. This was the man I came to know, and shall always remember, as Mr X. A moment later we heard him coming down the stairs.

Mr X opened the door for us and I noticed he was in shirt sleeves and braces, I also noticed something strange about him, that he had one blue eye and one brown. He welcomed us effusively in excellent English and at once produced some food and started straight away on plans for our onward journey. He was full of enthusiasm and confidence. It would not be the first time, he said, that he had taken Englishmen to Switzerland, and there would be no great difficulty in getting us safely through. In fact he expressed amazement that we had been left so long kicking our heels in Warsaw. We would be leaving, he explained, in a few days' time, but first he had certain arrangements to make, and completely new identity papers and travelling passes would be required. Then we would travel by express train to Vienna and thence on, also by train, via Innsbruck to a point in the area of the Swiss frontier: after that his arrangements must for the time being remain secret.

As I listened to all this my spirits rose. It all sounded so much more professional than anything I had heard in Warsaw, and Puffy too seemed visibly impressed.

During the evening Puffy received a telephone call which I could tell contained bad news. Before we left Warsaw we had been warned by the Underground that the Gestapo knew quite a lot about the escape organization, and there had been rumours, unsubstantiated, that 'The Hole' was being watched. Puffy was now being passed a message from his wife warning him under no circumstances to return to his flat. Much later I was to learn that he disregarded the warning and was arrested, along with his brother, eventually, after many terrible months in Auschwitz, to die or to be killed in the Sachsenhausen concentration camp near Berlin. My poor, dear, brave Puffy. Even now, after all these years, I cannot bear the thought of that good and gentle person being starved and beaten and finally dying under goodness knows what conditions.

All this, and much more, was to follow.

Meanwhile, though Weekes and I turned in early, Puffy and Mr X spent most of the night in earnest conversation. I have no idea what passed between them. Next morning Puffy and N returned to Warsaw.

We remained in Cracow for several days with Mr X and a young friend of his. He had a wireless to keep us amused, though the fall of Singapore was not exactly funny. The German papers naturally made much of it and I remember one headline:

Die stolze Zwingburg zeigt die weisse Fahne
The proud fortress shows the white flag

Occasionally Mr X would receive mysterious visitors but spent most of the day in the town. Either he or his friend would take us to lunch at a restaurant, and one day we were conducted on a tour and saw the famous university and many of Cracow's ancient and lovely buildings. Mr X and his friend always carried revolvers, and the former seemed to delight in picking quarrels with Poles on the tram and even, one day, with some Germans on the street: he did not have red hair for nothing.

Mr X also told us long stories about himself and his exploits as, to use his own words, 'an agent of British intelligence,' which at the time seemed most impressive but, in retrospect, some of the tales seem scarcely credible. At the same time he would firmly discourage us from mentioning our own experiences.

'Be careful what you say to me. You do not know who I am.'

It was not long, however, before we were on the move. T arrived from Warsaw to see us off and wish us luck. Mr X had continued to be vague about the journey which, from a security point of view, was sensible enough, and it was only on the eve of our departure that we were told the general idea of what our story should be if stopped and questioned. Despite the fact that Mr X kept assuring us that he had thought of everything ('I am an old hand at this game') and that nothing could go wrong, he neglected to provide us with a foreign worker's special permit to re-enter Reich territory. I left from Cracow station with certain misgivings: there was something about Mr X which seemed too good to be true. Would we really be in Switzerland two days hence?

We were equipped with identity papers as White Russians. Obtaining these papers in Warsaw had been taken as something of a triumph, for they were not easy to get. They were not false or forged but genuine documents issued by the White Russian Peoples' Committee in Berlin which had been established by the Germans to recruit émigré anti-communist Russians. We were to say, if questioned, that we were from Cracow (an address for each of us was provided) and were travelling to Vienna to work in a factory there. Even now I remember that the address of the firm was 19 Maria Hilfe Strasse. As well as our identity papers we had travel permits, and our tickets had been bought in advance. At the same time we had worked out histories of our past lives which had to explain why I spoke only German and Weekes only Polish. We agreed (and I was insistent on this) that, on the train, Mr X would travel reasonably near us but not actually with us, so that if we got into trouble, he would not necessarily be compromised.

The question whether we should be armed for the journey had been discussed, but I vetoed this at once. I could see no advantage in it at all, and it would lead immediately to our arrest if searched. Nor could I imagine any circumstances, until we came to the actual frontier crossing, when we could put up armed resistance to any purpose. Fighting our way across the frontier might be a different matter, and Mr X seemed to think we could obtain arms later on if we decided they were needed. This was one of the best decisions I have ever made.

After supper we walked to Cracow station, and T said goodbye to us on the platform. The station was full of people, the Vienna Express very crowded and only standing room in the corridor available to us. Weekes and I stood together, with Mr X several places away. The train was darkened and no one took much notice of us. In the gloom and crowd I felt fairly secure as the train pulled slowly away and gathered pace. 'Here we come,' I thought, 'Vienna, Innsbruck and beyond.'

It was only about seventy miles to the Reich frontier where we came slowly to a halt at a station which was probably Teschen, originally in Czechoslovakia, then seized by the Poles in 1938 and incorporated into Germany on the defeat of Poland in 1939. The journey so far had been without incident, and the inspection of papers which now awaited us would, we had been told, be fairly perfunctory.

At first nothing seemed to be happening. Then two policemen came walking down the platform and climbed onto the train at the end of our carriage. One started checking people in the compartments, the other those standing in the corridor. He worked his way quite quickly towards us, checking each person and passing on without much pause. As always at such times I felt anxious but not unduly so. Nevertheless it was most certainly a tense moment as he stood in front of me and held out his hand for my documents:

'*Ausweis, bitte.*' He took my documents, glanced at them, gave them back and passed on. With Weekes however, the language problem made difficulties and I heard the policeman ask him something about his destination which he did not understand. The policeman at once became impatient. Fearing a crisis I took the papers out of Weekes' hand and said, 'He does not understand German. I am travelling with him. Can I help?'

The policeman turned back to me and looked me up and down although in the gloom of the corridor he could not have discerned very much.

'You have a suitcase with you?' he asked.

'Yes,' I replied. 'Do you wish to look inside?'

'No, but you will both accompany me into the station.'

I protested at once. There was surely nothing wrong with our papers, I declared. It was most important, I added, that we should not miss the train, for our firm was expecting us the following day. It was to no avail.

'This is only a formality,' said the policeman. 'If you come quickly, then perhaps you can be back on the train before it leaves.'

My heart sank. This was one of the really bad moments of my life. It was not just the disappointment and the thoughts of failure after such a long endeavour; far worse was the fear, which had never been far from me all these months, that I should break down under interrogation and torture and spill the blood of all those gallant Poles who had helped, sheltered and befriended me. All this went through my mind as I picked up my little case and prepared to leave the train. Where was my lucky star and would it see me through?

Weekes and I got off the train, pushing past Mr X without glancing at him, and were led into a room just off the platform. First our handbags were examined: the food, medical equipment and a curious piece of rubber tubing which Mr X insisted on including in case a tourniquet should be needed ('You see, I think of everything, nothing is forgotten') created, I remember, a particularly bad impression. Then two largish men in civilian clothes, who I think had been sitting at a table in the corner of the room, took over. Immediately the chocolate ('Don't you realize that chocolate is only for German wounded?') and our ration cards ('How did you get these? They can only be obtained in the Reich.') became major points of interest. Our papers were then carefully examined and I had to face a barrage of questions fired at me first by one and then by the other. When our railway policeman remarked that we would miss our train unless matters were speeded up, he was told that we could always travel next day if necessary. Indeed, a few moments later I heard the train go puffing on its way. I felt as though my lifeline had been cut.

Then followed a real question and answer session for which my

German, out of sheer necessity, rose to the occasion: this was just as well, for I was representing it as my natural language.

'Where were you born?'

'Minsk.'

'When?'

'2 August, 1918.' (My actual birthday).

'Why did you leave Minsk?'

'Because of the Bolsheviks.' (A desperate attempt to win some sympathy.) 'They killed my father. My mother carried me away. But I was too young to know what was happening.'

'Then what?'

'We found refuge in Germany. We lived in Berlin.'

'Where?'

'*Friedrichstrasse.*'

'Number?'

'Twenty-one.'

'Number of flat?'

'Eight.'

So it went on. Out came the whole history of my fictitious life. No doubt my answers, some of which had to be made up there and then to meet unexpected queries, became more and more unlikely.

Then at last they both turned on Weekes. As he did not understand a word of what they said, I was told to interpret. Although this was awkward, our only common language being English, I had anticipated this very situation and did my best. I explained that as he spoke only Polish and I only German, we were unable to converse. Why were we travelling together then? Because I had been introduced to him in Cracow and been asked, as a fellow White Russian, to see that he got safely to Vienna as he had never been in Germany before and could not speak the language. Each question made further calls on my imagination and plunged me deeper and deeper into a fabric of falsehood. An interpreter was eventually produced who, after a few words with Weekes, said:

'He speaks Polish quite fluently, but with a marked accent which I would say was American or English.'

The fat was now completely in the fire. We were stripped and searched, then told to dress and made to get into two waiting cars.

'You will be taken to Cracow for a thorough investigation. If everything proves satisfactory you can continue your journey to Vienna in a few days' time.'

115

Weekes was shown into the first car, I into the second where I was put into the middle of the back seat, squeezed tight between two guards. Soon we were roaring through the night.

We made the journey back to Cracow in complete silence, but my mind was working hard. I had no illusions about our situation. What story should we tell and how could we get together to make sure it tallied? The Germans would obviously want to know exactly who we were and would probably stick at nothing to find out. Then they would want to know where we had been, what we had been up to and (worst of all) who had been helping us. During my time in Warsaw I had heard many tales of what the Germans did to people who would not answer questions: none of it was pleasant. Then, when it was all over, when they had squeezed out of us information to seal the fate of our Polish friends, we could be quietly finished off, and no one need ever know our fate. I prayed for strength and cunning and gradually evolved some kind of plan: it was not much but offered at least a possible line of action and a chance, however slim, of coping with all the likely pitfalls.

We drove into Cracow whence we had set out, only a few hours earlier, with such high hopes. We pulled up outside a large building which appeared to be a major police station of some kind. If it was the Gestapo headquarters then we were about to enter one of the most dreaded places in Europe. Trying to hold our heads high and keep our chins up ('His captain's hand on his shoulder smote, play up, play up and play the game') we marched in through the doors. Thinking of underground cells I glanced over my shoulder at the outside world behind and above me and took a deep breath of fresh air. Then we were inside.

Standing around in the entrance hall was a collection of individuals, whom I assumed were policemen. Some of them looked distinctly thuggish. A few were in uniform. As the only German uniform with which I had come into close contact was the army, I had no idea whether what I was now seeing indicated Gestapo, SS, ordinary police or what. They all stared at us coldly, without much interest. Our chief interrogator who had done most of the talking in the station at Teschen, now took us upstairs to what appeared to be his office, and our ordeal of interrogation recommenced at once. I have no idea what time of night it was, but it must have been pretty late, possibly 2 or 3 a.m. Now for as long as seemed advisable we stalled, argued, complained, protested our innocence and produced long and fanciful explanations and generally kept things going.

I had two aims. First to avoid saying anything which was likely to provoke the Germans into taking harsh measures against us which could prove irreversible and on which they might not embark if they discovered our true status as escaped prisoners of war. Secondly to avoid disclosing our true status until our train had reached Vienna and so give Mr X a chance of 'getting lost'. I felt sure that, as soon as we said who we were, there would be suspicion that a guide of some kind might well be on the train.

Thus I had to choose the right moment 'to come clean,' which would be essential to avoid having vital information about our friends dragged from us: not too soon, thus jeopardizing Mr X; not too late, in order to avoid being forced to 'spill the beans'. I could see no other alternatives, for by now we were far too compromised to be given back our freedom.

Danger and crisis sharpen the mind wonderfully, and I had by now decided on what line to take and how, with luck, this might safeguard my Polish friends. At last, therefore, when the patience of our questioners was clearly wearing thin, and when I reckoned that with luck our train would be in Vienna or at least have reached one or more of its stopping places, I made my announcement. I can recall my words exactly:

'*Ich glaube die Zeit ist gekommen, wenn wir die Wahrheit sprechen müssen.*' ('I think the time has come when we must tell the truth.')

'A-ah,' said my interrogator, in a voice disclosing both triumph and relief, '*Ich bin der selben Meinung.*' ('I am of the same opinion'.)

'We are,' I continued in German 'British prisoners of war who have escaped our prison camps.'

Weekes was whisked away at once, and I sat alone in front of the inquisitor. He wanted my full particulars, and I proceeded according to my plan. I held no cards of much value, but at least I could play them with such skill as I possessed. I gave him therefore my name, my rank of Second Lieutenant (there I was wrong for, as I later discovered, I had been promoted Lieutenant the previous August on completing three years' commissioned service) and my British Army number 77674. I also explained that I had escaped from Stalag XXID (the official designation of Fort VIII Posen) and that my prisoner of war number was 530.

'Good,' said my inquisitor, 'I see you are going to be sensible and

117

answer my questions. It makes it all much easier and nicer. So, first of all, when did you escape from your camp?'

This awkward question was bound to be asked and, fearing to disclose I had been on the run so long, I stalled. I wanted to avoid lying, if I could, as lies can so easily be found out, and I also wanted, if possible, to present myself as a perfectly innocent escaper: this I could hardly do if I admitted right from the start that I had been running for nine months. Thus I replied that I was not prepared to say when I had escaped. I sat back and waited to see how my first act of non-cooperation would be taken. The reaction was un-expected:

'The camp at Posen,' said my inquisitor, 'was closed down last year. You must therefore have been free for many months. Where have you been and what have you been doing?'

No reply.

'You had better tell me, otherwise we shall assume you have been spying. You know what happens to spies?'

'I am not a spy.'

'I think you are.'

'I give you my word as a British officer, my comrade and I are not spies.' (I wondered how Weekes was getting on).

'We shall see.'

I was not feeling very brave, but I managed to look stubborn. The German stared at me for a long moment which seemed an age. Then he shrugged and to my surprise completely changed the subject. He talked about the war; what did I think about it? I was a professional soldier, I told him, and did my duty like he did.

He spoke of the Jews and 'the conspiracy of international Jewry'. What was my opinion? I had none; as a Christian I took people as I found them, whoever they were, Jews, foreigners, it made no differ-ence. Then up came the matter of communism and the war in Russia.

'As a British officer you cannot surely like communism!'

'That's right: I don't like communism.'

'Yet you fight with the communists against us who are of your race, fellow Nordics and Arians.'

'Britain and Russia are allies.'

'You like Russians?'

'I've never met one.'

'The Russians are *untermensch* and barbarians, but we shall conquer and destroy them.'

118

'Perhaps.'

'The winter in Russia is harsh and makes special problems. But it will soon be spring and then the German armies will go forward again.'

He was, I suppose, softening me up, engaging me in reasonable and civilized conversation, putting me at ease, off-guard perhaps and with my having to struggle on in German, tiring me out. Suddenly he swung back to the point, 'Now where were we? Oh yes, you were going to tell me what you have been doing since your escape, all those months ago.'

Finally, wondering how late (or early) it was, and whether morning had arrived outside, I played, not a trump card for I had none, but the only card of possible value which I could produce. I spread, metaphorically, on the table between us my honour, the officer's code of honour, something which the British do not talk much about but which, I guessed, might have a special appeal to a German. This was my plan; thought up on that grim journey back from Teschen, the honour card, and play it I would for all its worth.

Fifty years later, sitting writing in my little Hampshire cottage, surrounded by family and friends, my dogs in the garden barking playfully at passers-by, and the village church visible through my study window twenty yards away, I find it difficult to transport myself back to that grim interrogation, with other people's lives depending on the answers I would give or withhold. The reality is recaptured only with an immense effort, and then the memories, all of them most unpleasant, come slowly drifting back. Certainly there were plenty of people in all the countries occupied by Germany only too willing at whatever cost, to help Allied prisoners to escape. Now, as I see myself seated in that room, far from home and in the clutches of my foes, I wonder whether the acceptance of such help can ever be justified and doubt whether I would ever ask for it again.

'I want to make myself absolutely clear,' I announced. (I was tired and, to be honest, frightened). 'I am not going to answer your questions. I am not going to tell you where I've been or who has helped me. It would be against my honour as an officer to betray my friends. You would not do so, nor would any German officer. You can take me out this very moment and shoot me but it will make no difference.'

There was a long pause. The inquisitor seemed undecided how to react or what to say.

'We shall take a break now,' he eventually declared, and immediately two particularly unpleasant uniformed Germans entered the room.

'Take him away,' said the inquisitor.

The two 'zombies' pushed me unceremoniously out of the room, shoved me into a dark passage and told me to walk down it. They followed. I came to the end of the passage, which was a cul-de-sac, and therefore stopped. I turned round, expecting any moment to be set upon and beaten up. Then, to my utter astonishment, one of the 'zombies' offered me a cigarette, which I naturally accepted gratefully. It was an anti-climax but a most welcome one.

Once back in the room my inquisitor stared at me a long time in silence. It occurred to me that he had been consulting someone about me. Possibly he had reported on the interrogation and received instructions.

'That is all for the moment,' he said.

I was removed, marched off to some prison (maybe I was taken by car, I cannot remember) and locked in a cell. There was no sign of Weekes. I fell asleep almost at once.

Next morning I discovered that my gaolers wore some kind of uniform. The building was a typical prison with iron staircases and iron platforms running along outside the cells: mine was on the upstairs level, very small, with a stove controlled from the passage, a basin of some kind and a WC. The guards did not seem very friendly (why should they be?) but were quite correct in their treatment and attitude, though I did hear other prisoners, whom I never saw, being shouted at from time to time. I was ordered to clean my cell and eventually received a cup of *ersatz* coffee and a slice of dry rye bread. Soup of a sort came later in the day. I was allowed no reading or writing materials, and smoking (not that I had anything to smoke) was forbidden. Once I had cleaned my cell, I had nothing to do except to sit on my bed or pace up and down, three paces each way. As before with solitary confinement I was able to ease my lot by my ability to recite the poetry I so greatly loved – Milton, Wordsworth, Shelley, Keats and Byron particularly and a few bits of Tennyson – almost indefinitely. I had learnt it at school and come to enjoy it enormously. I also had plenty of time for prayer. I prayed a great deal which helped to keep me surprisingly calm and quite resigned to whatever might turn out to be my fate.

There was little contact with my gaolers and none with anyone

120

else. I asked one guard how long I would remain in this particular place, to be told that those sent here did not usually leave! This was not exactly encouraging, and no, he knew nothing about my comrade. It was a wretched time.

During the following night I was woken (about 2 a.m. I should think) and taken back to face my inquisitor again. He came at once to the point.

'You look less tired. You are rested?'

'Yes, thank you.'

'You have had time to reflect upon your situation?'

'Oh yes. But what about my comrade?'

'Don't worry. He is all right. You have another chance, then, to answer my questions.'

I sat silent. I thought it best to say nothing. Would I describe my escape? Had I been helped in Posen? I said nothing.

'Are you not going to answer at all?'

'I have already explained why I can say nothing to endanger those who helped me.'

'Very well.'

He fished in a drawer of his desk. My silence, he said, was quite pointless. He thrust some papers at me.

'We have all the information we need. We know all about Poles helping British prisoners and have made a number of arrests. See the list before you.'

I looked nervously at the list. Most of the names meant little to me, but I noted some Posen addresses and the names of Puffy, Mrs M and Mr Wolf of Lodz. I had been anxious since Puffy's call from Warsaw, received in Cracow, that all might not be well. For several minutes I said nothing. Finally I looked up. I am sure the shock and misery showed clearly in my eyes.

'None of these names means anything to me', I said.

'Oh come now,' he said. 'As you have seen whom we have arrested you can do no harm by admitting everything. Would it not be better if you wrote out a statement, giving us all the truth?'

'I have nothing further to say.'

'You will write out a statement all the same.'

He produced a pencil and paper, told me not to hurry and to put down as much as I could. I wrote out a statement carefully, explaining who I was, where I had escaped from and where I had been recaught. I added that I could not betray those who had helped

121

me without dishonouring the officers' code. When I had signed it I was taken back to the gaol and locked in my cell.

I lay down on my hard bunk. It was not quite dawn. The lucky star, under which I had been born (the gift of my fairy godmother), the star which had shone so brightly for me at Calais, had shone again at least for me. For I had no doubt that, if the Germans had not already broken up the escape organization, they would have put me under the most terrible pressure which I could not have resisted for very long. My good fortune, however, was of little comfort to me as I thought of those arrests and the ghastly sufferings of so many wonderful and brave people. I have been thinking of them ever since.

Weekes, I at last discovered from one of the guards, was in a cell just down the passage from mine, but we were not allowed to communicate. With nothing to do the boredom soon became deadly and my future increasingly uncertain, but I managed to make friends with one guard who was to prove a great asset. I was never allowed out of the cell, but by standing on my chair (*streng verboten* naturally) I could see out of my heavily barred window, and the view included a distant barrack square with soldiers sometimes drilling on it. I could hear their marching songs.

Even my friendly guard could not refrain from gloating over the Japanese capture of Singapore (he showed me a magazine with that dreadful photograph of poor General Percival and staff marching out with the white flag and Union Jack to arrange the surrender) and he rushed into my cell one day with a newspaper report of the passage through the English Channel of the German warships *Scharnhorst* and *Gneisenau*. To this bad news from the outside world and the intense boredom of my cell was now added for me a further misery in the form of severe toothache. Under normal circumstances, when thus afflicted, one can reach for the aspirins or something stronger, perhaps have a double brandy or, in extremis, ring up the dentist. For the lonely prisoner in his lonely cell, isolated from the civilized world, there is no such comfort, and in my case the pain had to be endured, not cured. For some days it was almost intolerable, sleep impossible except in the smallest snatches, and appeals for help of any kind fell on deaf ears. But not all the ears were deaf, and at last my friendly guard, at that time the only friend I had, came to my cell one evening with five codeine tablets, which he had bought with his own money, and a cigarette. He had no matches, he explained, but would try to get me one next day. I swallowed two tablets and, after desperately trying to get the cigarette alight by putting one end of it on the warm stove and sucking on the other (all of course in vain) I had at last a fair night's sleep. The unlit cigarette remained a torment of frustration for two whole days before I got a match.

I have no idea how long I remained in that gaol, for time had ceased to count. No one would tell me how Weekes was faring nor whether he was still in the gaol, though I guessed from the kind of wink which my friendly guard gave me that he probably was. Meanwhile I hoarded my codeine and kept the toothache at bay. But it was a forlorn existence and how long it might have lasted I have no idea, had not my lucky star, after perhaps two weeks, suddenly shone forth again.

Although the food was neither plentiful nor tasty, it was adequate, and I do not remember feeling particularly hungry during this time. One evening after supper I was pacing to and fro as was my wont (I have hated zoos ever since) when the head guard came in and made an announcement.

'A General will be visiting the prison tomorrow.'

'I didn't know Generals would be interested in such a place', I said, suddenly alert.

'This is the first one to come in my time here. Now listen carefully. If he comes to your cell you will stand to attention and on no account speak, even if he speaks to you or asks you a question. If he does, one of us will answer for you.'

'But it would be impolite if I failed to answer him.'

'You will do as you are told or it will be the worse for you.'

He went out and slammed the door.

Like hell, I thought. Here might be a chance which I must not miss. If only the General would come to my cell. I feared he might be kept from me, yet if he did come I must on no account muff it. I spent the evening rehearsing what I would say.

And there he was, next day, standing in the open door of my cell, resplendent in his uniform, looking quite kindly and distinguished with his white hair and pale blue eyes. I stepped forward, my speech in German at the ready and, without the General speaking, and accompanied by shouts of 'keep quiet' from the guard, I fired away, 'Herr General, I am a British officer prisoner of war who has escaped and been recaught, and I have a comrade, a Corporal, also in this prison. I request we be returned to the custody of the German Army forthwith.'

123

The General looked at me for a moment, said nothing and withdrew. The door slammed, the keys rattled and turned. I was alone again.

For three days nothing seemed to have changed. I was not even reprimanded for speaking to the General. Then at last,

'You will be moving tomorrow.'

'What about my comrade?'

'He will go with you.'

It should perhaps have occurred to me that it might be a question of 'out of the frying pan into the fire' and our destination a concentration camp. We had been on the loose too long perhaps, seen too much, and now I had disobeyed and spoken to the General, I had become a nuisance, maybe, and better be disposed of. I should indeed have been worried over what was, in fact, a distinct possibility but, on the contrary, I felt sure my prayers were being answered, that all would be well. I was so excited at the prospect that I slept soundly that night.

One of the few good things about this gaol was that I had always been allowed to shave, albeit in cold water. On this particular morning I shaved early and with extra care. I then waited (there was nothing else to do). My *ersatz* coffee came as usual, which I drank. I continued to wait. They came for me about midday. I was taken downstairs and given back my belongings which consisted of my wallet, a pencil and my spectacles. My watch had disappeared and I never saw it again. Weekes was then brought down and received his belongings. There were about six German soldiers to whom we were handed over, and away we marched. Cracow was a beautiful city but I was thankful to see the back of it.

We travelled quite comfortably by train. Weekes assured me he had given no names away and I believe him for he was tough and courageous and anyway, like me, may not have been under any special pressure.

The journey took most of the day, so there was time for many bitter thoughts. All my efforts to escape, all the long months of waiting, all the anxiety inflicted on my family at home by my 'disappearance,' all had been in vain. Nothing had been achieved and I was back, as we say these days, to square one. But it was much worse than that as a lot of Poles must have been arrested when the organization was penetrated, and I could only guess at their fate. This is the trouble with 'underground' resistance. However carefully

124

information is restricted to small groups, each knowing nothing or little about the others, one arrest, one break in the chain, and untold damage is done, spreading further and further like ripples on a pond as each arrest is made. My only comfort, which has always remained with me, was that I had betrayed no one, and I always thank my lucky star that I was never put in a position where I might have been tortured and 'persuaded' to divulge.

Weekes and I spoke little on the journey and we were particularly careful not to say anything which could be useful to the Germans. Like me he had seen the list of names which the Germans had produced, but none of his particular helpers had been included except for Puffy and Mrs M whom he had not known well.

Eventually we came to a place called Lamsdorf in Upper Silesia, where there was a large camp for British Other Ranks, but I saw nothing of the camp itself, only the cell block. I was however to see Lamsdorf again later on. I have never seen Weekes again, though I understand he was soon to escape and return to Warsaw. I will always remember him as an intrepid and resourceful young man.

After a night in the cells I was collected next day by a posse of several soldiers under a rather pleasant looking *Feldwebel* with a black moustache and glasses.

'Where are we going' I asked.

'Oflag IV C, Colditz.'

Needless to say I had never heard of Colditz, now through books and television almost a household word.

'Where is Colditz?' I asked.

'Colditz is a famous castle, not far from Leipzig,' came the answer.

We took an afternoon train and trundled on through the evening and into the darkness. The *Feldwebel* was friendly and quite chatty. Colditz, he assured me, was a lovely place where I would have many comrades and be well looked after. I felt I knew the form well enough and was unimpressed. The Castle stood high above a little town, lit by a ring of many floodlights.

'Look out of the window, *Herr Leutnant*,' said the *Feldwebel*, as the train began to slow. 'Now you can see Colditz Castle. Beautiful is it not, just as I told you?'

Thus I first saw Colditz from the window of a train on a dark winter evening, early in 1942.

11

A VERITABLE LEAGUE
OF NATIONS

Colditz would later become famous through the writings of Pat Reid with a full length feature film being made of his first book *The Colditz Story* as well as a lengthy television series. This certainly never occurred to me as I tramped up the cobbled road towards the main gate, the jackboots of my escort beating a regular rhythm between the walls.

The nearer we got the more formidable this ancient castle seemed. Later I would read of its history and how it had been the home of the kings of Saxony and the birthplace of Maurice de Saxe (a son of Augustus The Strong) who was destined to become a Marshal of France and who defeated us British at Fontenoy during the war of the Austrian succession.

His father, Augustus, was well-named 'The Strong' for he was supposed to have had a fabulous number of wives and children. Indeed one of the prison blocks in the castle still bore the name on its outer wall of *Furstenhaus* or Princes' Nursery.

We reached the outer gate, which was unlocked with much clanking and creaking. I was taken before a German officer who listed my particulars, and I spent the rest of the night in a cell beneath the main archway.

Early next morning I was escorted through an inner gate into the prisoners' part of the castle. No prisoners were about, and I was confronted by an empty courtyard surrounded by high walls and many windows, all barred. I was taken by an armed Corporal across the courtyard to a shower block. Any prisoner arriving in the camp was deloused by being given a very hot shower, while his clothing was taken away and subjected to some form of heat-treatment. Fortunately there was no head-shearing as at Laufen. This was the first decent wash I had had since leaving Warsaw. Even the soap and clean towel which were provided seemed luxury indeed!

While I was drying myself who should turn up, at first a dim, vague figure in the steam but Mike Sinclair, bearing a large slice of bread liberally spread with margarine and real jam! I could hardly believe it.

'Mike,' I cried, 'Thank God you're still alive. Is Ronnie here too?'

'No,' he replied. 'I'll tell you about it later. Meanwhile I've brought you something to eat.'

'But I couldn't possibly take your ration,' I protested, 'So much marge and jam! You must keep it.'

I was thinking back to the hungry days of my earlier imprisonment but Mike explained that everything now was different and there were regular Red Cross parcels and plenty to eat. So I wolfed his offering down – the best bit of food since my recapture. I was then turned loose into the prisoners' compound and started my new life with new people in these new and strange surroundings.

Colditz, some twenty miles south-east of Leipzig, was a small country town on the River Mulde, amidst pleasant rolling country of fields and woods. The castle, which stood on a cliff and towered above the town, was described by Pat Reid in *The Colditz Story* as, 'beautiful, serene, majestic and yet forbidding – a real fairy castle of

127

childhood story book'. It housed the camp designated Oflag IV C, a special officers' camp (or *Sonderlager*) for escapers and trouble-makers. An International camp, highly volatile and therefore always interesting and often exciting, it was in no sense a punishment camp (or *Straflager*) as has been alleged, rather a high-security camp. At the time of my arrival it housed some 200 French officers, 150 Polish, sixty Dutch, fifty British and around thirty Belgian officers; a veritable League of Nations. There were also, I remember, two officers of the Royal Yugoslavian Army who were actually White Russians. Apart from Mike I really knew no one in the camp, although among the British was that stalwart party which made the first escape from Laufen, but I would soon be making many friends, It was certainly more comfortable in Colditz than in Laufen or Posen, mainly because we were considerably less crowded, and the morale of the inmates was, under the circumstances, very high. Food was plentiful, as Mike had told me, and I was amazed to see shelves well-stacked and to hear that messes could actually keep parcels in reserve, held under German supervision in the parcels office and issued on request. The German parcels staff were in fact extremely accommodating and absolutely honest. Germany was never really short of food, but luxuries such as tea, coffee, chocolate, jam, cigarettes and tobacco which came in our parcels were difficult or impossible to obtain. Yet never to my knowledge were any of our parcels ever pilfered. I am no great Germanophile, but I pay tribute where tribute is due.

I soon discovered Colditz was for those Allied officers whom the Germans considered tiresome or troublesome, either persistent escapers or those considered to be particularly anti-German (*deutschfeindlich*). There was also a war correspondent named Giles Romilly who was related to Winston Churchill and consequently designated a 'prominent' prisoner. He was treated like the rest of us, except that at night he was locked up in a separate room with an armed guard outside the door. Later other 'prominent' prisoners would come to Colditz. Giles, I remember, like Micky Burn who would arrive in due course, was one of these ex-public school intellectual communists whom one often encountered during the thirties. Micky, whom I came to like enormously, actually told me one day that I was a typical barrier to all social progress and would undoubtedly end up one day, nice fellow though I might be, hanging from a lamp post! I reminded him of this when we met at a Colditz reunion some forty years on and had a good laugh together.

For meals we grouped ourselves into small messes, and I was accepted by Mike's. At that time it consisted of a chap called Pemberton-Howe, who was a Territorial Army captain in the Royal Army Service Corps, Alan Orr-Ewing, known as 'Scruffy', a forestry student commissioned into the Argyll and Sutherland Highlanders, Bertie Boustead of the Seaforth Highlanders, Captain Mazumdar, an Indian doctor in the Royal Army Medical Corps, known as Jumbo, 'Scarlet' O'Hara of the Royal Tank Regiment, a rather mysterious chap called Howard Gee and, finally, Mike and myself. Others would join us later.

'Pembum' as Pemberton-Howe was known, was a model prisoner who had decided to sit back and make himself as comfortable as possible. In peacetime he ran a well-known pub in Oxford called The Abingdon Arms. At his first camp he had quickly become chairman of the canteen committee and had established himself in an active bridge four and he also succeeded in finding a source of parcels from the United States which added some variety to our mess diet. He was a nice friendly person, typically and insularly English. I remember him coming into the room one day and finding a Dutch and a French officer sitting chatting with us at our mess table, 'What's this?' he exclaimed, 'an 'effing League of Nations?'

Pembum liked curry and had persuaded his benefactor in the United States to include curry powder in the parcels. He liked it strong and tasty, as only Jumbo could make it. One day, when Jumbo was our mess duty cook, Pembum ordered curry for supper, and Jumbo looked around to see what might form a good basis. This was a problem, as we were out of tinned meat at the time. Then Jumbo's eyes, searching the shelves and cupboard, fell on a jar marked mincemeat, which in fact Pembum had put away at the back of the cupboard so that we could have mince-pies on Christmas Day. Alas, that was not to be as Jumbo, thinking it was minced meat, served it up as curry. In recalling this occurrence I am reminded of Pembum's elaborate preparations before eating his curry which included a head-band to prevent the sweat running down into his eyes and a special scarf round his neck.

One might wonder why Pembum, so good and domestic a prisoner, had landed up in Colditz, and indeed I always understood that his presence among us was due to a German misunderstanding. At

129

his previous camp someone had been tracing a map of the Swiss frontier when Germans burst into the room to conduct a search. The mapmaker, caught unawares, had stuffed his work into the nearest available hiding place, namely under Pembum's mattress, where it was inevitably found. Pembum, unaware of this incident, was therefore extremely indignant when he was woken up that night and told he was moving to another camp.

'We have suspected for some time, Captain Pemberton-Howe, that you have been behind the escaping activities here, so we are sending you to a place where you will be kept properly under control and from where escape is quite impossible.'

Howard Gee was supposed to have been captured returning from Finland, where he had volunteered to fight against the Russians during the winter war of 1939 and 1940. I remember him at Laufen where his civilian status had landed him up as one of the orderlies. Somehow he had been elevated to officer status and sent to Colditz, possibly because of his suspicious circumstances. He was a strange person who had worked for some tourist firm before the war and travelled widely in Europe and spoke absolutely perfect German. I always assumed he had been working for our Intelligence.

Like most people in Colditz, our mess was made up of a group of individualists. They proved good companions.

The reasonable living conditions in Colditz, at least when compared with other camps, and the fact that there was enough to eat, certainly made life bearable. Our German rations, however, apart from the bread which, though made from rye, was quite palatable once one was used to it, were as bad as ever and often totally ignored. Incidentally, the Concise Oxford Dictionary describes rye as 'cereal used for bread in northern Continental countries and for fodder in UK.' Similarly the Dictionary describes Kohlrabi, which later in the war became a main item of our German rations as 'cabbage with turnip-shaped stem, used in England as food for cattle.' Two-tiered bunks (they had been three-tiered at Laufen) and straw palliasses provided reasonable comfort at night. The sheet with which we were issued, however, was usually required by the escape committee to make rope, while the wooden slats, on which one's palliasse rested, were frequently required for shoring up the various tunnels which were always being built somewhere. Thus one often had to sleep precariously balanced on about three slats and liable at any moment to fall through onto the floor or, if occupying a top bunk, onto the unfortunate sleeper below.

The foreigners provided welcome diversions, opportunities to learn their languages and much interest and pleasure. I made friends with a charming Dutch officer called John Smit who had escaped from Colditz the previous year and been caught very close to the Swiss frontier. He and his companion had been locked up in a cell with a clear view of the frontier near Schaffhausen and brought back the most detailed information about it. This information was to prove invaluable. John was one of the KNIL (East Indies) Army officers as were the majority of the Dutch in Colditz and thereby hangs an interesting tale.

When the Dutch Army capitulated in 1940 the Germans declared they would release all prisoners provided that every officer would sign a declaration promising to take no further part in the war. The Dutch Commander-in-Chief, I understand, either recommended or ordered all to sign, and most of them did so with the notable exceptions of those KNIL officers who happened to be in Holland at the time. These decided that to sign such an order, even when recommended by the Commander-in-Chief, would be an act of treachery when their Queen had gone abroad to carry on the war. Instead of going into hiding and trying to make a getaway, which might perhaps have been the most obvious course of action, these officers put on their best uniform (boots, breeches, spurs and Sam Browne belts), marched in a formed body under their senior officer, Major Engles, reported to the German military Headquarters and announced they would sign no declaration and demanded to be taken prisoner! The Germans, with great reluctance, took them in and, in due course, they found themselves in Colditz. Unfortunately, certain members of the Dutch Home Army, who had signed the declaration but had nevertheless, due to the position they had held, been taken into custody, had also been sent to Colditz. A few of these, in the view of the KNIL officers and some of the others, were traitors and were treated by them as such and denied them normal social intercourse, even though they were treated by the Germans as one group and lived together in the same quarters. Naturally we British took no sides in this dispute, and I remember John Smit telling me that it upset him and his comrades very much when they saw British officers talking to traitors.

The French officers, many of whom were splendid people, were much inhibited by the difficult political situation in which they found themselves. Most of them disliked the Germans intensely, yet their country under Pétain, the much revered victor of Verdun and Commander-in-Chief of the French Army on the Western front from 1916-1918, was actively collaborating with Germany. In their confusion, which was very real to some of them, they resorted to a soldierly loyalty to 'The Marshal' who, they believed, would have the interests of France at heart and must surely know what he was doing. A representative of the Vichy Government had actually been sent to Colditz, and probably to all the other camps where Frenchmen were held, to explain the situation and was generally well received, certainly listened to with great attention. While many of them, at this time, considered de Gaulle and his Free French to be traitors, there were some who secretly admired the continuing resistance and despised the Vichy lot. Under these circumstances we British had to be tactful, and once, when the RAF bombed Paris, our relations with them became very strained. Later, when the first Free French officers arrived at Colditz and were treated by the Germans as if they were British, the French officers refused to speak to them but all this gradually changed as the fortunes of war swung round.

All Colditz inmates admired and liked the Poles and were amused at the way they took every opportunity to show how much they hated and despised their captors. These Poles were naturally interested in the experience of Mike and me in their country, though for obvious reasons we had to be careful what we said.

The differing characteristics of the national groups showed up clearly in attitudes and behaviour on the roll-call parades. These parades were held first thing in the morning, last thing at night and at any time, without warning, in between. The Dutch, always smartly turned out with headdress, boots and breeches, were very disciplined and correct. The French, in all kinds of uniform, often with no buttons on their tunics and breeches unlaced, delighted in teasing the Germans and were sometimes extremely clever and witty in doing so. The Belgians generally kept quiet and unobtrusive. We British delighted in being casual and unmilitary, never wore hats or caps and in winter often wore pyjamas under a greatcoat: we usually kept fairly quiet but, if provoked, reacted strongly. The Poles behaved in a military fashion but only had the uniforms in which they had been captured. No Pole, except their senior officer and adjutant who acted officially, would speak to a German and, when counted, they would turn their heads away as the German officer or

Feldwebel came down the line and would object violently if a German touched them.

Strange to relate, for the Germans are not noted for their sense of humour, there was one officer on the camp staff who had one. This was Captain (*Hauptman*) Priem. He also had a liking for the bottle and sometimes came to take roll-call slightly the worse for wear. On these occasions he would try to turn the tables on the prisoners, who so enjoyed teasing the Germans, by teasing them, particularly the British and the Poles, both of whom were the easiest to provoke, the Dutch being too correct and the French too subtle to fall into so obvious a trap. One day he decided to have a go at the Poles and was so successful that the Polish adjutant lost all self-control and actually hit Priem in the face. He thus broke the rule that, whatever else one might do, one never laid one's hands on a German which was a court-martial offence resulting in very severe penalties, even possibly death. It was hardly surprising therefore that the adjutant was immediately arrested and dragged off through the gate into the German part of the castle. This exciting incident threw the whole parade into confusion with the prisoners breaking ranks and shouting and jeering at the Germans. Priem dismissed the parade and quickly withdrew. After we had all fallen out the Senior British Officer (SBO) accompanied by his Polish equivalent, went down to the gate and rang the bell, which was normal procedure if one wanted to speak to the Guard Commander. They demanded to see the Commandant immediately. Eventually, after a prolonged and heated argument, first with the Guard Commander and finally with a German officer, who had to be fetched, our own SBO was allowed through, but not the Polish Colonel. It all ended happily and the victim was released and all charges dropped. It was understood that our SBO threatened to inform the Swiss Government (our Protecting Power) and the International Red Cross that Priem was in the habit of being drunk on duty.

Roll Call Parades (*appell* in German) were seldom dull, usually amusing and occasionally exciting: they provided many excellent opportunities for annoying or confronting the Germans or, if some escape activity was contemplated or in progress, of thoroughly confusing them. The French were always good at this, and I have had much pleasure over the years in recalling what I have always considered to be the best story from Colditz. It was on a roll call taken by *Hauptman* Püpcke, who was the German officer we most

133

respected; he never tried to ingratiate himself with us but was always fair and correct. Püpcke that morning looked nervous and shifty as we were called to attention. This was so unlike him that we knew something must be up. Sure enough, having counted us and instead of dismissing us, he explained he had an announcement to make. We were all attentive, and you could have heard a pin drop. He then asked us to hear him out. We would not, he thought, be very responsive to what he had to say but, as officers, we would surely understand that he had his duty to perform. He then informed us, rather hurriedly, that 'Herr Hitler' had made a special and most generous offer to all Allied officer prisoners and they could volunteer to be employed and use their own particular skills for the benefit of the New Order in Europe. Püpcke knew only too well that such an announcement would normally spark off some violent reaction from Colditz prisoners, so when he had finished he saluted quickly, muttered, '*Danke, meine Herren,*' and turned away, amidst the expected jeers, catcalls and howls of laughter. Then suddenly an amazed silence as a French officer stepped forward and marched up to Püpcke.

'I would like,' he said, 'my services and professional skill to be placed at the disposal of the German people.'

'You mean,' gasped Püpcke, 'that you actually want to work for us, for Germany?'

'Certainly. And the more work I am given the better I shall be pleased.'

Püpcke pulled himself together, as the German sentries leaned forward to hear this extraordinary exchange. 'And what is the work that you offer so generously to do? What is your profession?'

'I am an undertaker.'

He was immediately arrested and led away amidst clapping and cheers.

Until just before my arrival the SBO had been Lieutenant Colonel Guy German, a Territorial officer of the Leicestershire Regiment, but the Germans had removed him for being too intransigent and uncooperative and sent him to another camp. His place had been taken by the quieter and very charming 'Daddy' Stayner who had commanded a Territorial Dorset battalion in France. The Escape Committee was run by Pat Reid, the leader of the first Laufen escape who would eventually write the famous trilogy *The Colditz Story, The Latter Days at Colditz* and finally *Colditz – The Complete*

Story. I registered with the committee as being keen to escape and willing to do all I could to help others get away.

Meanwhile I was the most newly arrived prisoner and must adjust myself to these new surroundings, new people and new conditions as best I could. I was anxious to hear Mike's story.

Having left Warsaw in August of the previous year Ronnie and Mike reached Budapest successfully. After some delays and difficulties they had proceeded towards Turkey but towards the end of November had been arrested and been taken to Sofia where the Bulgarians handed them over to the Germans. They were held for some weeks there under extremely unpleasant conditions but finally their move back to Germany began. They must have been desperately depressed and disappointed, having got so far, and with the Turkish frontier almost within reach, but they were not beaten yet. When their train slowed down to enter Prague they managed to jump clear. Ronnie, Mike thought, had made a complete get-away, while he himself had twisted his ankle and was recaught almost immediately. He had then been brought to Colditz.

We discussed at some length the arrest of so many Poles which my interrogator had claimed, and I told Mike of the warning Puffy had received on the telephone in Cracow. He was very concerned and felt the claim was probably correct. This was later confirmed by some Polish officers in Colditz who received coded messages in their letters. They also told us that Mr X was thought to have been a Gestapo agent who had infiltrated the escape organization. I have never been able to discover the truth with any degree of certainty, but the case for this explanation of these tragic events is undoubtedly strong. There had been those rumours before I left Warsaw that Mrs M and others were being watched. What more natural, one might think, than that the Germans, anxious to make a maximum haul, should have stayed their hand and used an agent to find out as much as possible. Puffy loved gossip and intrigue, and if Mr X was really a police agent, I dread to think what passed between them that night in Cracow when they talked together for hours. Then again there seemed in retrospect something fishy about the arrest, for no obvious reason, of Weekes and myself on the train, and why were the two plain-clothes policemen from Cracow, who took us into custody, so conveniently waiting on the station?

On the other hand, why the cat-and-mouse game with us and all the rigmarole of the journey and the intricate preparations for it?

The arrests were already in process, so why were not Weekes and I bundled straight into gaol before we left Cracow or even on arrival there? Why were we allowed to meet Mr X at all? If we had become suspicious, which was quite possible, we could quite easily have given him the slip in Cracow and warned all concerned.

For a long time I discounted the agent theory despite the arguments for it, but many years later came across a report from the Warsaw underground to the Polish Government in London which included the opinion that the arrests were due 'to the successful establishment of a Gestapo agent into the escape organization'. On balance I now accept this theory. It was a tragic incident in the long, sad story of the war.

Ronnie Littledale turned up in Colditz during July. He had managed to find help and shelter in Prague by the simple expedient of approaching the first likely-looking person and saying in English, 'I am an escaped British officer prisoner of war on the run: can you help me?'

Subsequently he made his way, mostly by train, to the Austrian-Swiss frontier. Once again he trusted to luck and accosted someone who looked friendly and asked him for information on the local frontier crossing routes, explaining carefully who he was and why he wanted to know. The man took him to his house, gave him a meal and told him that, until the snow had begun to melt, he did not have a hope of getting across, as the few crossing points available in winter were too closely guarded.

'Come back in the spring,' said this helpful and friendly acquaintance, 'and I will then be able to help you, but on no account stay here in this very sensitive frontier area.' So Ronnie went back to Prague.

Ronnie was devoutly religious and had always insisted on having his army issue New Testament with him on his escape travels. This had understandably outraged Mike Sinclair's sense of security! When they had jumped from the train in Prague and Mike had been immediately recaught they invoked a tremendous hue and cry with German police, some with Alsatian dogs, rushing about in all directions. Ronnie had hidden on the outside platform between two carriages, and just as some police were about to reach his hiding place, with Ronnie no doubt praying fervently not to be discovered, there was a loud hissing noise and a jet of steam shot out from under the carriage and completely hid him from their view.

Soon after returning to Prague he was rounded up during the mass street arrests which followed the assassination by Czech agents from London of the Nazi governor, Heydrich. Heydrich, a particularly evil man even by Nazi standards, thoroughly deserved to die, but the reprisals which followed were appalling. Ronnie never spoke of his ordeal at the hands of the Gestapo, but when I first saw him in Colditz he looked ill, strained and much older than when I had last seen him in Warsaw.

Meanwhile plans and efforts to escape dominated the lives of most of us. Two months before my arrival Airey Neave and a Dutchman had made a clever breakout through a tunnel which took them, via the guard house, over the moat and they reached Switzerland successfully. There were usually several tunnels concurrently under construction. During the previous year ten French, four Dutch and one Polish officer had made 'home runs'. The first success during my time in Colditz was achieved by Squadron Leader Paddon who escaped from a cell at Thorn in the Polish Corridor where he had been sent to be court-martialled for 'insulting' a German warrant officer.

Escape from any camp, and especially from Colditz where German security was tight, was never easy and required a lot of ingenuity and luck. At Colditz too it was complicated by the unusually high proportion of inmates determined to escape if they could, and there had been an occasion, I was told, when British tunnellers, aiming at a buttress from the third floor, had fallen through onto some Dutch tunnellers operating similarly on the floor below! As a result, a much closer tie-up between the various national escape committees had been arranged with great success.

In the interests of everyone, a decision by the escape committee had to be final. It was quite possible, for example, and indeed happened frequently, that one might put up to the committee quite a hopeful scheme, only to be told that one's plan must wait, as that particular part of the castle had already been allocated to another venture, which must not be prejudiced.

There was, about this time, a really ambitious French tunnel in progress which began right at the pinnacle of the castle, actually in the clock tower, and was working its way slowly down to ground level. I was told that it had its own air-conditioning, electric light (usual with tunnels) and a trolley to help remove the spoil. There was so much of the latter that it could not be hidden or secretly disposed of, so it was dumped quite openly in one of the attics, where it was regularly inspected by the Germans, who hoped it would provide clues to the tunnel's whereabouts. Like nearly all long tunnels, it was eventually discovered before completion.

While life of course was not pleasant in Colditz, it was a great improvement on my previous prison experience. Indeed it was as frustrating as ever but, with so much interest and activity provided by the international aspect of the camp and the feverish escaping motif, it was never boring. Furthermore, I found the fantastically high morale of the prisoners somehow carried me along. I was later to write a chapter entitled 'A Load of Rubbish' for *Colditz Recaptured*, the book compiled by the German Security Officer, Eggers:

> The inmates, at the time of my arrival, were mainly French and Polish officers, but there were representatives of most allied countries, and the whole place was a veritable League of Nations. Life went on against the background of never-ending contest between the prisoners and the Germans. Apart from physical violence by the inmates, no holds were barred. The prisoners' aims were, first to outwit the Germans and escape; secondly to harass and annoy the Germans as much as possible; and thirdly to demonstrate their absolute confidence in final victory. The Germans' aims were, first to prevent prisoners escaping; secondly to avoid becoming annoyed; and thirdly to demonstrate their own absolute confidence in final victory. This all-in contest raged unceasingly. Sometimes the prisoners were successful, sometimes the Germans. I do not know who really won the game.

It was difficult to like our gaolers, given the circumstances of the time, but of the three officers with whom we came mostly into contact, we preferred Priem because he had a sense of humour; we respected Püpcke because he was dignified, fair and soldierly, while of Eggers opinions varied. Personally I never went along with the prevailing view that Eggers was a 'baddie' and, in the very long run (as I shall in due course record) be became, in rather an unexpected way, a 'goodie' par excellence, a kind of Colditz folk hero.

In no way am I attempting to write a history of Colditz and all the various excitements, achievements and failures which were part of our daily lives. These have already been fully and ably chronicled in numerous books, especially those by Pat Reid, and dramatized on film and television. I shall merely be telling of those things which I specially remember or which affected me the most.

Mike Sinclair, whose determination to escape never faltered and who thought of little else, had been suffering for some time from chronic sinusitis. The Germans were reasonably conscientious about health and normally made hospital treatment available when required, even though no prisoner in Colditz was ever prepared to give his parole. There were exceptions, some of which are recorded by Pat Reid, though I do not recall them. Douglas Bader may have given his parole when taken out of the camp to have his false legs repaired or maintained and, on one very special occasion, under the orders of the Senior British Officer, I gave mine, but that comes later. The Germans considered our stance on parole, when matters of health were concerned, to be unreasonable but had to accept it. Anyway, at the beginning of June Mike was taken under escort to a Leipzig hospital for a sinus operation. I believe he had been once before and had no doubt taken every opportunity for reconnaissance. This time, while still in hospital, he managed to escape and actually reached Cologne where his luck (never his strong point) ran out, and he was arrested during a major search for parachuting RAF pilots and crews, following a heavy air raid on the city.

As the summer wore on the war news grew steadily worse. We had not yet acquired a wireless set, though we learnt later that the French had one all the time, and so we relied on the German newspapers. We soon learnt how to sort out the propaganda from the real news and became very good at reading between the lines. The best source was the official High Command Report which was short and factual and printed each day in all the papers, in heavy type and surrounded by a border. It started off with the words which became so familiar to us, '*Das Oberkommando der Wehrmacht gibt bekannt*' (The Headquarters of the Armed Forces announces). Following the Japanese conquest of Malaya, Singapore, the Philippines and all the Dutch East Indies, with in consequence a direct threat to Australia, we now had to read about the rapid advance of the Germans in southern Russia until they had reached the River Volga and the Caucasus mountains. This, combined with Rommel's defeat of our Eighth Army in Libya and his rapid advance to Alamein, placed the whole of the Middle East and India in jeop-

139

ardy. I recall Rommel's proud boast, headlined in the press, '*Wir haben das Tor Aegyptens in der Hand, mit der Absicht hier zu handeln.*' (We have the gate of Egypt in our hands with the aim of settling matters here). We should have found it more depressing than we did, but our minds were too much concentrated on our own affairs to allow any ware of pessimism to sweep over us.

In September our spirits were raised by a successful escape by three British and three Dutch officers who tunnelled out from the office of the senior German Warrant officer onto the terrace and then marched out dressed as a party of Polish orderlies under German escort. Four were recaught, but Flight Lieutenant Bill Fowler and the Dutchman, Van Doorninck, reached Switzerland safely. Sadly, Bill Fowler was killed later in the war.

This success was quickly followed up. In October four British Officers, Pat Reid, Hank Wardle (a Canadian), a Lieutenant Commander called Billie Stephens and Ronnie Littledale, carried out a brilliant escape across a roof and over the moat, and all reached Switzerland. Ronnie then made his way through France and Spain back to England, alas to be killed in September 1944 when commanding the 60th's 2nd Battalion in northern France. Such successes were highlights as thereafter the record was less impressive, though not for want of trying.

As we approached Christmas 1942 our spirits, fortified by these escape achievements and by the German defeats at Stalingrad and Alamein, were reasonably high. Yet for many of us it would be the third Christmas since capture and, although it was obviously far worse for those who were married, I and most others were beginning to find the going rather heavy.

It was now nine months since I had arrived in Colditz and, although quite a number of British had made various escape attempts, I had achieved nothing. Mike Sinclair had however made a successful break in November when he and a Frenchman, Captain Charles Klein, dressed as German soldiers, had worked their way through the German headquarters building and managed to walk out of the camp without being challenged. They then separated, which must have been a mistake, Klein being caught in Plauen and Mike some fifteen miles from the Swiss frontier. Mike's error had been to walk across a major river bridge, instead of wading, swimming or finding some other route. He was caught at the far end of the bridge which he must have known would be guarded, being in a frontier zone. When one is lonely, cold and hungry one takes risks which a party of two or more might avoid by mutual encouragement. In due course I would experience this myself.

All the same, I had not been entirely idle. I had worked on a tunnel and volunteered for many hours of 'stooging' which means being on watch to report the movement of all German guards and staff and, if applicable, to give warning of their approach. I forget how this tunnel was discovered, but I remember very vividly an amusing incident when helping with a tunnel which began under the chapel pulpit, which I shall now relate.

Colditz was probably the only camp in Germany which could boast of its own real chapel, rather than a mere makeshift one. This chapel had originally been monopolized by the large number of French and Polish Roman Catholics, and it was not until a British padre had arrived that the Protestants achieved, so to speak, a foot in the door. When not in use for services, or when (as was frequent) it was closed by order of the Commandant as punishment for some misdemeanor, the chapel was placed out of bounds and kept locked with the key being held in the guardroom. Someone got the bright idea of starting a tunnel under the pulpit, so a very skilful entrance was constructed from the stairs of the British quarters through to the chapel gallery. During the periods when the chapel was closed and locked three officers would go through the makeshift entrance, two to work inside the tunnel while the third would be in the tunnel but remaining with his head out. A fourth officer would get into the mini-tunnel between the quarters stairs and the chapel gallery and the camouflaged trap would be closed behind him. There was another camouflaged trap on the gallery side which would remain open, laid flat on the gallery floor. Then, if the stooges reported Germans approaching or likely to approach the chapel, they warned the man in the gallery entrance who would pass the word orally to the man in the mouth of the tunnel by saying clearly but as quietly as possible, 'Red' or 'Amber,' as most applicable, and 'Green' when the danger had passed.

If the warning was 'Red', then the one in the tunnel mouth would close the trap over his head, while the one in the gallery entrance, having delivered his warning, would reach forward and close the trap on the chapel side of him, thus concealing himself.

On this particular occasion, one dark winter's evening, I was the chap in the gallery entrance, 'the fourth man'. Suddenly without any

'Amber' warning, I received the 'Red Alert' from the stooge on the stairs behind me who, in turn, had received it either from the one at the foot of the stairs or from a watcher at one of the windows. Having passed the warning on I lent forward, picked up the trap in front of me and started trying to fit it into position. Now this was an awkward procedure but one we had practiced pretty thoroughly so all should have been well. Unfortunately the Germans entered through the main chapel door below me too quickly, and I had no alternative but to leave the trap lying flat where it was and keep as still as possible, with my head and shoulders framed in the entrance which was too small for my total concealment. There were two German corporals searching down below, having turned on the chapel lights, and using their torches to look into all nooks and crannies. They were being quite leisurely about it all, and I realized it was only a routine check, but I was going to look an awful ass if they came along the gallery and shone their torches at me as I would be lit up like some statue in an alcove! I heard them coming slowly up into the gallery and one of them flicked on his torch and came walking toward me. I held my breath. But my usual good luck held firm. 'Come on,' said the other German, 'there's nothing here. Let's go,' and off they went. The pulpit tunnel was eventually discovered before it reached the outer wire, and the chapel was closed in retribution and only reopened several months later.

Christmas came and went. Our two excellent padres, Dickie Heard of the Queen Victoria's Rifles (in peacetime Dean of Peterhouse, Cambridge) and Ellison Platt, a Methodist, laid on the usual programme of carols and services, and a few extra parcels were drawn from store to make some sort of Christmas dinner. Some home-made wine, from raisins if one had any, otherwise from German *ersatz* jam or even potatoes, and occasionally some distilled hooch added to the jollity. Our own mess dinner was slightly marred by Jumbo who, as I have already told, had used up our carefully hoarded tin of mincemeat, from which we had hoped to concoct mince pies, by currying it.

Jumbo, our Hindu doctor, was an officer of the Royal Army Medical Corps, and thereon lies a tale. I cannot remember exactly how he came by his commission, but I imagine he was finishing his medical training in England when the war came and he volunteered. Anyway, be was taken prisoner in France and, having shown himself to be *deutschfeindlich,* was sent to Colditz. His real name was

Captain Mazumdar. He may have been anti-German, as indeed we all were at the time, but he was certainly anti-the British Raj which, with hindsight, sounds reasonable enough. Certainly he was a very likeable person and popular with us all.

Chandra Bose was trying to raise a 'national army' from among Indian prisoners of war to fight alongside the Japanese and help drive us out of India. Jumbo was therefore extremely excited when Chandra Bose arrived in Germany and was highly gratified when summoned to meet him in Berlin.

'Goodbye, Jumbo,' we all said, 'have a good war in Burma,' and 'don't be too hard on the poor old Fourteenth Army,' and similar valedictory chaffing. We never expected to see him again; yet, in a few days he was back.

'Good heavens,' we exclaimed, 'didn't he want you after all?'

'Oh yes,' said Jumbo, 'he wanted me all right, and I would very much have liked to accept his offer to join him. He's such a wonderful man. But then of course I couldn't, could I?'

'Why ever not?' we asked.

'Because I hold a British Commission, and I therefore owe my loyalty to the King, whatever my political views and private feelings may be.'

Jumbo was subsequently moved to a camp for Indians and, I understand, escaped and reached Switzerland successfully in 1943. He came back into my ken in 1985 when he joined the Colditz Association.

The close of each year always sparked off massive conjecture among the prisoners as to how much longer the war would last, the final verdict always being 'home by Christmas'. All the very understandable euphoria over the Allied victories in Russia and Africa, which made 1942 the turning point of the war, gave many of us grounds to believe that 1943 might see the end. Such optimism was essential to our morale and personally, if I had really thought that I would still be in Colditz in 1945, I should have felt something akin to despair. One does not, however, harbour thoughts which one knows one cannot face. On then to 1943 with our hopes undiminished that the year would bring either final victory or our own escape or, with luck, perhaps both. 'Hope springs eternal in the human breast.'

12

FRANZ JOSEPH

There had been a number of abortive escape attempts towards the end of 1942 but, if my memory is right, the early part of 1943 was comparatively inactive. Our hopes may have been undiminished but it was not a cheerful time, despite the good news from North Africa and the Russian front via our recent acquisition of a wireless set from some of the departing French, I believe. It was brilliantly concealed and operated under conditions of the strictest security, as described in detail by Jim Rogers in his excellent book *Tunnelling into Colditz*.

The news was listened to each day, consolidated and read out in certain rooms after the evening roll call by two or three specially selected readers. All this meant a lot of extra duties for the stooges. I am glad to say that, despite all the difficulties and complications, and the special risk of a sudden unexpected roll-call while the listeners were in with the wireless, the Germans remained to the very end in apparent ignorance of the whole business.

Jim Rogers himself was the BBC news reader in our quarters. Known as 'The Horse' at Colditz (I hope if he reads this, he will forgive me). I always thought his nickname came from his appearance, but in his book he explains it came from some equine stories which he used to tell. He was a large and very amiable Sapper, a civilian engineer in private life with connections in South Africa. Always a great enthusiast Jim undertook this role with the greatest relish. Indeed one always knew whether the news was good or bad by watching his face and general attitude during the evening parade. If 'The Horse' looked glum it would be bad news, but if he looked happy (and later in the war he could sometimes scarcely control his excitement) then the news was good. This faithful wireless team, working under the supervision of Dick Howe, who had succeeded Pat Reid as head of the Escape Committee, did much to maintain the high state of morale which was a hallmark of the Colditz camp.

In particular I have a vivid memory of the way Jim would announce some great new Russian victory on the Eastern front; 'Marshal Stalin,' (and here Jim's face would break out into a wide grin) 'with a two hundred gun salute, announced the capture of . . .' The first important town to be captured, or I suppose 'recaptured' one should say, was Wielki Luki, and the following morning on parade the French were in their best form. 'Wielki Luki,' they whispered loudly, 'Wielki Luki,' followed by one voice crying; '*Où sont les Allemands?*' and the answering chorus, echoing and re-echoing round the courtyard, '*Les Allemands sont dans la merde.*'

All this sounds exciting and almost fun yet, when I think carefully about it all, I recall it as a particularly dreary time, though I kept busy with my stooging duties and even, for a time, became the official Adjutant of the British contingent. Some time during the spring or early summer I also joined Mike Sinclair in a plan to cut the fence which surrounded part of the walk area in the park. The idea was to sit leaning our backs against the fence, prepare a panel by holding a saw under our arms and working away surreptitiously. It would all take some weeks, and the idea was that, when the panel was almost completed, we would finish it off, crawl up a bramble-covered bank and quickly slip over the wall to freedom, hoping to achieve a start of some forty-five minutes before the count which took place at the end of the walk time. The chances of success were slim enough, but Mike's enthusiasm carried me along. Alas, when the sawing was almost complete the Germans found the cuts and replaced the panel. However, Mike and I would soon be frantically busy on other and more hopeful schemes.

In July I started my Colditz diary which I managed to maintain and eventually take home with me. I decided it would be totally irresponsible to write anything which the Germans should not see because, however careful one might be to hide it, there was always a chance of it being found. It contained, therefore, mainly my comments on the progress of the war (using only material and conclusions from the German newspapers) as well as a summary of events in the camp which I did not mind the Germans reading.

In fact the Germans soon discovered the diary, as I made no attempt to hide it, and now and then removed it to check it through.

Thus I could use it to inform the Germans on things we thought it good for them to know, or perhaps what the Senior British Officer or the Escape Committee wanted them to see.

It became a real source of pleasure to me, something into which I could retreat when the going seemed tough. It would eventually fill seven thick exercise books, using both sides of every page, in tiny but very clear writing. I called it *A Journal of Prison life, looking at the war through iron bars*.

The first entry discloses an aspect of prison life often forgotten, namely occasional outbreaks of bickering. 'Another row on the table this morning at breakfast as to whether we should have jam or not. As usual I took no part and had a peaceful breakfast in the bedroom. A frightful record of Spanish music (very noisy) has just been played about four times over – almost enough to drive one mad. It's still raining, not that it makes any difference to us here whether it is wet or fine.' It was often a trying life.

On 13 July the last batch of French officers was moved from Colditz, and new British arrivals began. A party of nine came from Eichstatt who had escaped dressed as a group of German officers including one General. The real group had arrived for an inspection and, while it was at one end of the camp, the false lot walked out at the other end but they did not get very far. The 'General' was Lieutenant Colonel 'Tubby' Broomhall, a Sapper who had been captured when Senior Operations Staff Officer of our Armoured Division and would one day be a proper Major General and Engineer in Chief. Others of his party who came with him included Tony Rolt and Tony Bamfylde, both Rifle Brigade (the former had been a member of my mess at Laufen), Hector Christie, a keen racing man, and Peter Greenwell who had been at school with me. Two of my 60th friends, Martin Gilliat and Phil Pardoe who, with a number of others, had escaped through the successful wire job at Warburg and got quite a long way across the country before recapture, had arrived in June. Other people who came to Colditz with them included two more of my Rifle Brigade Laufen messmates, David Fellowes and Charlie Weld-Forester, Peter Parker of the 60th, the famous Gentleman Rider, Jack Fawcus, and Frank Weldon who would later become a very famous event rider and Badminton fence builder. It was good to see old friends again but sad in many ways that Colditz would be losing its international character.

Later in July my diary records a visit by a representative of our Protecting Power (Switzerland) and, as Camp Adjutant, I saw something of them:

A change from the usual routine. The Swiss came down for their three-monthly visit, and we had our private discussion with them lasting from 11 o'clock until 2.20 with half an hour's interval for lunch. At 2.30 Colonels Broomhall and Stayner, with John Hyde-Thompson as interpreter, went off to the Commandant's office for a discussion with the Mixed Commission (representatives of the German High Command and Foreign Office and more Swiss). Afterwards they came round the camp and were, I think, from our point of view, impressed. I was able to talk not only with the Swiss but also with the German Foreign Office representative who seemed quite reasonable. I don't suppose the camp will improve much as a result of the visit, but it made a change and gave one something to look at.

Another new arrival was Charlie Hopetoun, son of the Marquis of Linlithgow, Viceroy of India who was declared a 'prominent prisoner' and treated like Giles Romilly.

On 22 July the German newspapers reported the resignation of Mussolini 'on health grounds,' which caused us all great excitement, especially when we got the details from the BBC news that night. On the same day there was another resignation – mine from the adjutancy of the camp, mainly because the possibility of my making an escape bid had arisen, as I shall explain later.

The arrival of a new prisoner, recently captured, provided much interest, as he was able to bring us up to date on many things. He was a Lieutenant Colonel who had commanded a tank battalion in Sicily. He told us an amusing story which was not very kind to the Americans who, lacking battle experience at this stage of the war, were still rather green. When the Americans in Tunis broke before Rommel's sudden attack in the Kasserine Pass, this Lieutenant Colonel and his battalion were sent down to help. On the way he kept meeting American tanks and trucks going rapidly in the other direction. Finally he managed to stop a Lieutenant Colonel:

'What's happening?' he asked.

'Gee,' exclaimed the American, 'it's hell down there and we've taken a real beating.'

'I'm sorry to hear that,' said our man. 'Have you had many casualties?'

'No,' came the answer, 'but we would have.' Needless to say the Americans soon learnt.

A popular option for would-be escapers was to change places with people being moved to another camp, and the departure of the French contingent provided such an opportunity which three of our number took up. They reached the new camp all right but were eventually discovered and returned to us. At the same time the three Frenchmen who had swapped with them and remained at Colditz were similarly unmasked. Our three were Lieutenants Barrott (Canadian Black Watch), Hamilton and Sandbach, none of whom I knew particularly well. Giles Romilly also tried to make use of the French departure by hiding in their luggage but was discovered.

Towards the end of May, while Mike Sinclair was becoming involved in what would be known as the Franz Joseph attempt, a possible idea was given me by one of the British orderlies, a very nice young chap called Hamilton (not to be confused with his namesake referred to earlier). I was sitting sunbathing in the courtyard one hot afternoon when Hamilton came up and sat down beside me. This is what he said, 'I believe you are very keen to escape. Well then, what about this? Each week two of us have to collect rubbish from the parcels office and take it in a small handcart to a cellar in the outer courtyard underneath the German Sergeant's Mess. We do this under the strict supervision of 'Dixon Hawke' (*Unteroffizier* Schädlich nicknamed after a famous detective of fiction). Now, as I see it, we could take someone like you in the cart. The cellar is not locked and you could then have a go at getting right out of the camp.'

It was certainly the germ of an idea, and we discussed it together for some time. It appeared that the rubbish had only once been poked by the Hawke's long French bayonet and, although he normally watched while the rubbish was emptied into the cellar, Hamilton was fairly confident that his mate could distract the Hawke's attention long enough for him to bury me quickly in the deep pile of rubbish which was a permanent feature of the cellar.

Dick Howe and his Escape Committee agreed with me that the idea definitely had possibilities, but there were a number of particular difficulties, and a lot of thought and planning would be required. For the time being however, Dick explained, the Committee's attention was entirely monopolized by another major escape plan, and I would have to wait until the autumn. This would give me time to work things out and start some preparation.

What was absorbing the Committee's energies was the Franz Joseph business, one of the most exciting and ambitious escape plots ever to be tried out. This has been fully described elsewhere, so I will confine myself to a few comments and the very minor part in it allotted to me.

The plan centred around a *Feldwebel* of the guard, named *Stabsfeldwebel* Rothenberger, who had a huge ginger or blond moustache which made him resemble the Austrian Emperor Franz Joseph. I am not sure where the idea came from originally, possibly Dick Howe himself or one of the Committee, but here was an obvious case for an impersonation and his colouring and build made Mike Sinclair the most suitable choice for this role, especially as he could speak German almost perfectly.

The plan, as I have said, was an ambitious one, as it envisaged not just a small party under 'Franz Joseph' bluffing their way out, which would almost certainly have been successful, but the opening of a way for a large party, and possibly two large parties, to follow through. Mike, accompanied by two German speakers, Lance Pope and John Hyde-Thompson, both dressed, armed and equipped as sentries, would get through a specially prepared window, out of view of the German sentries, onto the parapet at the back of the castle, but still within the wire. Mike would then replace the two parapet sentries with Lance and John, on the pretext that some prisoners were thought to have escaped and they were required to make a report in the guardroom.

Mike would then order a third sentry in position by the gate in the wire, to follow the first two back to the guardroom, giving the same reason. The way now being clear the first follow-up party would descend down a rope from a window in the old British quarters (now empty and kept locked), followed, if all continued to go well, by a second party, and the whole lot would then make their way to the park and over the wall. If they were seen en route, which they might be, they were to keep running while Mike Sinclair would give the impression of chasing the party and shout orders that there was to be no shooting. If a stray German appeared Mike would send him to the guard room for reinforcements.

Preparations were fascinatingly thorough and intense. Every time the real Franz Joseph appeared (and stooges were permanently on

149

duty to watch for his approach), Mike would be advised. He would then study everything about him, the way he talked, the way he stood, the way he moved and so on. Others would be taking in the details of his uniform and equipment, while the make-up expert, Teddy Barton, would examine the moustache, the hair and complexion. Meanwhile the 'tailors' were getting busy while a special party were manufacturing the rifles, bayonets and equipment, the whole operation being covered by intense stooging.

During all these preparations the facade of normal life went on. At the beginning of August I received interesting news from home about my old prep school friend, Jack Anderson:

> **Sunday, 1 August:** I started the month well by getting two letters, one from my sister, Gwynedd, who wrote, 'We are thrilled to the marrow over the popular newspaper hero – Lucky Anderson VC, DSO. Close ups in all the dailies, briar pipe, beetling brows and six foot of harris tweed revealed none other than Jack of Copthorne days.' Apparently he is married (Gwynedd says the wife looks pretty) with a daughter aged two. When mummy wrote about him she said, 'It all makes me think how desperately you must have longed for a chance like his!'
>
> I attended Communion in the Saalhaus, the chapel being closed for the same reason it was closed when I first arrived here.

The following day was my birthday, and my entry for the day seems to be reflecting thoughts following my mother's comment:

> **Monday, 2 August:** My birthday! Actually my fourth as a POW. How frightful to think I am twenty-five. I was only just twenty-one when the war started, and I was so full of hope as to what I would do.

Soon afterwards Jack Anderson's luck ran out and he was killed. Our living accommodation was rearranged at this time:

> **Tuesday, 3 August:** On early 'Appell' we were told to move all our belongings over to the first floor in the French quarters and to evacuate our own quarters permanently. This we refused to do until an armed guard was brought in, and then we complied.

The new accommodation was very crowded, and we made ourselves so unpleasant that the Germans admitted there was some mistake and allowed us (1) to reopen the top small bedroom and (2) to continue using our old dining room until the top two floors of the French quarters could be made available to us. This allowed considerable thinning out, and I found myself finally in an extremely pleasant room (pleasant on these standards), 30 foot long and 16 foot wide, with only seven others in it including, Mike Sinclair and Alan Orr-Ewing. Furthermore the room has ample table and chair accommodation and enough cupboards and shelves. The two windows are of course barred, like all windows in the camp, and they overlook the town and the fields and woods on rising ground beyond the river.

This move, apart from an emergency shuffle in the closing weeks before our liberation, was to prove our last, and my most vivid memories of Colditz are centred on that room and the one on the floor above where we fed.

The Poles left during August, much to my sorrow, and eventually landed up at a camp near a place called Dosse.

Thursday, 10 August: We gave a farewell tea party for the Poles today, and Colonel Broomhall made a very good little speech of farewell and, at the end of Appell, he gave us 'Left Turn, three cheers for our Polish allies.'
Wednesday, 11 August: The first Polish party left for Lubeck today. One of our officers tried to go in place of a Pole but was discovered. 'Black' Campbell and Peter Allan were found in a tunnel yesterday and taken off to jug.

My diary frequently gave vent to feelings of frustration and nostalgia.

Thursday, 12 August: The glorious twelfth! Visions of Blair (Blair in Ayrshire, the home of Colonel and Mrs Blair, parents of my mother's old friend Cecily, where we used to shoot as boys) and the grouse moors, the wind and the rain in one's face, the feel of heather and peat beneath one's feet. Wonderful days!

Then two more entries in similar vein:

Saturday, 14 August: Spent the morning walking in the park with Pembum – the Germans as usual nervous, pushing us around and shouting. It was one of these fresh, cloudy mornings when the downs at home would look so beautiful.
Monday, 23 August: Today a steady drizzle, but we managed to get an afternoon walk in the rain. Martin, Phil and I trudged round and talked of old 60th days. Will there ever be such days again?

The Royal Air Force were now operating at night quite frequently over our part of Germany. Their main targets were thought to be the oil refineries at a place not far away called Leugna. These raids caused us intense excitement. First the floodlighting around the castle would be extinguished, meaning that there were RAF planes round somewhere; next stage was a wailing siren, meaning that the planes were heading towards us; finally there would be short, sharp panicky-sounding blasts on the siren, meaning that the RAF were overhead. At the first sign (lights extinguished) most of us would scramble out of bed and congregate by the windows so that, after the final warning, we would be able to hear the raid. First one would detect a faint humming, and this would gradually grow and increase until the sky above us became one great roar. Then there would be lights shooting upward and the crump of bombs exploding. All this was a help with our morale, though I, and no doubt others, continued to suffer moments of depression.

Saturday, 28 August: I find that people, even nice people, are very apt to get on one's nerves, especially those who are noisy by nature. One has constantly to guard one's temper. The trouble is that prison life is one long fight: a fight to get food; a fight to get a smoke; a fight to get a light for one's pipe; a fight to get enough room, enough quiet, enough exercise etc. Sometimes I seriously think that the ones who were killed were the lucky ones. Luckily, on the whole, I bear up fairly well.

By this time all was ready for the launching of the great Franz Joseph escape, and the attempt took place on 2 September. The plans and preparations I have already described: I took little part in them, except for extra stooging, as I was hard at work preparing my own attempt scheduled for early October. I was however given a front line stooging role, watching and reporting the progress of the operation. Together with the two main escape groups, I and some other stooges were let into the ex-British quarters, now kept locked and empty by the Germans, which overlooked the park. This was immediately after the evening 'Appell' at 9 p.m. Right from the start therefore I was crouched against a window watching the first of the parapet sentries due to be relieved from his post by Mike in his Franz Joseph role. It was breathtakingly exciting.

There followed a long, tense period, waiting for a report from the stooges on the other side of the castle that the real Franz Joseph was safely in the guardroom. It was tense enough for me, with my comparatively safe, easy and routine role, but infinitely more so for the two big escape parties and most of all for Mike and his two companions waiting for the word to go.

At last the message came, and I strained my eyes down on the parapet and the German parapet sentry whom Mike would come to first, having already passed two sentries on the way. Then suddenly they were there, Mike addressing the German, while the two false sentries stood to attention behind him. Would the German accept Mike as Franz Joseph and would he obey the order to report immediately at the guardroom? There was a ghastly pause, and then I could hear Mike raise his voice. At last, with relief mingled with rising excitement, I saw the sentry march away and Lance Pope took his place. I reported 'so far so good' but was unable to watch the rest of the drama because it was for me out of sight. The next sentry was apparently more amenable and marched off straight away 'succeeded' by John Hyde-Thompson. The third and last sentry due for relief was however made of sterner stuff and refused to move. I heard one of our watchers whisper, 'Oh God, he won't go: why the hell won't he go?' I learned afterwards that Mike had tried everything, repeating and explaining the order and finally threatening and shouting in true Teutonic fashion but to no avail. Although he clearly accepted Mike as Franz Joseph and willingly handed over his keys of the gate, so that our three principal actors could easily have made their own escape, this stout-hearted sentry simply would not budge. His orders, he said, were such that he must never leave his post unless told to by an officer: a *Feldwebel*, even if he was the guard commander, was simply not enough. Furthermore, he had, unbeknown to us, an alarm button, and this he was pressing all the time of his argument with Mike. Thus, the next thing I saw was the arrival of the real Franz Joseph with the NCO, whom we called 'Big Bum' (*Gefreiter* Pilz) and, I think, two armed sentries. They passed out of my sight as I made my report, and there followed a lot of noise, shouting and finally a loud bang.

'Mike's been shot,' I heard the whispered words, and then we were all told by Dick to disperse at once to our own quarters.

I had been unable to see the last act in the drama but, later that evening, heard it all described. What a confrontation it had been! Two identical Franz Josephs, each with drawn pistol (Mike's of course an imitation) and each accusing the other of being a fraud! Then came the shot, fired by Big Bum.

At first we were too busy standing everyone down and hiding all incriminating evidence and 'valuables' such as maps, compasses and the real German money to worry unduly over the fate of our three impersonators, though I naturally felt great concern over Mike. Happily the wound, though nasty, was not a dangerous one and after being taken to hospital he returned two days later and was sent to the sick bay for convalescence. His two companions were locked up in the cells.

It had been a brave attempt. Afterwards one felt it might have been more sensible to have limited the plan to getting the three impersonators clear away, which as things turned out would have succeeded. On the other hand it might have worked and very nearly did, and what a triumph it would then have been!

Mike was in quite good form on his return but unable to move very much. At least he was not dead, which could not be said for one of our other comrades, one Pop Olver who had recently died in hospital from heart trouble. We held a memorial service for him in the camp on 5 September, taken by Padre Platt.

This was a time of great excitement for us over the war news and especially the Allied landings on the Italian mainland:

Monday, 6 September: The landing on Italy seems to be going according to plan. Part of the Italian communiqué runs as follows:

On the Calabrian front the enemy, with strong airforce protection and a reinforced stream of troops and tank forces, has penetrated farther into the hinterland. Between Palmi and

154

Bagnara the defending troops, after they had repulsed a preliminary British troop contingent which had landed, had to withdraw. In the area east of Bagnara and in the mountain fastnesses of Aspromonte furious fighting is in progress.

Again on 8 September:

The OKW report states 'very heavy defensive fighting in the southern sector of the East Front.' I think the first time the word 'very' has crept into the communiqué in this connection. Ages ago Colonel Young (Colonel George Young RE, one of the first of our Commandos operating in the Near East) said he would shave off his moustache when the Second Front came. He had an enormous one. Now it has gone and he looks almost unrecognizable.

For some time, since Italy had been in the forefront of the news, I had been wondering about my brother John. In 1941 he had been captured during the Battle of Sidi Rezegh while serving with his regiment, The Rifle Brigade. Subsequently he had made a magnificent escape across the desert but, in the following year, had again been captured during the Battle of Knightsbridge. He had managed to swap identities with his batman with a view to further escape from his camp in Italy. On 8 September I received a letter from my mother, dated 15 August, saying it looked as though John had been moved to Germany. John was three years my elder, but my eldest brother David was also in Italy, commanding the 3rd Battalion, Welsh Guards.

Then came tremendous news of Italy's departure from the war. I recorded our reactions:

Thursday, 9 September: TREMENDOUS NEWS TODAY. Italy is out of the war, unconditional surrender! I was sitting in my room, reading, when David Wheeler (Lieutenant David Wheeler RN, one of our submariners, the others being Mike Harvey, Geoffrey Wardle and Trevor Beet) said:
'What on earth is all the shouting for in the courtyard?' I went out and saw excited groups standing reading newspapers over each other's shoulders, others shouting and the windows crowded with figures behind the bars. Someone was blowing a trumpet. I rushed up like a maniac to the nearest group and saw

155

the glaring headlines – *Feiger Verrat Badoglios*[1]. (Badoglio's cowardly betrayal.)

Meanwhile, amidst all the excitement, I was quietly but very industriously preparing my escape.

Note:
1. Badoglio, Italy's most successful soldier, took over the Government after Mussolini was deposed.

13

THE LOAD OF RUBBISH

The camp security officer during most of my time at Colditz was Captain Eggers. He survived the war and some years of tribulation afterwards to produce two books, *Colditz – The German Story* and *Colditz Recaptured*. The latter was a collection of stories, some told by prisoners and others by members of the German staff, of their experiences at Colditz. I wrote for him the story of my escape from the Castle, under the heading *A Load of Rubbish*.

This chapter is devoted to that Load of Rubbish and what became of it.

Throughout the summer of 1943, and especially during the build up for the Franz Joseph attempt, I was busy with my own preparations. The plot for my escape, described briefly in the previous chapter, sounded simple enough, but the more I thought about it and began to plan in detail, the more complicated it became.

There would be three phases. First the trip in the handcart from the parcels office and prisoners' courtyard to the Sergeants' Mess cellar in the outer courtyard; second, getting out of the camp; and, third, my journey across Germany to freedom.

The main difficulty in Phase 1 was how to gain access to the handcart, how to get into the cart without being seen by German eyes and how to be sure it was big enough, not only for me but also for my luggage and sufficient rubbish to conceal me. The parcels office was normally cleaned twice a week by the two orderlies under the supervision of the German corporal known as 'Dixon Hawke' or more usually as the Hawke. They carried the rubbish, mostly paper, cardboard and straw packing, through the gate leading from the prisoners' quarters and courtyard and down to the Sergeants' Mess cellar. I would have to be smuggled into the parcels office and packed into the cart while the Hawke's attention was distracted. He would also need distracting while I was 'emptied' into the heap of rubbish accumulating in the cellar. Hamilton and his friend were confident they could do this and told me (reassuringly?) that the Hawke only occasionally used the long French bayonet to stab into the handcart.

The Escape Committee already had a key to the parcels office and were able to provide one to the Sergeants' Mess cellar, though I forget how they obtained it. The Committee could also ensure that I could be smuggled into the parcels office unobserved by the sentry in the courtyard. Here I must explain that a number of German soldiers in the guard companies had been deliberately and systematically compromised by a small group of German-speaking prisoners who spent most of their time doing this invaluable work. To give just one example; there was an inner circle of sentries guarding the perimeter, each circle having its own password in the form of a number changed each day. By about 9 a.m. every morning the two passwords would be known by the Escape Committee, as they would be tapped out slowly by compromised sentries in full view of a prisoner watching from a window.

This subversion of German soldiers was a necessary though distasteful business. It would start with normal fraternization and be pursued slowly through the process of photos being produced showing 'my wife' and 'the children,' then 'cigarettes for you and the wife' and 'chocolate for the children' being offered and invariably accepted. Then, eventually, would come the pay off; the request for specimen passes, German money, maps, items of clothing, uniform cap badges and buttons, even parts for wireless sets and certainly passwords and information of any new security measures. It was done so skillfully until the hapless soldier, threatened if necessary with exposure, became hopelessly entwined. To my knowledge, however, such threats were never carried out. Escape was by no means only a sport but also a game played in deadly earnest, and we prisoners could be ruthless in our efforts to be free. For me there would thus be no difficulty in making certain that the courtyard sentry would be round the corner out of view of the parcels office door at the crucial moment as we only had to choose a time when the right kind of sentry was on duty.

As far as the measurements of the cart were concerned, I got them from the orderlies and calculated that it would be just big enough.

For Phase 2, when I would leave the cellar, and subsequently the camp, I would need to be dressed as a German soldier in uniform. A pathway from the outer courtyard wound its way between buildings to a gate in the main wire fence, with access beyond to the park down a very steep slope and thence to the outer wall which in places could easily be climbed. Those being taken down for the daily walk in the park passed fairly near this gate, thus providing possible scope for measuring the lock and making a key, though getting to the gate for this purpose would be difficult.

Once clean away over the wall I would remove my German uniform, hide it in a ditch or bushes and proceed dressed as a Belgian worker with false identity papers and travel and work permits which the Escape Committee would provide. I planned to go to Holland rather than Switzerland where the crossing points had become so well known both to us and to the Germans. Sufficient information to give me a reasonable chance of getting help in Holland could be made available to me, and escape routes there were believed to be well organized.

The whole operation would need a director to coordinate and control all the arrangements for stooging, reporting, timing, having all concerned in the right place at the time, ensuring everyone knew exactly what to do and, finally, at the critical moment, either giving the go-ahead or the standdown as appropriate. For this job, on which so much might well depend, I chose Tony Rolt who had been with me at Sandhurst, had joined the Rifle Brigade and had been a member of our little mess in the bad old day at Laufen. He willingly undertook the responsibility for masterminding my escape.

The immediate task was to prepare my clothing. This was bound to be a lengthy process, particularly when it came to the uniform and, in fact, took me nearly four months, even with the help of a number of the self-made experts. Cloth had to be obtained, cut, tailored, sewn and of course dyed but prisoners can do anything if they get together and pool their enthusiasm and skill, and the final results were quite good. The first attempt to dye the uniform field-grey shrank the tunic, which I had made with such labour and loving care, to about half-size, and I had to start all over again on a new one. As for the gate key, an ingenious Dutch officer undertook to manufacture, mainly from powdered milk tins, a complicated device which, if momentarily placed against the keyhole and some knobs were turned, could gauge the innards of the lock and provide the measurements required.

159

There remained however the problem of how my Dutchman could get close enough to the gate. This problem was also overcome by the Escape Committee which stage-managed a violent disturbance by the park walkers as they were being escorted down the path at the point of their route nearest the gate which was in fact about eight yards from it. In the ensuing confusion the attention of the guards was successfully diverted for the necessary five or six seconds, and the deed was done. A few days later I was presented with the key.

'Although I make no promises,' said the Dutchman, 'I believe it will work.'

By late September I was ready. My uniform and civilian outfit were finished, also my dungarees to keep me clean in the handcart. My equipment and supplies had been collected and hidden with the clothing in a searchproof cache deep under a floor. Only the actual day for the attempt would remain uncertain until we knew which sentries were due for duty in our courtyard. It was an exciting and anxious time.

The Escape Committee, which under Dick Howe had been so helpful and encouraging, gave me the green light for Monday, 4 October. I attended the morning roll call as usual and then disappeared to get myself dressed up, protected as I was doing so by the normal system of stooges. First, I put on my civilian clothes – a non-descript jacket and trousers with a workman's peaked cap in the pocket – then the German uniform, the dungarees and finally I covered it all up by putting on my British military overcoat, to wear just for crossing the courtyard. Into a small case I packed my food for the journey, consisting mainly of chocolate, raisins and biscuits, and a small, rather thin overcoat, inadequate for a German autumn but the best I could do. I also remembered to have with me a small mirror and comb, so that I could easily tidy myself up before leaving the Sergeants' Mess cellar and keep my hair in order during the journey. Needless to say I had removed my moustache, and my hair was cropped German army style. I also secreted about my person such things as maps, extracts from railway timetables, German money and forged travel and work permits as well as my faked identity document.

Any prisoner hoping to leave Colditz in an unauthorized fashion needed a great deal of luck in order to overcome all the many precautions which the Germans took to thwart such an enterprise. I prayed that Fortune would smile on me that morning and give me at least a reasonable chance of the freedom for which I had worked so hard for so long.

As I stood waiting for a signal to cross the courtyard I could see that the sentry had moved out of view of the parcels office and was being 'chatted up' by, I think, a big Czech RAF pilot called Chalupka ('Czecho'), while two members of the Escape Committee, probably Dick Howe and 'Lulu' Lawton, were unlocking the door. I saw my signal, walked across and slipped inside.

I was packed quickly into the handcart. It was no easy fit, and I ended up on my back with my knees somewhere round my neck. I was then completely covered with paper and packing. I felt like a trussed chicken and never, before or since, have been quite so uncomfortable. I began to wonder whether I would be able to endure the journey to the cellar. To make matters worse the Hawke then appeared and told the orderlies to put the cart down in the centre of the courtyard while he went off on some short errand. I was assaulted by agonies of cramp and confinement as the minutes slowly passed. I could just see out through a crack in the cart some of the prisoners walking round, and I noticed Martin Gilliat pass by close to where I lay. At last the Hawke returned, and I was carried through the gate. No stabs from the long French bayonet! On we went, tramp, tramp, tramp over the cobbles. Suddenly I heard Hamilton gasp, 'I can't hold him,' and his comrade's whispered reply, 'for God's sake keep going, man, we're nearly there.'

At last I was set down and the cellar door unlocked by the Hawke who remained outside, as was his wont, to enjoy the morning air.

They tossed me out into the pile of rubbish and buried me completely in it.

'Good luck,' whispered Hamilton, 'remember me to Blighty.'

The Hawke came in, glanced at the pile of rubbish which concealed me, and then they all went out. The key was turned in the lock, and I was alone.

For a full ten minutes I lay completely still. I then emerged quietly, stretched my numbed and aching limbs, took off my dungarees and stuffed them into my case and, using my comb and mirror, tidied myself up, smoothed over the pile of rubbish and, door-key in hand prepared to move out.

One often hears people say, 'I remember it all as if it happened yesterday'. Yet, strangely enough, that walk from the cellar to and through the gate in the wire, which was the most crucial part of the whole escape and one of the most exciting things I have ever done, I cannot remember at all. I can only imagine how I passed among the German soldiers, dressed like me and coming from their morning 'break', hoping no doubt that I looked suitably carefree with no resemblance whatsoever to a British officer dressed as a German soldier.

The anxiety and embarrassment which I must have experienced, or any incident en route I just cannot recall; it remains an unaccountable blank in my memory. I reached the gate, opened it with my miraculous key, relocked it behind me, probably resisted a strong temptation to glance back over my shoulder, walked down into the park and across it, clambered over the wall and disappeared into the woods. I was free! And with freedom memory returns and a sudden feeling of triumph and achievement still comes flooding back to me down the years and with it the lovely smell of woods and grass and earth. Nowadays, I spend much time walking through the countryside with my dogs and, whenever I smell these things, I am transported back to those moments long ago.

Such thoughts were quickly banished when I heard the shooting. Mike Sinclair, back in the castle's sick bay still recovering from his wound, also heard the shooting and sat bolt upright, full of anxiety for me. Several shots rang out in the woods to my right and, after a pause, one or two more. Shotguns, I realized at once, and not far off. A large hare came running past me, and I waved him on, thinking we were in much the same boat. Some Germans were obviously enjoying a morning's sport, and I smiled to myself as I imagined them totting up the bag at lunchtime, 'Ja, Ja, wunderbar sport today; forty-seven hare, three pheasants und one British officer.' But they must do without him, and I hurried on until the sounds of shooting died away behind me. I buried my German uniform and dungarees in a ditch and covered them with autumn leaves. I became a Belgian civilian worker and, hoping I looked the part, walked on up the hill.

The country was certainly very beautiful, particularly as I was no longer seeing it through barred windows. There were apples on the trees along the roadside, and the leaves were gorgeously autumnal.

There was no time to hang about. I had planned to reach the small town of Bad Lausich, some fifteen miles away, and catch the evening train for Leipzig. This was not so foolhardy as it sounds, for the Escape Committee had arranged to cover up my absence from the Castle. This they would do by using the 'ghosts' to take my place on roll calls: these were in fact two supernumerary prisoners, Mike Harvey, a submarine officer, and Jack Best, RAF, who had voluntarily gone into hiding when a Dutch RAF officer by the name of Van Rood had been caught back in April trying to bluff his way out dressed as a German captain. The Germans, after a prolonged search of the camp, had assumed that the escape attempt had comprised three prisoners and they had only caught one, which was exactly what they were supposed to think. The 'ghosts' were used to stand in on roll calls for someone like me who had escaped and needed a little start before the hue and cry began, or for someone working down a tunnel who might otherwise be caught out by a surprise unscheduled roll call. Naturally as there were two 'ghosts' they could thus cover two people if necessary. They gladly undertook this highly important task, despite the discomfort of much time spent in 'hidey-holes', disruption of their daily lives, and communication with home and the anxiety inevitably caused to their relatives. All praise and thanks to them. I was told I would be covered for about one week but should not count on anything longer. It meant I could catch a local train without fear that the station would be specially watched for me. I plodded on.

Once in Bad Lausich I had difficulty at first in finding the station and eventually approached a harmless-looking old lady, using one of the many phrases taught me by Lance Pope and practised in the camp, 'Der Bahnhof bitte, welche Richtung?' She told me straightaway.

Similarly I aroused no suspicion when buying my ticket at the booking office; my documents passed muster, and I caught a train for Leipzig, the one which I had selected before leaving Colditz. There were lots of people about but none took the slightest notice of me, even when I was drawn in conversation. This was most encouraging, as my foreign accent and home-made clothing were evidently arousing no suspicion. Germany by 1943 was teeming with foreign workers from almost every country in Europe, and I was posing as one of them with my faked documents showing me to be a Belgian on transfer from Saxony to the area of Rheine not far from the Dutch frontier. I knew all about the job I was supposed to be going to and had been fully rehearsed in how to answer questions about it.

So far all had gone according to plan. I intended to travel by train as far as I would find it safe to do so, and I hoped to get at least as

163

far as Rheine in this way. Walking and boy-scouting across the countryside would be too slow and too conspicuous for so long a journey. Much better, I had been advised, to travel by fast, long distance train, provided one was confident about one's travel documents. I had therefore worked out a route via Leipzig, Eisleben and Hildesheim. My regimental motto bestowed on us by General Wolfe before Quebec, was '*Celer et Audax*' (Swift and Bold), and this was how I intended to proceed.

Leipzig would be a headache. If my escape had been discovered the main station would certainly be watched, and I had decided, despite the 'ghosts', to avoid it. I knew from the timetable that my train would stop at a small suburban station south of the town and that I could continue my journey from the northern suburbs, catching a fast train to the north at Eisleben, some thirty miles on. I had a town plan of Leipzig with me and a small torch and I would spend the night crossing the town on foot.

It was a very slow train, and we were well into the evening by the time I got out, left the little station and, clutching my small case, walked off into the darkness.

Leipzig was, of course, totally blacked-out and I began to think it might be difficult to find my way. Fortunately (my usual luck was holding) it was a wonderful clear night and all the stars were shining. Checking by Casiopeia and The Plough I fixed my sights on the North Star and used it as my guide. Ever since, whenever I am out walking after dark, I look for the North Star and remember how it led me through the Leipzig black out.

It seemed a long, slow walk. Few people were about. Soon after midnight I found a low wall to sit on, while I ate some food and rested. Dawn came slowly, and I had to search around for the station but, thanks to the town plan, I found it without too much difficulty. It was full of people and my train, which turned up after considerable delay, was packed with early morning workers. Once again I had no difficulty in buying my ticket, and my travel permit was evidently in order. For some reason, however, the train did not take me as far as I had expected, and I had to walk some twenty miles to Eisleben. I must have rested on the way, and I remember picking apples off the trees and even once picking up an old chewed core and finishing it, presumably when I could no longer find an apple to pick and was feeling particularly thirsty. Anyhow, I probably missed my connection at Eisleben, for I discovered from the lady in the booking office as she handed me my ticket that the next train for the north would be leaving in the morning. This was a serious setback, as no escaper should be seen hanging around. There was however an excellent and heated waiting room, where I was able to buy a cup of *ersatz* coffee and some biscuits. After a time I settled down comfortably for the night and quickly fell into a deep sleep.

At midnight I was rudely woken by the attendant and told in no uncertain terms to clear out, as the waiting room was being closed. Where on earth could I go? I shambled off, still half asleep and fortunately wandered into the station garden, or it may have been a small park. There were some quite thick bushes scattered about, and I lay down behind one of them. I was soon once more asleep.

At 3 a.m. I was woken by the intense cold, and further sleep was impossible. Never before nor since have I ever felt as cold as I did during the next three hours, and often these days, as I lie cosy and snug in bed, I remember how miserable I was that awful early morning. Somehow I had to keep moving about to stir up my circulation without attracting the attention of some wandering police patrol.

The morning express was punctual but soon became as hot and stuffy as any modern commuter train, and as crowded. At least it was a change from being frozen stiff. I stood jammed up against the end of a compartment, as the miles slipped rapidly and beautifully by. Colditz was receding satisfactorily into the distance.

'I'm taking you home, I'm taking you home,' rattled the train, and I began to believe it really might be true.

First stop was Halberstadt where people got off and others got on. No one bothered about me and all seemed highly satisfactory until two uniformed policemen stepped abroad and ordered all documents to be produced for their inspection. With maddening thoroughness, examining papers carefully and asking questions of each traveller, they worked their way slowly up the compartment towards where I stood. At last only I and one elderly woman remained to be checked. They chose the woman first (my luck still holding) and immediately an argument began. The police soon started shouting, the woman shouted back, and suddenly the train began to move. The police abandoned their task at once, ran from the compartment and jumped down onto the platform. The train gathered speed and rumbled on its way.

We reached Hildesheim around midday. I had to change here and wait for some hours for another long-distance train which would take me west via Bad Oeynhausen to Osnabruck where I would change again for Rheine. I had intended to leave the station at Hildesheim, perhaps to go to a cinema or anyway make myself scarce and then return. It was too small a station in which to remain all day without arousing someone's curiosity, if not suspicion. As I went out through the barrier, however, I received such an inquisitive stare from the ticket collector that I changed my plan. I looked carefully again at my timetable and saw that my train would be stopping at Elze, only about ten miles away, so decided I would make my way there on foot. I do not know whether this was a good or bad decision, but it seemed sensible at the time. After all, the escaper, alone in a world of enemies, cold, hungry and tired, can only do what his instincts tell him is best. Here a companion would have helped and we could have discussed the options together and weighed up the pros and cons.

The road stretched endlessly before me, and I suddenly felt in need of rest and relaxation as well as a wash and a shave. Fortunately I had time to kill. Many years later I would drive down this very same road with my wife beside me in the car but now I was very much alone. I looked carefully round; the road was empty, and I could see no one in the fields. I walked down a track into a cornfield which had not yet been harvested and, hidden by the tall, strong German rye, I shaved, washed in water from a ditch and slept in the warm sunshine.

Then, late in the afternoon, my mental alarm clock sounded, and I woke. It was time to be getting on. Back on the road, still strangely empty, I soon found myself approaching a small village, a mile or two from Elze which I could see in the distance. I considered for a moment whether I should avoid the village and take to the fields but thought it would be more natural to keep to the road, I walked straight on.

As I entered the village I suddenly saw in front of me two policemen sitting on motor cycles chatting together. They looked fairly harmless, though they both turned to watch me as I approached. Now obviously under scrutiny I was beginning by this time to feel fairly happy and natural in my role as Belgian worker, and I gave the police a reasonably cheerful, 'Good day, lovely weather.'

They nodded amiably enough, and on I went. I had covered a good hundred yards or more when I heard both motor cycles start up, and down they swooped on me from behind.

'*Halt.*'

I stopped. They sat on their machines, one each side of me.

'What's the matter?' I asked.

'Where are you going?'

'To Elze.'

'And why are you going to Elze?'

I noticed that the one who was not doing the talking was looking at me very carefully up and down, from head to foot and back again.

'To continue my journey to Rheine. You see, I missed my connection at Hildesheim,' I explained.

'And why are you going to Rheine?'

'I am on transfer to work there,' and I gave details of the job awaiting me.

'Papers.' I produced them.

The two of them pored intently over my documents.

'Everything is in order.' I said.

They continued their study. Then suddenly, with a triumphant '*Ach*,' one of them waved my travel permit in my face.

'This paper,' he said, with great emphasis in that loud, staccato, slightly hysterical voice so beloved of German officialdom, 'is false!'

There is no doubt that the German language is extremely expressive. The word '*Falsch*' (false) seemed to be echoing back at me from walls of the houses in the street.

'*Falsch – falsch – falsch.*'

'It can't be,' I replied. 'It was what was issued to me for my journey. You can see the stamp on it.'

'No. It is false – false,' how he loved the word. I suppose, really, I must have looked suspicious, dusty from my walk, carrying my little case and out in the middle of nowhere, but I had to keep my end up. 'Look,' I said, 'I'm sure everything's OK and I really must go on. I shall be in real trouble if I miss my connection at Elze.'

It was no use. I found myself suddenly looking down the barrel of a pistol and, turning round, down the barrel of another.

'You are under arrest,' they said.

14

LAMSDORF REVISITED

To the escaping prisoner, recapture meant the difference between success and failure, triumph and disaster, freedom and captivity. Much has been said and written about freedom, but only those who have lost it and have had to live without it can have any idea of what it really means. Recapture is therefore a shattering experience, though not a new one to me. I tried again.

'Under arrest?' I exclaimed. 'Why should I be under arrest? I have done nothing wrong. I have come from Belgium to work in Germany. I am working with the Germans for the New Order in Europe and now you arrest me. That just isn't on.' *(Das geht ganz und gar nicht)* (A favourite phrase of mine). 'There must be some mistake'

'There is indeed a mistake,' came the reply, 'on your papers.

'What kind of a mistake, then?'

'A spelling mistake. Now MARCH.'

I marched. I marched with these two policemen, each on their motorcycles, one in front of me, one behind, and each with his pistol drawn. One or two passing villagers stopped and stared at our procession, and one cried out, 'What is it then?'

'He has false papers. We are investigating him.'

They took me to the village police station, a small building on the other side of the village and immediately started to question me. They explained that one of my documents had an obvious spelling mistake, though they would not show me what it was, and I realized I would not be able to maintain my role as a Belgian worker once they began to check seriously on my story. I therefore decided to try a new line, which I had thought out in advance and I told them I was

Sapper Brown of the Royal Engineers who had escaped from Lamsdorf in Upper Silesia. I chose Lamsdorf because it was there I had been taken from Cracow, so I could if necessary describe it.

'So English,' they said, and their voices betrayed that feeling of respect which foreigners strangely seem so often to show us. I have encountered it in many countries. Indeed the whole atmosphere of the police station immediately became relaxed and friendly. Nevertheless I was locked up for the night in a very dirty cell with a cup of *ersatz* coffee and a slice of bread.

If I could be accepted as Sapper Brown there would be three advantages. First, I would be protecting the Colditz 'ghosts' who would be standing in for me for a maximum of ten days; secondly, the long journey to Lamsdorf should present opportunities for escape; and, thirdly, an 'other ranks' camp was usually far less secure than one for officers. Meanwhile I had the dirt and discomfort of my cell, and my intense disappointment at being caught, to brood upon during a long, dark and rather dismal night. Much of the time in fact I spent trying unsuccessfully to remove the stout boarding over the windows with a view to getting away.

Next day I was taken in a car to Hildesheim and handed over to the military. Again my story was taken down, and I was led off to the cells. At midday I was marched off and put in yet another cell, this time at the headquarters of a 'Prisoner of war (French) Work Commando' situated elsewhere in the town. The air-raid siren sounded while we were en route. I had no contact with the French at the Work Commando. Later that afternoon I was taken to the station and thence by train (standing room only) to Hanover. There we were joined by a large group of rather smart looking prisoners, well-dressed in civilian clothes, each with a suitcase and most wearing 'homberg' or 'trilby' hats. Some of them were crowded in with me. I spoke in English and, getting no reply, then in German to the one standing next to me, 'Who are you?'

'We are Italian officers.'

'Italians? But I thought you were on the other side.'

'The Germans are arresting all the Italian officers they can get their hands on.'

'Good heavens. What are they going to do with you?'

'I understand we are going to Stalag XIB at Fallingbostel.'

I had never met an Italian before and the impression I formed of these nice and friendly people has been with me ever since.

There was also a Russian soldier with us who spoke a little German. Why he was there I have no idea, but we were heading for a place called Fallingbostel where a lot of Russian prisoners were held. He told me his work was hard, the food bad and cigarettes unobtainable. I gave him the day's ration of bread, which had been issued to me, and a slab of chocolate from my escape ration which, surprisingly, I had been allowed to retain. My poor Russian friend wolfed it all down in the greatest haste. I had no cigarettes to offer.

Fallingbostel is some thirty miles north of Hanover on the edge of the great Luneberg Heath, and we arrived there late at night. There was the usual shouting and cursing from the German NCOs as we all 'fell in' along the platform and were marched away. The camp, or what I could see of it, seemed to be a great sprawling sort of place and hutted. I was removed from my newly acquired Italian comrades, questioned rather perfunctorily and shoved into yet another cell, this one made of concrete and icy cold. It contained a small wooden plank bed which stood only six inches above the floor, two very light blankets and no mattress or pillow. I was frozen, and my limbs ached in protest at the hard bed planks so that, tired as I was, I could only sleep in snatches. Then, quite suddenly, an air-raid siren blared away and, after a little time, I could hear distant thuds and bangs as bombs rained down on Hanover. I was just dozing off again when an appalling crash, seeming to come from just outside my window, jerked me into very full consciousness. I thought perhaps an anti-aircraft gun had loosed off nearby, but I heard next morning from a Serbian soldier, who took the *ersatz* coffee round, that a British bomber had crashed just beyond the camp perimeter. Meanwhile another grimly uncomfortable night dragged slowly on.

At 6 a.m. next morning, Friday, 8 October, a whistle blew somewhere outside and a loud voice screamed, '*Aufstehen*,' (get up). Nothing more seemed to be happening, so I stayed beneath the blankets. At 7 a.m. my door was unlocked and in came a rather aggressive German corporal. At the sight of me lying in bed he flew into a rage, yelled obscenities at me and kicked my shoes right across the cell. This was too much. I had not really slept properly, and I was foolish enough to allow myself to react. German is such an expressive language for curses, and I did just as well as the corporal who stormed out, slamming and locking the door behind him. It was a bad mistake on my part and it was probably from this moment that they began to have doubts about Sapper Brown and to check more closely on my story.

Later I was allowed out of my cell to visit the lavatory down the corridor (time strictly limited), empty the bucket which served as my urinal, and wash (hands and face only permitted). Then it was back to the cell where a Russian soldier brought me a mug of that nasty mint-tasting stuff which sometimes serves as tea in Germany, saying, 'Kaffee, Kamerad.'

It was hot and I drank it gratefully enough. All my food, such as it was, had been removed from me, and I was hungry. It was also cold in the cell, which had no heating of any kind, and I had to stamp around to keep warm. Then at 11 a.m. a mug of thin vegetable soup arrived, and the same again at 5 p.m., after hours of interminable boredom.

In fact I had long ago come to terms with the boredom problem when one is locked up with no books, cards, writing materials and so on. My experiences in Laufen and Cracow had taught me how to cope, partly by endlessly reciting the poems which I loved and knew so well by heart and party by pacing endlessly up and down or doing physical exercises. Prayer too was always a help. The importance of keeping as fit as possible is obvious, though I found this difficult to achieve when one had so little to eat.

During my visits to the lavatory, limited to once a day, I soon discovered that the door from the corridor out of the cell block was always carefully locked whenever a prisoner was out of his cell and, according to a Russian who brought me my soup, the same applied whenever a cell door was for any reason unlocked. Any attempt, then, to dodge out of the cell when the soup came in would be fruitless. Equally frustrating was the size of my cell window – far too small for me to squeeze through, even if I could somehow have removed the bars. All I could do was to stay alert in case some opportunity presented itself, but the outlook was pretty bleak.

On the Saturday morning I was informed by a German NCO that Lamsdorf had failed to identify me, and I must therefore make a new statement. However, I stuck to my story despite threats that, if my true identity could not be established, I would remain where I was until 'the authorities came to a decision about your future.' In short, if I persisted in 'such folly' no one could say what might eventually become of me.

I was able to make various contacts with my fellow prisoners. A

171

Russian used to bring round the bread and soup, and we managed to exchange friendly remarks in German. Another Russian, a charming middle-aged grey-haired man who came, he told me, from Smolensk, appeared one day and gave all us cell-block inmates a welcome shave and hair cut. So few Russian prisoners survived the harsh treatment meted out to them that I have often wondered whether my charming barber was among them. Then there were several elderly-looking Serbs who were rather jolly, some very charming Poles, quite a few dirty, tough-looking and highly-spirited French, one insipid Italian, one stolid Dutchman and a very cultured Belgian. They were all extremely good to me; hatred of a common enemy can bind together in friendship peoples of different nations, customs and outlook.

Yet as I look back down the years I often wonder whether I ever really hated any German. I do not believe so. Some I disliked of course, and some I liked. Certainly I hated many of the things they did, particularly the atrocities committed on Poles, Jews, gypsies and so on, often by quite ordinary Germans who like to shelter behind *'Befehl ist Befehl.'* (Orders are orders). But I am glad to say I do not remember ever actually hating the individual Germans whom I met.

'Love your enemies, bless them that curse you, do good to them that hate you, and pray for them which despitefully use you and persecute you.' St Matthew Ch. 5 v. 44 – what a difficult command!

After nearly a week in this strange place I was suddenly informed by one of my gaolers that I had been issued with an American Red Cross parcel! Wonders will never cease! I was not actually allowed to see it, but small quantities from it were given me each day, including, particularly welcome, a few cigarettes. I was also at this time allowed to go on walks with the other cell-block inmates in the yard; half-an-hour in the mornings and the same again in the evenings. We were made to walk round in a circle, three yards apart, with our hands behind our backs, undignified perhaps but better than always being in a cell. We still had no books, no reading or writing materials of any kind, no cards. Yet in the silent loneliness of this solitary confinement it was easy to experience a spiritual presence with all the comfort and reassurance it can bring. 'Be still and know that I am God.'

One day we were paraded with our two blankets, marched off to a shower block and thoroughly deloused. My clothes, which had now been on me for some ten days were absolutely filthy and smelt vile. They were also deloused with the blankets, though I had not been conscious of having any lice. It was marvelous to get right out into the glorious October sunshine and afterwards feel clean and fresh again.

The days dragged slowly, oh so slowly by. On the Wednesday, it must have been 13 October, I reckoned that the 'ghosts' in Colditz would have been withdrawn in accordance with the plan, and I began to consider my options. I had already on several occasions been re-questioned about my identity, and the sergeant in charge of the cell block (I never saw a German officer at Fallingbostel) was continually advising me and pressing me to say who I really was. By the Friday, eleven days after my escape, I decided to 'come clean'. Why I made this decision I have no idea, because it was undoubtedly a wrong one, as events were to prove.

I can only assume that a mixture of cold, boredom and hunger managed to persuade me that I was achieving nothing by staying put and that the journey back to Colditz might provide an opportunity of getting away. Anyhow, rightly or wrongly I volunteered on the following day to make a new statement, gave my correct name and rank, admitted I had escaped from Colditz but naturally did not disclose the date and method of escape. The German sergeant showed absolutely no surprise.

'I always thought you were an officer,' he said, which I suppose was a kind of compliment.

Later that day the crew of our bomber which had crashed during my first night at Fallingbostel was brought into the cell block. There were seven in all. From my limited contact with them I thought they sounded cheerful enough though flabbergasted by the rations! They stayed two days. On Sunday, 17 October, there was a daylight air-raid alarm, and a large number of bombers, presumably American as the RAF bombed principally at night, droned by directly overhead, making a steady roar that was music to my ears. From my window I could just see the Italians in the next compound staring up at the sky and pointing at them, but my cell was on the wrong side of the block for a view.

Despite the disclosure of my true identity there was no immediate reaction, and the boredom dragged on over a very long weekend, unrelieved even by a row with the German corporal who had taken a special dislike to me since that first morning when I had failed to get up on time. My second row came when he had struck me with a broom, though not very hard, and I had pulled it from his hands. Afterwards we had exchanged some rather cross words.

On the Monday, however, exactly a fortnight since my escape, the sergeant came into my cell and told me to get '*marschbereit,*' (ready to leave). Colditz had claimed its own, or so I thought. I was however entirely wrong for I was astonished to discover that one solitary middle-aged German soldier had been sent to collect me. Colditz prisoners were usually considered worthy of a substantial escort. I picked up my case and, accompanied by this genial-looking 'Fritz,' walked out of the camp. It all seemed very friendly and relaxed, and I obviously wanted to keep it that way until I could give him the slip. I sniffed the clear, cold autumn air with considerable pleasure and opened the conversation. 'And how was Colditz when you left this morning?'

'Colditz?' he replied, 'What is that Colditz?' I cottoned on immediately.

'Where are we going?' I asked.

'Lamsdorf of course,' came the answer.

Lamsdorf! Obviously the rigid, efficient administrative machinery of the Germans had proved even more inflexible than usual and had been sparked off into action by my first mention of Lamsdorf and would take some time to slow down, stop and get into reverse. 'Hast thou appealed unto Lamsdorf? Unto Lamsdorf shalt thou go.' I was Sapper Brown again.

Needless to say, my circumstances would now have been far more favourable if I had kept my mouth shut about Colditz: however I believe it had been my belated admission that had been responsible for my move from Fallingbostel and, that without it, I would still have been sitting in that cell. Be that as it may, the net result was good in that I was now being presented with a reasonable chance of escape, nor had I compromised the 'ghosts,' though this was more by luck than judgement as I was later to learn.

We reached Fallingbostel station without incident, and the short walk had given me a chance to think out my strategy. I had no identity documents or papers of any kind which totally precluded normal railway travel, for without them I could not even buy a ticket. Equally out of the question was travel entirely on foot, as I was too far from any frontier or seaport to make it a practical pro-position. I must therefore aim at illegal and highly surreptitious boarding of a train, and a goods train would offer the best chance, one that was heading in the right direction: which direction would depend on where I was at the time.

At Fallingbostel we caught the train for Berlin, arriving at the Charlottenburg station in the fairly late evening where, 'Fritz' explained, we would have a long wait. He proved friendly and co-operative, taking me to a large waiting room full of soldiers bound for the Eastern front, some no doubt returning from leave, others perhaps reinforcements for the southern front where the battle for Stalingrad was approaching its climax. He even bought me a cup of *ersatz* coffee and some biscuits and the same for himself. It was warm and comfortable, and Fritz soon became drowsy. I pretended to be drowsy too, and eventually he fell asleep. This was my obvious chance.

I got up very quietly and left the room. The problem however, was how to leave the station. Still in my civilian clothes and, with my case, I cut a reasonably natural and inconspicuous figure and set about reconnoitering the various exits, all of which appeared to be guarded and controlled. An air-raid alarm might have helped, but none occurred. I was just wondering whether I should try to find a railway siding where there might be a goods train, or whether concealment in a lavatory would be best, when the hue and cry began. I was soon spotted, which was a bit unlucky, and rearrested by Fritz and two armed police whom he had summoned to assist him. He was naturally most aggrieved, 'I buy you coffee. I am nice and friendly and I treat you well. Why do you do this to me?'

I tried to reassure him, as I did not want him too much on the alert, by explaining that I had not been trying to escape but merely looking for a lavatory, but he was unconvinced.

Late that night we boarded a large and crowded troop train. We found standing room only and took up a position in the corridor. We steamed slowly out through the blacked-out suburbs. Some time during the night I tried a very old trick, 'May I go to the lavatory?' I asked.

'Yes, down that way,' said Fritz, and to my utter astonishment I was allowed to wander off down the corridor on my own, pushing my way past sleeping, sprawling soldiers, until I was almost at the end of the train. Once in the WC I locked the door, opened the window and waited for the train to slow down. Alas we hurtled on, and as the minutes passed by so the calls of nature brought others to the door. They knocked and waited. Then they rattled and even

175

shouted, while the train roared on, much too fast for me to contemplate a jump. Finally they banged until, frustrated beyond endurance they heaved until the flimsy door gave way. Fritz stood furious among the soldiers outside.

It was really rather unfortunate that the train never slowed at all during the ten or fifteen minutes I was alone in the WC with the window wide open, but to jump would have been suicide, or certainly well beyond reasonable risk. There is a world of difference between what might be acceptable if one was within striking distance of the frontier and safety and what could be justified in the centre of enemy-held territory. It was most frustrating.

I was now placed in a compartment and wedged between two large soldiers. I watched an angry Fritz as he sat opposite me with pistol at the ready. The nice, easy relationship between us had been replaced by open hostility. Coffee and biscuits were no longer on the menu, and indeed there was no menu at all, not even a drink of water, and Fritz ate his rations unaccompanied by me. Under the circumstances it was fair enough.

Our route had taken us through Frankfurt-on-the-Oder, Sommerfeld, Liegnitz, Sagan and Breslau. Today some of these places have been transferred to Poland and have other names.

At about 6 p.m. after what had seemed to me a very long day, we pulled into Oppeln where we got out. Here I was disagreeably surprised to find that Fritz had somehow obtained an assistant and that I now had two guards instead of one. We boarded a local train which reached Lamsdorf at, according to my diary written up later, 7.10 p.m. We walked up to the camp, just as I had done with Weekes at the end of my Polish adventure. On arrival I was received by a most unfriendly corporal, who had probably heard from Fritz of my behaviour in Berlin and on the train. He became even more unfriendly when I refused to tell him whether I possessed any German money. In fact I had quite a lot of German money, together with a miniature compass, a map of Germany and a railway timetable, all carefully and neatly packed into a small container and concealed within my body. A vigorous search, to which I was now subjected, consequently revealed nothing. My civilian clothing was then taken away and I was given a pair of shorts instead and then shoved into a cell. Sapper Brown was once again under lock and key.

Whether Fritz had brought with him a report from Fallingbostel regarding my identity I do not know but, although I seemed to be accepted as the sapper, I realized that my Colditz past would catch up with me sooner or later. There was no time to lose.

With so little clothing and not much in the way of blankets or bedding I spent a fairly unpleasant time. I was delighted, however, when I discovered in the morning that the cell next to mine was occupied by Rifleman Stokes from my own Company whom I had last seen in the streets of Calais. Several other prisoners in the block seemed free to walk about in the passage; they were all splendid people, most kind and generous to me with cigarettes, chocolate and other items from Red Cross parcels. I noted down the names of some others who wandered in from the camp (security seemed very lax) and came to see me, word of my arrival having apparently got around very possibly through Stokes, as I had told him who I was. My visitors included Colour Sergeant Nix, Sergeant Phillips, Corporal Walker, Rifleman Searle and Rifleman Truepenny – all from my battalion, and two Warrant Officers from Queen Victoria's Rifles. They spoke to me through my cell door and left me useful things like soap and toothpaste. Then to my great surprise, appeared Hill, our groom from Annington, our family home since 1938, with whom we had lost touch. I did not even know he had joined up, let alone been captured. Finally, along came Tony Stallard, our Battalion Medical Officer, to give me a check-up, and we talked much together. It was quite a reunion!

Escape, however, remained the primary consideration, and I asked my visitors whether there was any organization in the camp which could help me. Accordingly a sergeant came to my door later in the day.

'I understand from your message,' he whispered through the door, 'that you have come here as Sapper Brown but that you are actually an officer and wish to talk about escaping.'

'That is correct,' I replied. 'I understand I am allowed to walk in the courtyard for a short period each day. I believe I can escape from there into the main part of the camp. If I do this successfully, can you hide me and help me get out of the camp?'

'We can do this without difficulty. Supervision in the camp is not strict and we have three tunnels under the wire.'

'Three tunnels? Do many escape then?'

'Not really. One or two have got away, but the tunnels are used mainly by soldiers who visit the Polish girls working in a nearby factory. They meet the girls and then return through the tunnels.'

'What about tomorrow afternoon?' I said. 'I can make a recce today and let you know if it's on. I shall need food, documents, money, maps, anything you can let me have.'

'I think we can manage all that, but the documents will take some time. We can photograph you all right, but I doubt if the papers we produce are all that good.'

'Never mind. I'll have to take my chance.'

'Right Sir, but,' the sergeant's voice dropped to a whisper, 'there is one difficulty. Can you wait for a day or two? There is one of our chaps locked up here who has been court-martialled for sabotaging some industrial machinery, and he's been sentenced to death. We are planning to spring him as soon as we can and hide him up permanently in the camp. We would like to get him away first.'

Naturally I agreed at once. I realized that my time was running short and I could ill afford to wait, but I had no choice. Nothing must jeopardize the plan to save this man from execution.

They came for me the next day; a large and formidable posse from Colditz, and on the following morning, very early, I was marched away.

I never heard what happened to our gallant saboteur.

In *Colditz Recaptured*, the collection of prisoners' tales edited by Captain Eggers, I was to write:

My last memory of Lamsdorf was surprisingly a very happy one. Some thirty members of my Regiment and the Rifle Brigade had turned out to cheer me on my way. Dressed in their best battledresses and all wearing smart green sidehats, they were lined up like some guard of honour. I was allowed to walk down the two lines and say goodbye. The Germans were visibly impressed and talked about it all the way to the station. I have been granted quite a number of quarter guards and similar honours since then but none has given me such pride and pleasure as this one.

Eggers was later to write, 'The Germans recognised Grismond Davies-Scourfield as one of their more dangerous prisoners. He was not only an experienced escaper but had worked with the Polish Underground Army.'

This was a tremendous though undeserved compliment, but if this was really their opinion of me it would account for the unusually strict way I was guarded on the journey from Lamsdorf. Back at Colditz I was relieved to find that the 'ghosts' who had stood in for me had been safely withdrawn, though only in the nick of time, and were once again hidden away. It was some time, as we shall see, before the Germans discovered why it was they had failed to notice my absence.

And so it was all over; the load of rubbish had been finally swept up and disposed of. I had been a little unlucky for once in three ways; first, the mistake on one of my documents; secondly, the continued high speed of the train during those precious moments in the lavatory; and, thirdly, the delay in my attempt at Lamsdorf owing to our saboteur. But never mind. There is no room in the escape business for painful post-mortems or regrets of any kind, provided the lessons are learnt. Anyway I had survived and could always try again.

15

WIND ALONG THE WASTE

My first task back at Colditz, having given to the Escape Committee all relevant information of my travels, was to re-establish communication with home. My monthly ration of three letter-cards and four postcards was still intact, so I could write to my mother, my two sisters and also to Margaret Miller, my CO Euan's wife, with news of all the Riflemen I had met at Lamsdorf. Otherwise it was a question of settling down once more, sorting myself out and preparing, as far as I could, for yet another winter, my fourth as a prisoner and hopefully my last.

At all costs, I felt, one had to remain master of one's fate and not lapse into feeling one was at its mercy, as described by Omar Khayam:

> Into this Universe, and 'Why' not knowing,
> Nor 'Whence', like water willy-nilly flowing;
> And out of it, as Wind along the Waste,
> I know not 'Whither,' willy-nilly blowing.

This chapter, then, tells of how I tried to control my unenviable fate. I doubt if I succeeded very well.

The Escape Committee had allowed Alan Orr-Ewing to attempt, on 10 October, a repeat of my escape but he was quickly caught, I believe, when still in the cellar under the Sergeants' Mess. Even so, when I was interrogated it was clear that the Germans had no idea of how or when I had left the castle. Indeed, Eggers was to write and tell me years later that my account for *Colditz Recaptured* had solved a mystery which had never ceased to worry and intrigue him.

180

The Red Cross parcel store was at this time well stocked, which counter-acted the gradual deterioration in the rations provided by our captors. My diary recounts in generous detail a number of so-called dinner parties which sound far more scrumptious than they really were. Much of our existence was full of make-believe, none more so than in the matter of food and meals. On one occasion, for example, we apparently sat down to 'tomato soup, salmon cutlets, fried spam with gravy, mashed potatoes and peas, American orange juice, apple tart and cream, American biscuits and cheese, ending up with coffee'.

On another occasion I noted, 'Alan made a cake yesterday out of ground millet, crushed biscuits, raisins, oatmeal, margarine, treacle, the whole covered with chocolate icing'.

The diary also tells of considerable and prolonged toothache from which I suffered at this time. We had a new British dentist who was excellent but very short of dental supplies for which we relied on the Red Cross, and at one critical moment I remember his drill breaking down. He managed to get me right after several weeks of discomfort and pain, some of it severe.

Mike Sinclair had made a good recovery from his wound, and I noticed he was spending most of his spare time, night and day, staring out of our bedroom window; he was obviously concocting some new escape plan. Early in November Mike spent some time in the town cells for his part in the Franz Joseph attempt while, for my escape, I received the fairly mild sentence of ten days. I appealed against the sentence on the grounds that I had already spent so long in confinement at Fallingbostel and Lamsdorf, but the General in Dresden confirmed it.

Most of us found a spell in solitary confinement, if no longer than fourteen days, a pleasant change from the hurly burly bustle of the camp. Unlike my experience of confinement at Laufen and Posen (not to mention Cracow) we were well treated in the Colditz cells, mainly owing to the nice little Warrant Officer in charge. Although one was not supposed to take any Red Cross supplies, this amiable fellow pretended not to notice, provided one was sensible and did not try to bring too much. Reading and writing materials were permitted, and the cells were reasonably comfortable. There were two daily walks round the little courtyard, from which I believe there had once been a successful escape over the wall during a PT session. All the same, at the end of one's stint, one was usually quite glad to be back once more in circulation among friends.

When the International Red Cross representatives visited us in November (my diary records, 'They had appallingly long hair!') I inquired about my brother John who was having quite an adventurous war. While with the Rifle Brigade's 1st Battalion in North Africa he had been captured in 1941 during the battle of Sidi Rizegh. He had successfully escaped and rejoined his unit, only to be captured again the following year at 'Knightsbridge'. Now I had heard from Mrs Stilwell, who lived in Portugal and organized a service of small parcels to certain POWs including, for some reason, myself, the disappointing news that John was now a prisoner in Germany.

Later I was to learn that he was in a large camp at Brunswick, and, as Alan also had a brother there, we both applied to join them but without success. Nevertheless I was able to send him a parcel which he actually received and acknowledged. He signed himself IAN (in capitals) which was something to do with swapping identity with his batman for some purpose of escape. My elder brother, David, was fighting in Italy at this time, commanding 3rd Battalion, Welsh Guards.

During November a new Senior British Officer arrived, Lieutenant Colonel Willy Tod of the Royal Scots Fusiliers, who was a most admirable man and a great SBO. It was said that he had been on leave when the German offensive of 10 May, 1940 began, and his request to be returned to his battalion was refused by the War Office, on the grounds that men like him might be in short supply later. He therefore went to Dover and persuaded the commander of a torpedo boat to take him over, so that he was able to reach his unit and reassume command. He was captured during the retreat to Dunkirk. Soon after arriving at Colditz he heard that his only son had been killed in an accident somewhere in North Africa.

Bad news reached me from home in letters received during my ten days in the cells. These told me that two of my closest friends, Jack Anderson VC and Ambrose Greville, the Earl of Warwick's younger brother, had been killed in action, while Michael Ham, my very great friend from Winchester days, had been killed on flying training.

Bad news of this kind was of course terribly depressing and is reflected in my diary. For example:

182

Tuesday, 7 December: After three and a half years the old life recedes further and further until it is only a dim recollection, something wonderful which happened once and, one is told, may happen again, but is all far too vague to mean very much. I have even forgotten what the voices of my family sound like.

As we approached Christmas the Allied air raids hotted up, with frequent alarms at night and occasional ones by day. This could be helpful to escape plans which often depended on the floodlighting being switched off. Mike, as he stood watching by the window, would always keep careful note of the frequency and length of the blackouts and how the sentries reacted. Whether he had some definite escape plan in his mind or was merely brooding on his long and tedious captivity I was soon to know.

Meanwhile Christmas 1943 was celebrated more lustily than any other during my captivity. The fortunes of war were certainly on the turn, but the end still seemed a very long way off. Nevertheless some people had become adept at making wine and even spirits out of almost nothing, and parcels were reasonably plentiful, so there was much feasting and merrymaking. One might call this period, with apologies to Surtees, one of Jollities but without any Jaunts. Yet, apart from the religious aspect, which was important to most of us, there was really nothing to celebrate and our parties were attempts to get away from harsh reality. Even our letters from home were taking longer and longer to get through.

I shall let the Diary tell my Christmas story:

Thursday, 16 December: I haven't made an entry for some days as there has been nothing worthy of record. Papers still come in very spasmodically and several days old, and little is to be gleaned from them. There is a lot of pow-wow about 'the bluff conference at Teheran' between Churchill, Roosevelt and 'Marshal' Stalin, but they do not give us much of a picture of what happened there. We are still attacking in Italy, and the Russian battle continues as before. The Germans here are being particularly bloody about hot water. . .

Monday, 20 December: Yesterday we had our carol service in the Chapel which went off quite well. Warmish weather. Not much news. Papers still come in spasmodically and late. . . Dentist again today: I seem to have an awful lot to be done. Got

183

a letter from Margaret, my younger sister, yesterday, the first letter for a month, but it was an old one written 13 Oct, but anyway very nice to get.

Sunday, 26 December: Boxing Day! Christmas 1943 is over. My 4th Christmas as a POW is now completed. On Christmas Eve the lights were left on till one o'clock. At six-thirty two plays, each of one act, were presented in the theatre, one by the orderlies, one by the officers ('The Man in the Bowler Hat'). We then had a large and excellent supper with the spirit of Christmas already coming to life.

Christmas Day seems to have been extremely busy with church services, 'cocktail parties', large meals, four-a-side hockey in the yard and much noise and banter.

At the end of the day my diary notes, 'Poor old Alan Orr-Ewing put his hand through a pane of glass, cutting it and his forearm to the bone, but it did not seem to spoil his exuberant evening. He spent the night in a chair beside the stove.' In fact he had to have an enormous number of stitches in his hand and arm, which brought home to him that he was perhaps beginning to enjoy his home-made booze just a little too much. He kept a hoard of bottles under his bed and used to tell me that he was merely following a family tradition of heavy drinking. Perhaps he was pulling my leg.

'I really think,' he said to me one day, 'I shall sign the pledge.'

'An excellent idea' I replied.

Accordingly Alan went along to Padre Dickie Heard (Padre to the QVRs at Calais and before the war Dean of Peterhouse, Cambridge) and explained his needs.

'Fine,' said Dickie, 'I'll prepare a pledge for you.'

'There's just one proviso,' said Alan, 'it's to last only until we are liberated, just until the first Allied soldier arrives here.'

'Oh, no,' replied Dickie, 'you can't make conditions like that.'

So Alan tried our Methodist Padre, Ellison Platt. 'Certainly' said Ellison, 'sign what you like.'

Later that evening Alan gave me the news.

'I've signed the pledge' he said, rather coyly.

'Splendid!' I replied.

'Ah, yes,' said Alan, 'but as I signed it generations of Orr-Ewings were turning in their graves!'

*   *   *

1944 came in with a gale and heavy snow which made deep drifts in the courtyard. On New Year's Eve I had a party which included Frank Weldon, who became the famous event rider and Badminton fence-builder, Phil Pardoe of my Regiment, Douglas Bader the legless air ace, Peter Dollar the well known polo player and David Walker who became a famous novelist, writing *Geordie, Harry Black* and many other books. At last I received a good batch of letters from home.

> **Tuesday, 11 January:** At long last some letters! I got five today, two from Mummy (John has definitely been moved from Italy and is in this wretched country), one from Gwynedd, one from my old governess and one from Diana Davidson. No-one who has not been cut off from the world and everyone whom he loves can know what it can mean to get letters after a long period of awful silence. I was given them on the 4 p.m. Appell and, feeling that, as I had waited so long for them, I could wait a little longer, I put them resolutely into my pocket and devoured their contents at tea time.

Gwynedd was my elder sister. Diana Davidson's letter should perhaps have meant more to me than it did. I had no idea that I was to marry her soon after the war!

Sometime during the Christmas period Mike Sinclair told me of his latest plan to escape. After many weeks patiently and meticulously studying the air-raid blackouts and timing exactly the movement of sentries, he and the Escape Committee had worked out a detailed scheme. It involved getting through an upper window above our bedroom the moment a blackout began, descending by rope onto the terrace behind the guardroom, then by another rope to ground level and across an orchard and through the wire into the town. The scheme allowed for two; would I go with him?

I naturally agreed at once with great enthusiasm, and my spirits soared. They did not soar for long and a cryptic diary entry for 16 January reads, 'Excited, then violently disappointed today.'

The disappointment was caused by a decision of the Escape Committee that Jack Best, rather than I, should be Mike's travelling companion. Dick Howe explained that I had just had a run for my money, and it now seemed only fair that one of the 'ghosts' should have a chance. The decision was indeed fair and sensible and, while I accepted it with good grace, it was a grievous blow.

As in the case of most escapes, the arrangements were going to be pretty complicated and would have to be worked out with meticulous care and precision. There had to be an air-raid blackout of sufficient duration. Three sentries were involved, and each had to react in a specific way to provide the circumstances in which the attempt would have any chance of success. The bars of the exit window would need cutting in advance and then camouflaging back into place. A second rope and wire cutters would have to be taken down the first descent as well as the requirements for the journey. Stooging, reporting and strict coordination and control would be vital. Everything, right up to the moment of the final decision to launch, might have to be repeated several times, perhaps many times, before the right conditions were achieved. Mike had in fact worked out, from his many weeks of observation, that the desired conditions could only be expected once in every thirteen blackouts! The nerves of Mike and Jack, and indeed of all concerned in the operation, would therefore be tested to the limit, and a lot of people were involved. There would be a launch party under Dick Howe, and a large number of people stooging and forming communication links under me, while Tom Stallard of the Durham Light Infantry would be in overall charge as controller and coordinator.

Accounts of this nail-biting escape have already been published, including a detailed one by Jack Best himself in *Detour*, but I must record the almost unendurable excitement each time we tried to get them off. I cannot now recall the number of false starts when the right conditions failed to materialize, sometimes at the very last moment. In the almost pitch-dark room, my position was behind the launching pad which was a table pushed up to the window, and near the door through which the stooge reports would come. I can see now, quite plainly in my mind, Dick Howe by the window, and the figure of Mike lying prone on the table, his head and face covered by a balaclava, wire cutters strapped to a leg, a rope coiled round his waist and socks over his shoes: one could almost feel the intensity of his fierce and single-minded concentration on all the many things he would have to do and remember from the moment he was pushed out through the window. Anchored to a bed-post was the first rope, made of sheets tied carefully together, ready to be lowered down two stories to the terrace some thirty feet below.

Jack Best described the last moments before the 'go', 'The room was dead silent, but you could feel the atmosphere throbbing with excitement, and my heart was going nineteen to the dozen.'

It could, should or might have been me, I thought, not Jack, but there can be no 'might have beens' in our escaping world, just the task on hand to be done as best one can.

At last, on the night of Wednesday, 19 January, all went well. The messages flowed in to me. I passed them on to Tom.

'Sentry A. moving right.'

'Sentry C. now at point 3.'

'Sentry B. no movement.'

'Sentry A. now at point 1.'

'Sentry B. OK.'

'Sentry C. OK.'

'Guardroom no movement.'

'Sentry A. OK.'

'All OK now,' from me to Tom Stallard.

'Get ready – OK. LAUNCH,' from Tom to Dick. The rope of sheets was rolled out of the window and lowered, and away they went, one after the other.

For several moments all was silent. Then we heard someone come out of the guard room and shout something followed by more silence, and eventually the floodlights were switched on. Meanwhile Mike and Jack had reached ground level by the second descent from the terrace, crossed the orchard, cut the wire and were away.

We heard nothing of them for several days, and our hopes were just beginning to rise when, on 24 January the Germans came for uniforms in which to bring them back. They had got as far as Rheine aiming for Holland, like I had, when they were arrested and, as in my case, their papers declared to be false.

Jack Best had assumed the identity of another prisoner, Bob Barnes, for the escape, while Bob became Jack Best, the 'ghost'. Mike and Jack therefore went into the cells as Mike and Bob. The 'ghost' saga, however, was not to last much longer. Towards the end of March Mike Harvey, the other original 'ghost', was caught trying to escape and went into the cells as one Bartlett who immediately became a 'ghost' called Harvey! The whole puzzle was eventually unraveled by Eggers who noticed a discrepancy between the photo on the papers of the real Bartlett. Eggers has recorded how difficult it was to explain all this muddle to his superiors!

Jack and Mike's escape was followed quite quickly by further excitement when a Canadian, known as 'Dopey' Millar, escaped. I never knew exactly how he did it, though some skilful climbing and the use of a rope were, I think, involved. I remember him coming to see me a few days before he left, asking me about contacting resistance movements, and I got the impression he was aiming for Yugoslavia and Tito's partisans. He was never heard of again and is thought to have been recaught inside Germany and executed, an infringement of the Geneva Convention and an act of cold-blooded murder.

At the beginning of February Alan made what turned out to be his final bid for freedom, his third attempt since reaching Colditz in 1941. This time he managed to take the place of one of the French orderlies who were occasionally taken for walks under guard outside the castle. He made a dash away into the woods but was pursued by a sentry down to the river, into which he plunged and swam across. He was unfortunately caught while emerging onto the farther bank.

Alan used to tell a story of one of his earlier escapes before coming to Colditz. He managed to hide in a horse-drawn cart which took rubbish away to a dump out in the country. He made a hole in the rubbish above him through which he could see, peering up it through his thick-lensed glasses, for he was very shortsighted. He thus hoped to see when the best moment arrived for him to debouch from the cart and slip away into the woods. On this occasion, as bad luck would have it, the cart in which he was concealed stopped outside the kennels where the guard dogs lived, and a mass of soiled and stinking straw was hurled onto the cart. Alan, looking up through the hole he had made, trying to see what was going on, received a splash of dog mess on his glasses, depriving him of any real vision, being able to see nothing either through his smeared glasses or, because of his shortsight, without them. He was, however, a forester by profession and could tell by the smell of the trees at what moment the cart entered the woods so he was thus able to leap from the cart at the right sort of place but unable to get very far for fear of running into a tree! He was quickly recaught.

After these various excitements life seemed to settle down into a steadier, if monotonous, routine.

Tuesday, 15 February: Thawing slightly. Everything very wet and mushy. No papers today. Had a letter from Lady Davidson (Destined to be my mother-in-law). She is now Aunt Iris, rather

188

funny after all these years of formality. I have always liked her very much, so kind and thoroughly intelligent.

Sunday, 20 February: Last night there was a very big raid, not far away, probably on Leipzig. The alarm went about 4 a.m. and lasted one and a half hours. Loud explosions, which shook doors and windows, went on, and very bright flashes. We thought we could hear two planes being shot down. Today at midday there was another raid, and explosions could be heard.

Dickie preached today on Faith, Hope and Charity. Having lost my favourite, indeed my only, mug, an enamel one sent out from home, I have offered a slab of chocolate to the man who brings it back to me.

Monday, 21 February: Alan brought me my mug this morning and so got the chocolate. One of the De Gaullist messes had it. There was an air-raid alarm at 2 o'clock.

I am beginning to realize now that I have been a prisoner for far too long. My nerves seem to be all to pieces these days. I say things I do not mean and am continually having rows and bursts of fury against even my friends, particularly those I see most often – I who was always so easy to get on with and was always reckoned good company in those happy, carefree days in far off England. I have these outbursts (three today alone) and am left bitterly repentant. I simply must try to take myself in hand, but it is not easy.

Such feelings of depression never lasted long with me. It was the war seemingly dragging on endlessly and frustration through inability to think up any good escape plan.

We were eating extremely well at this time, because a large consignment of parcels tempted us to let ourselves go a bit. It was, in fact, the last normal consignment of Red Cross parcels to reach Colditz, and from now on we were to eat progressively less well until the end of the war. Prisoners and their various messes could be classed into two distinct groups, bashers and hoarders. The former quickly ran out of everything, while the latter, like our mess, were careful and eked out their dwindling reserves right up to the end. This difference in policy naturally led, in due course, to some awkward situations.

In March we had a new kind of experience, the arrival of a British 'stool-pigeon'. His name was Purdy, and he was introduced into the camp by the Germans in order to spy on us. I remember his arrival and, as he looked rather a miserable sort of chap, we went out of our way to give him a warm welcome. Unfortunately, as it turned out, he was able to see some of our tunnellers emerging from a hole and then concealing their tools and working clothes in a hide. Both the tunnel and the hide were 'discovered' by the Germans a few days later. He was in fact recognized by one of our officers who told Willy Tod that he had left the Naval Camp under very suspicious circumstances, and Willy acted at once, ordering George Young, our security officer, to interrogate him. George did a good job and obtained a complete confession from Purdy that he had been working for the German Propaganda ministry in Berlin. While Willy was negotiating with the German Commandant for Purdy's removal, I was approached by Dick Howe who told me the traitor was to be hanged as, if we merely threw him out, he would be sent to another camp and continue his misdeeds, so it was our plain duty to dispose of him. Did I agree?

I thought for a moment and then said, I supposed that I did. I was then taken by Dick up to an attic, where he had assembled some fifteen of our toughest characters. He proceeded to harangue us and made us all say, albeit I think with some reluctance, that Purdy should be fetched immediately to the attic and hanged. He even produced a rope and called for two volunteers to do the deed. There were no offers. Dick pressed us, so we suggested that perhaps he should be the hangman. No, he said, he was too well known to the Germans who would suspect him immediately. As it turned out no one was prepared to do it, although I suppose it should probably have been done, but the idea of doing it in cold blood was too much for us. The Germans almost immediately removed him. After the war he was prosecuted for working with the Germans and sentenced to death, the sentence being commuted to life imprisonment. He served some eight years.

Various escape activities, all ultimately abortive, continued to occupy our attention and the tunnel, which was almost certainly given away by Purdy, had been making excellent progress. Mike Sinclair, already depressed by the failure of his recent escape, received news at this time that his younger brother had been killed in Italy with the Scots Guards. This affected him profoundly and, from this moment he became extremely moody and difficult. I noticed that he would bite through a pipe stem in a month's smoking. Our comradeship became strained and I failed him really just when he most needed my help. Any attempts I made in that direction were rebuffed.

At least the war news was fairly good. The great Russian winter offensive was carrying the Red Army right across the Dniester and well into Poland and Romania, while our ever more frequent air-raid alarms in Colditz, both by day and night, bore evidence to the greatly increased bombing by the United States Air Force and the RAF. No longer was the outcome of the war in any doubt, and already it was Easter.

> **Sunday, 9 April:** Easter Day. I was up early and immediately after 'appell' went to the theatre for the celebration of Holy Communion. It made me realize how bad tempered, intolerant and uncharitable I have become. It was a gloriously hot sunny day. At 11 a.m. we had the Morning Service, quite well attended and some good singing: Platt preached a rattling good sermon. The air-raid alarm went during lunch. After lunch I wrote a letter to Mummy and then sat in the yard reading *War and Peace*. No change from the fronts today, the heaviest fighting going on just north of Odessa. Mike made a marvellous cake with butter for Easter: it was flavoured and iced with milk chocolate.
>
> **Monday, 10 April:** There were no papers today, being Easter Monday. There is a tremendous undercurrent of tension in the camp, people feeling that we are on the eve of great events. . .

These events would follow soon enough; some would be very good, others very bad.

16

DEATH OF THE RED FOX

Winter gradually gave way to spring, but the war dragged on, or so it seemed to us. The seasons in Colditz just came and went: one moment I would look out of the window and see the leaves just coming into bud and think it was spring at last. Then, after what seemed to be only a few days the leaves would be falling and it felt as if winter was on the way. Yet, paradoxically, the interval between felt endless.

It was a particularly trying time for those still anxious to escape, including myself who could think of nothing with any real prospect of success, and those who could fared little better.

> **Saturday, 29 April:** Last night David Wheeler (Lieutenant D. E. Wheeler RN, Submariner and a member of my mess) and Duggie Moir (Lieutenant D. N. Moir, RTR, with me at Sandhurst, captured at Calais with 3RTR) were caught trying to escape. Otherwise life goes on much as usual.
> **Tuesday, 2 May:** John Beaumont (Lieutenant J. W. Beaumont, DLI, became a parson after the war) escaped but was recaught half an hour later.
> **Wednesday, 3 May:** Geoff Wardle (Lieutenant G. Wardle, RN, Submariner and a member of my mess) has got seven days for being caught trying to get out through the orderlies' quarters.

John Beaumont's escape on 2 May was rather intriguing. He made a camouflage blanket which, when placed over him, made him look exactly like a heap of rubbish. Not only was the design and making of this blanket a work of art in itself, but the skill, achieved after intensive practice, with which he learned to snatch it from beneath his coat and twirl it over himself, was quite fantastic. Accordingly, on the day chosen for his escape, he went down on the Park Walk and on the way back, while the attention of the guards was suitably diverted, stepped out from the walking column, and the next moment, hey presto, there was no John Beaumont, only a heap of rubbish beside the path! Then, as soon as the coast was clear, he climbed into a tree, which he had previously selected for the purpose, and there survived the search which inevitably followed. From there he made a getaway but was caught soon afterwards.

Meanwhile, escape or not, I was determined to keep fit, and my diary at this time is full of reference to Physical Training and running round the cage in the Park. On 4 May I apparently did fifteen laps with Alan; on the 10th some twenty laps ('the best part of four miles') with a further twelve the next day and some fencing too. I believe the fencing equipment had been sent from Holland to some Dutch officers, one of whom was the Army Sabre champion. This burst of activity indicated a plentiful food supply, a situation which was not to last much longer, and a continuing determination to escape again. The parole outings, which had been started during the previous winter, might have helped ones well-being, both mental and physical. Pat Reid mentions in *Colditz – The Complete Story* two games of rugby on the village green, two bathing outings on the river and a visit to the town cinema. I can remember nothing much about these privileges and, like many others, felt it was wrong in principle to give one's parole and certainly never took part in them. There is a relevant diary entry:

> **Monday, 8 May:** An icy day but great amusement as the German reprisals have fallen. There wasn't much choice, and it's the theatre as usual – closed for a month. Personally I don't care one jot. I have always maintained that it is best to have as few privileges as possible (hence my not going on any parole) so that the enemy have few levers on me.

That entry is a typical example of my use of the diary to let the Germans know our feelings. This particular reprisal was for our bad behaviour during the visit of the Repatriation Board, a curious incident in itself. The names of six officers due to appear before the Board, which was made up of representatives of the International

Red Cross and of the German Government, had been crossed off the list by the Germans, either because they knew too much or were simply classified as *deutschfeindlich*. An example of the former was Kit Silverwood Cope, who suffered from thrombosis caused by typhus in Warsaw and who had been seriously maltreated while in Gestapo hands. Colonel Tod therefore refused to allow any of the British to appear before the Board unless all on the list could do so. After a fearful row the Germans gave way.

> **Saturday, 6 May:** A scuffle with the Germans today as they would not allow certain people to go before the medical board. Guards were sent into the courtyard to clear by force a space around the door. There was an extra parade at 9.0 a.m. and at 2.0. Eventually the Germans gave way completely. The following passed the Board: Kit (Lieutenant Colonel Silverwood Cope), Harry Elliott (Captain Harry Elliott, Irish Guards), 'Skipper' Barnett (Lieutenant Barnett, RN), Julius Green (Captain J. Green, Dentist), one Frenchman, 'Errol' Flynn (Flying Officer Flynn, RAF), and two of our orderlies.

The splendid and witty Irish Guards officer, Harry Elliott, who had been a member of Pat Reid's team in that very first escape from Laufen, was always in cracking good form and good for a laugh at any time. He once told me an extremely vulgar but rather amusing rhyme:

> *Captain Carter*
> *Was a wonderful farter*
> *Until a martyr*
> *To the bleeding piles:*
> *And even now, Sir,*
> *Can let a rouser*
> *In his trouser*
> *That can be heard for miles.*

Harry always roared with laughter himself when telling one something funny, indeed I can hear him now after this recitation, and I laugh with him even today when I think of it again, though he died some years ago.

All this time the war, which had seemed so remote to us prisoners, was beginning at last to creep closer. On 11 May my diary records the Russian recapture of Sebastopol; on 19 May the fall of Cassino; and many references to air raids in our vicinity, both by day and night, including 'sounds of explosions'. On 26 May (the fourth anniversary of the fall of Calais) I wrote: 'Our bombing is now so extensive and practically continuous that to record details would be too big a job.' On 28 May, however, I was moved to write:

Today was the most exciting one I have had for 4 years. The air-raid siren went at 1.15, and at about 2.30 Rupert, who was reading on his bed, suddenly looked up and said, 'Hullo, what's that noise?'

Kenneth Lockwood, and I were the only two others in the room. Kenneth said, 'Sounds like bombers' and we rushed to the window.

It was a very hot day, and the sky, though cloudless, was hazy. The air was filled with that heavy roaring sound we had sometimes heard during raids at night; yet, though we stared through the bars we could see nothing.

Suddenly a voice from another window, almost hysterical with excitement, screamed, 'Look! Straight above us!' We pressed harder against the bars but still could not see them. Then the eyes focused: one, two, three, four, five, six . . . forty-eight powerful looking planes, all in formation, were flying overhead, probably at 15,000 feet. We gazed fascinated; we had not seen a friendly plane for four years. As they passed over, another great formation betrayed its presence by glinting in the sun.

Someone appeared and shouted that more could be seen from the courtyard. I raced downstairs. The yard was full of people, shouting, pointing and staring upwards: only the German sentries looked stolidly ahead. Then excitement rose to fever pitch as one, two and three more great formations could be seen and then more following on. The noise of their engines, added to their grim relentless flight, was very inspiring.

Later we saw three parachutists drifting slowly down and disappearing behind a hill. It was all tremendously exciting, not much to people outside but to us, who would run to a window if anything out of the normal routine was going on outside, even if it was only four men marching across the village, it was a fantastic thrill.

Again, on the following day:

> This afternoon they came again, slow moving formations flying down the valley on the western side. They were higher this time and less easy to see, but now and then they caught the sun and shone brilliantly.

On 31 May I began a seven day 'stretch' of 'solitary' for being late on roll call. As the town cells were full I was put into a cell just outside our courtyard near the guardroom, actually the very one where I had spent my first night in Colditz, twenty-seven months before. This meant I was not entirely out of touch with my comrades, and there was much speculation that the invasion would come at any moment. I arranged with Rupert Barry that, if it did start, he should shout down to me during our walk on the terrace, the codeword 'THUMBS UP' and, if all seemed to be going well, 'WHACKO'. Thus, on 6 June, my last day in the cells, I got both codewords from him and the additional information that we had captured Rome.

It is difficult to recapture the euphoria in the camp during this time, so I shall let my diary tell the tale:

> **Wednesday, 7 June:** THE SECOND FRONT HAS COME!!!
> All morning the rumours flew around the camp like wildfire, and when the German papers came we saw the huge, red headlines in the *Völkischer Beobachter*, the Nazi Party's official daily paper, for example, 'The battle in the West has started,' and 'The beginning of the Invasion on the coast of northern France'. Smaller headlines in the *Leipziger* told the same story. The communiqué reads as follows, 'Last night Mon/Tues the enemy began his long-prepared, and by us expected, attack on Western Europe . . . Bitter fighting is in progress.'
> So much for the actual news. Now for the camp. It is difficult to describe our feelings. We have waited so long for this moment that most of us are almost unable to realize that the Second Front has really come. We are in a kind of daze, a daze mixed up of joy, excitement and anxiety. There are optimists who seem to think that the war is as good as won already; and pessimists who talk of the Germans' tremendous strength. Most however feel very confident but realize we still have a long way to go.

In the days that followed we all watched the papers with minute care and naturally awaited our wireless bulletins each evening with feverish impatience, but already by 9 June I was noting that feeling in the camp was sobering up. A week later we had quite a different kind of distraction:

> **Wednesday, 14 June:** The other day an advertisement for the British Free Corps was slipped into our letters! This is typical of the way in which the Germans seize every opportunity of insulting and annoying us. Apparently these 'British patriots', whose sole idea is 'the preservation of the British Empire' and 'the destruction of Bolshevism' wear German uniform with ENGLAND on the shoulders, and I wouldn't be surprised to learn that they were officered by Germans. Anyhow I sincerely hope they are all caught by the Russians (or us) and shot.

It is difficult to image what the Germans thought this advertisement could possibly achieve but presumably they hoped that at least some British prisoner might volunteer. I never heard of anyone doing so. They did have some minor success with the Free Corps idea in one or two of the occupied countries with recruitment from the civilian population, but prisoners of war would undoubtedly be a most unlikely source of volunteers. These Free Corps were supposed to be raised to fight, mainly in Russia, but I suspect they never got that far.

Excitements and distractions, though momentarily uplifting and diverting, did little to counter-act our frustration at being unable to escape and forced into idleness, especially when great events were in progress in the outside world. On that same day (14 June) I also wrote:

> People are now at such a loose end that they occupy their time minding other people's business. Someone who went to Communion this morning was asked why he had gone! One has only to wear a new piece of clothing to be asked why one is wearing it, or to have about half a dozen people making some such remark as, 'Oh, I see you are wearing a new so and so.' If one goes and stands looking out of a window for a few minutes, up comes somebody and asks what one is doing. The truth is that people who like their own company, who appreciate peace

and quiet and who prefer individual to communal existence, are being gradually driven dotty by being forced to live in a crowd which hasn't enough to do or sufficient room to spread itself.

Yet it never ceases to surprise me, in retrospect, how well we really got on together, and instances of bad temper or rows were amazingly rare. Nor did I ever come across or become aware of any instances of homosexuality throughout my entire time as a prisoner, and if such behaviour did occur, as was alleged in one book on Colditz (but not Pat Reid's), then it must have been very rare indeed.

On 17 June we saw in the newspapers the first mention of the V1s or 'Doodlebugs' as they were nicknamed in England. In Germany they were officially named *Vergeltungswaffen* (Retaliation weapons).

'The papers,' I recorded, 'are full of their answer to our "terror attacks" which appears to be some form of self-propelled or possibly wireless controlled aeroplane.'

On the same day I also recorded an incident in the continuing escape saga.

> Yesterday six people were caught in the castle drainage system, three of them under the outer courtyard. Eggers gave them a direct order to show him where the entrance was. They naturally refused. A tiresome *Unteroffizier* (Under-officer) investigating the drains of the inner courtyard, drew his revolver on some officers who were laughing at him but, when he found this only made them laugh the more, he put it away, looking very stupid.

Towards the end of June the Germans suddenly declared that all Canadian Army officers were now classified as Prominent Prisoners, while the original three (Charlie Hopetoun, Giles Romilly and Michael Alexander) would henceforth become 'Special Extra-ordinary Prominent Prisoners' without any change in their conditions: the new Prominent Prisoners, who also included Kenneth Sutherland, either because they thought erroneously that he was closely related to the Duke of Sutherland or because he had been maltreated while in Gestapo hands, would continue to be treated like the rest of us, except that they would sleep in the old

Polish long room and be locked up there at 10 p.m. each night.

July and August continued to be full of interest, though all the excitement over the battles in Normandy, Italy and Russia merely increased our frustration.

Tuesday, 27 June: A PC from Mrs Stilwell (in Lisbon) has told me that dear old David (my eldest brother) has been awarded the MC for service in Italy – tremendous news.

Thursday, 29 June: This morning there was a large air-raid, and we saw a dozen groups of Flying Fortresses, some directly over-head. At one moment there were three groups (each of sixteen planes) above us, the groups flying in different directions. They seemed to be bombing the oil works forty kilometres due West, for we could see a lot of flak bursting among the planes, and a huge smoke cloud rose up which eventually became about forty miles long. The local flak gun (a standing joke here and known as 'the Colditz cannon') let fly once, but there was something wrong as the shell was seen to land and explode in a nearby field! We only saw one German plane, nowhere near ours. The Fortresses were flying at about 15,000 feet, according to my RAF friends, and were very distinct. It was extremely thrilling to see them.

Friday, 30 June: There is an amazing story (if true?) of an agent who was fitted out with papers taken off a German prisoner captured in Africa. Unfortunately the prisoner's brother was a railway policeman, saw his brother's name on the papers when controlling them and had the agent arrested. What rotten luck!

There was a big search today in our quarters. Half the year has gone, thank goodness! My tour as mess caterer has come to an end.

Rumours were beginning to reach us via a newcomer to Colditz that a large number of RAF officers, who had escaped through a tunnel from the Sagan camp, were shot on recapture. My diary of 5 July notes that we had just heard some of the names of those executed. I believe that this bit of German barbarity figured in the Nuremberg trials after the war.

Friday, 7 July: Very hot. Allied planes were over in great strength and we got splendid views this morning, great formations of planes circling and cruising around, quite unmolested. They gleamed in the sun like great beautiful things.

Thursday, 20 July: After an interval of four weeks I heard from home today, one letter from Gwynedd, one from Margaret (my younger sister). Margaret writes, 'Isn't it splendid about David's MC? I believe he was simply marvellous, too; people writing home to say so.' Gwynedd writes, 'By the way, David has done very well and got the MC. We only heard through a young chap writing home who said they all felt that when David was there nothing could go wrong, which is a tribute to be proud of.'

The attempt on Hitler's life caused an intense flurry of interest. The Horse (Jim Rogers) was shaking all over with excitement when he read out the BBC news on 21 July, and I remember that, as I listened, I turned and looked out of the window as if to see rioting in the streets of the town. My diary records:

'Yesterday an attempt was made to kill Hitler. The *Leipziger*'s headlines are '*Mordanschlag gegen den Führer. Der Führer unverjetzt*' (Murderous attack on the Führer. The Führer unhurt). Apparently a bomb exploded during a conference. Hitler himself was burnt and bruised. Badly hurt were one general, one colonel, and one official; slightly wounded were six generals (including Jodl), two admirals, a naval captain and a lieutenant colonel. It is said to be the work of Germany's enemies.'

Later the search for Goerdeler, an ex-mayor of Leipzig and a principal conspirator, centred round our area with the local papers each day carrying his photo and a big notice, '*Wer kennt den Aufenhalt Goerdeler*'? (Who knows Goerdeler's hide-out?) He was eventually recognized and betrayed by a servant on someone's estate, or, as later reported, he was recognized in a restaurant by a member of the Women's Auxiliary Corps.

Monday, 24 July: The German army now gives the Nazi salute instead of the military salute. This is presumably as a result of the 'putsch' and one of Himmler's measures to instill army loyalty to Hitler. They look very stupid and self-conscious doing it, and it looks most unsoldierly.

200

Tuesday, 25 July: News of the adoption by the Wehrmacht (Armed Forces) of the Nazi salute is given out as follows: 'The Reichsmarschall of the Great German Reich, as the senior ranking officer of the German Wehrmacht, at the same time in the name of General Feldmarschall Keitel and Grandadmiral Dönitz, has reported to the Führer that, in recognition of his escape, all parts of the Wehrmacht have asked to be allowed to introduce the German salute into the Wehrmacht as a sign of unbreakable loyalty to the Führer and the firmest connection between Wehrmacht and Party. The Führer has granted the Wehrmacht's wish.'

These exciting events, even if their outcome proved disappointing (and, to the brave German resisters, absolutely disastrous), seemed to bring the end of the war much closer. On 25 July I was writing:

I got four letters today, two from Mummy (29 May and 27 April), one from Margaret (4 May) and one from Lady Davidson (4 May). Mummy tells me that David has written saying he is now a Lieutenant Colonel – 'Isn't it frightful?' is his own comment. Mummy writes. 'Dear old Gris, it can't be so very long now till you get back. You need not dread any preparations, you will find Annington and us just the same.' And in the earlier letter she writes: 'I don't think it will be long now before you are home and only wish you could see Annington at this moment – a glorious day and all the blossom out, including the pink cherry trees I planted along the wall and David's tree that he planted the first year we were here. David writes of the wild flowers in Italy, how marvellous they are. He has done so well. Here is an extract from a letter one of the officers wrote to his mother – 'I am terribly lucky as I am working with David Scourfield again. He is, we all think, the best soldier in the Regiment and very popular with everyone, as well as being extraordinarily competent: I don't think things could ever go wrong with him present.' Lady D tells me that Drummond (Her son, my future brother-in-law, drowned when sailing in 1948) is on a destroyer in the Med and very happy. I bet he is, the lucky devil! She goes on: 'There is one long round of meetings: I believe your mother thinks I like them. This spring seems more lovely than the others, the blossom is certainly a sight. . . As for the birds they have never sung so lustily or in such numbers.'

Tuesday, 8 August: I had a May letter from Margaret today and one from Mummy (11 June). She tells me the sad news of Pip Bankier's death in action in Italy, Micky (his twin brother) being wounded, and of Mervyn Mansel's death of wounds in Burma. Both Pip and Mervyn were very good friends of mine from schooldays at Winchester. She had also heard that David was wounded on 26 May (4th anniversary of my being wounded) but remained on duty. It is just like David to remain at his post. She also wrote, 'I hear all the men were so pleased D got the command as he is very popular with them!'

Saturday, 12 August: The glorious Twelfth! What wonderful memories are brought back, memories of the moors and butts and the thrill of the first grouse of the year. When I think of that and then look around – well, I feel like laughing.

Wednesday, 23 August: Livelier activity has been noticeable on the Colditz front today, caused by the arrival of a British Brigadier by name of Davies captured in Albania, five other British officers and three US officers (the first Americans in Colditz). All are 'Balkan bandits.'

The Americans and British (including the Canadians and the Free French forces), having broken out of their Normandy bridgehead, were now sweeping across France while, at the same time, the Russians too were gaining tremendous ground. It began to look as if the war might suddenly end. Mike Sinclair dreaded that this would happen while he was still a prisoner of war; a failure after all the efforts he had made. He became even more morose and introspective than before. Even I, his old friend and comrade, just could not get through to him at all, and, to be frank, after a number of rebuffs I ceased to try very hard.

It came as no great surprise to me therefore when, on 28 August, Mike, who had gone off on the Park Walk for the first time in months, was arrested on returning to the castle, searched and found to be wearing civilian clothes underneath his uniform. I was to be honest, a little hurt that he had told me nothing of any escape plan, and when I asked him he merely shrugged and said, 'you never know when an opportunity might suddenly arise'. On 4 September he went into the cells for fourteen days.

202

Mike was by no means alone in thinking that the war might be drawing to a close. With Allied bombers almost permanently overhead and the German armies being forced back to their frontiers both in east and west, a great wave of euphoric optimism was sweeping through out camp. Arnhem would soon bring us back to earth with a bump.

On 18 September, the day Mike came out of the cells, there was an unsuccessful attempt by (I think) Cyril Lewthwaite (Royal Warwickshire Regiment, now deceased) to dodge the column on the way back from the Park. I had a slightly similar idea forming in my mind and was not best pleased to have been upstaged. Mike also seemed annoyed when he heard about it and I was soon to find out why. It was a difficult time really, with morale soaring and plummeting on the slightest pretext. The cut in our rations (we were now down to one quarter of a parcel per head per week) and complete cessation of all private parcels did not help. I began to feel hungry again even after meals, and the mere possibility of yet another winter in Colditz was discouraging to say the least.

The Germans chose this moment to issue an official warning to all prisoners of war about the dangers of escaping, partly no doubt with the object of discouraging future attempts and partly to justify, or at least excuse, the Sagan murders. I have never seen it reproduced since then, though it has been referred to in books on Colditz and, as it is of some general and possibly even of historical interest, here is my relevant diary entry:

Saturday, 23 September: The Germans have stuck up on the notice board and distributed round the camp a notice in large red and black print with headlines, under linings etc. It reads, 'To all prisoners of war. The escape from prison camps is no longer a sport!'

It then went on to say that, in view of British commando activities and the contents of a British pamphlet espousing what it called 'a non-military form of gangster war in spheres of operations including the enemy's own country,' Germany was determined to protect its homeland. Certain forbidden zones, known as death zones, had therefore been created in which all unauthorized trespassers would be shot on sight. To avoid such a danger all prisoners of war were strongly advised to stay in their camps.

This German threat to execute or murder all escaping prisoners showed their abandonment of all pretence at civilized and honourable behaviour. It undoubtedly weakened the resolve of many would-be escapers who felt, the war being so near to an end, that even if they succeeded in getting home there would scarcely be time to be retrained and sent to the front. Indeed, Colonel Willy Tod had said that he would only approve future attempts if they provided a real chance of success. For myself I was certainly affected to some extent but, like most of us in Colditz, would never have abandoned efforts to find a good way out and felt that, at any costs, it was our duty to maintain all practical pressure on our captors, right up to the end.

Certainly nothing would ever have deflected Mike Sinclair's determination to achieve his aim; for him, the greater the danger the greater the challenge. On 25 September he made his last and most daring escape of all.

I might have guessed that this threat to shoot escapers would merely act as an additional spur to his endeavour, an extra challenge which he would almost certainly accept, indeed one which he would be unable to resist. Furthermore I knew he had some plan of sorts connected with the walk, though he had never discussed it with me or anyone else. Nevertheless, for some reason or other, I was surprised to see him that day fully clad in his French khaki cloak waiting for the Park walk to assemble. I thought to myself, 'Dear old Mike, he never gives up, and now I suppose he is still hoping for a chance to slip the column.' As he stood there he looked very much in his 'I don't want to talk to anyone' mood! Even so, I thought he needed company and tried my luck.

'Hullo, Mike,' I said encouragingly, 'I see you're going on the walk. Would you like me to come with you?'

'I'd rather go alone thank you,' he replied in a peculiarly deadpan voice.

'I don't mind coming, honestly.' I said.

'No!' I felt the intended rebuff.

This worried me. He had been very strange, ever since he had learnt of his younger brother's death at Anzio, and increasingly so as time went on. He had been wearing an almost perpetual frown, he seldom smiled, looked well beyond his years and, I particularly recall, the stems of his pipes were always quickly bitten through. Of course, in retrospect, I see how much I had failed him and now was

204

failing him again. I should have insisted on going with him or begged him to be careful or done something. Instead, as he so obviously did not want even my company, and I am sure still less my advice or admonition, I felt he must do as he wished. After all he might have some wonderful scheme with, for all I knew, the blessing of the Escape Committee, or maybe he just wanted to go for a walk without having to make conversation. At all events, I mentally shrugged my shoulders, wandered off and sat down in what was then our room to write a letter home. The room looked out over the Park, though one could see nothing through the trees and shrubs.

Suddenly, just before 3 p.m. there was a fusillade of shots and much shouting from the Park. Those of us in the room leaped to our feet and rushed to the window. 'My God, it's Mike,' I said to myself, 'it must be him.' I went down to the courtyard and stood by the main gate awaiting the walkers' return. I was filled with dread and fore-boding.

Eventually, after what seemed an age, the gate was opened. I saw Lance Pope, our camp interpreter, and asked him what had happened.

'Mike Sinclair,' he said, 'is dead.'

17

COUNTDOWN TO FREEDOM

Mike Sinclair was indeed dead, having made his final throw. Yet he had been so much a part of my life during the last four long and weary years that at first I found the reality hard to accept. This is what had happened.

Walking round the Park enclosure by himself, Mike had suddenly thrown off his cloak revealing his civilian clothes and, wearing thick leather gloves, had started to climb the high double barbed-wire fence. Immediately the nearest German guards unshouldered their rifles, yelling, 'Halt, Halt, prisoner escaping.' 'Halt or I shoot,' and similar excited cries. Counter cries from the prisoners in the compound of 'Don't shoot' added to the noise and confusion. Mike continued to climb, balanced on the top strand, stepped across to the outer fence and prepared to jump.

It so happened that the nice little *Feldwebel*, who was normally in charge of the town cells and knew and admired Mike greatly, was supervising the walk that afternoon: shouting to his sentries not to fire, and drawing his pistol, he ran round on the outside of the wire, arriving just as Mike jumped down.

'It is no use, Herr Sinclair,' he said, but Mike struck the pistol aside and ran for the cover of the trees. At least three of the sentries and the machine gunner positioned halfway up the slope towards the castle immediately opened fire. Just as Mike reached the cover of the trees a bullet struck his elbow and glanced off into his heart. Pat Reid was to write in *Colditz – The Complete Story*:

He lay still as the sentries rushed forward, swooping on their prey. He did not move when they reached him. A sentry, bending down, turned him over, while another quickly opened his shirt and felt with his hand over the heart. He was dead. He had made a home run.

Whether Mike would have claimed it as a home run is something we shall never know. What I am sure of is that he had achieved what he had set out to do, namely to escape or perish in the attempt. Yet he was not the sort of person to take a risk without carefully calculating that it was worthwhile, provided some prospect of success and therefore not only justifiable but actually, in the exercise of his soldierly duty, obligatory. His calculation would have taken into account the similar escape of a French officer, Pierre Lebrun, in the summer of 1941. Lebrun had been heaved over the wire, run the gauntlet of the sentries' fire and got clean away, eventually to reach North Africa and rejoin the French Army. If Lebrun had done it, then Mike would have reckoned, so could he. This was in no way a suicide attempt, as for Mike, suicide would be contemptible, cowardly and totally out of character.

The funeral took place a few days later in the town cemetery:

Thursday, 28 September: Mike's funeral took place this morning in the town cemetery. At 8.45 we left the Castle. Püpcke led the way, followed by the Colonel and Dickie Heard, Martin and Phil, Corporal Nugent and myself, Peter Parker and Jack Courtney, Riflemen Cowan and Le Gris. Then followed the German contingent of a *Feldwebel* and twelve men. The regimental contingent all wore battledress, the officers with regimental badges of rank, black buttons (where showing) and lanyards, and all had gaiters and boots. We marched down 'at ease'. It was a fine morning but no sun. The Service went off very well. The coffin was draped in a Union Jack and a 60th peaked hat lay on the top; it was carried to the grave by the cemetery staff. Martin read the lesson (St John xiv.1.) and also the passage from *Pilgrim's Progress* (chosen by me) about Mr Valiant-for-Truth . . . The grave itself had a small lime tree at one corner. The whole service was quiet and dignified, as I am sure Mike would have wished.

Whenever now I hear or read that famous passage from *The Pilgrim's Progress*, and particularly the words, 'and though with great difficulty I am got hither, yet now I do not repent me of all the trouble I have been at to arrive where I am,' I think specially of Mike for whom it is so apt. He would have no regrets; he had done his duty, as he saw it, right up to the end.

The same day after lunch we held a memorial service in the chapel, complete with Last Post, Reveille and the National Anthem, with 'Abide with me' and 'For All the Saints,' as our hymns. Dickie Heard gave a moving address, ending with the following passage:

> Finally Mike was a believing Christian, and one who'd known suffering and turned it to use. That's why, although his death is a tragedy for his parents, it isn't just a wasteful tragedy of a life. We say in our Creed that we believe in the resurrection of the Dead and WE KNOW that Christ's promises are sure. Mike was the kind of man who wouldn't be confident about himself, but we who know him know that he is all right, and that he's met up with his younger brother who fell at Anzio, and the countless others who in their Country's service have gone before us on the way that leads through death, but comes out in a brighter eternal world.

On the previous morning the Roman Catholics had held a special Mass for him. On the day after his death I had written:

> **Tuesday, 26 September:** Life in prison seems very different without dear old Mike pottering about, either making the coffee or mixing cocoa. Many people have come up to me and expressed their sorrow, saying how much they liked and respected Mike and what a brave chap he was.

When Martin Gilliat, Phil Pardoe and I went through Mike's belongings we came upon a note he had written and hidden among his clothes and which showed he realized how it all might end. It read, 'I take full responsibility. Safe home to you, all you good chaps.' A few days later I wrote to his father; it was a difficult letter, but I hope it helped.

Still, life had to go on. As the Allied armies on all fronts battled and bludgeoned their way slowly forward towards the frontiers of Germany, life in Colditz continued much as before. We braced ourselves for another winter and the prospect that we might not be home for Christmas after all. I wrote, 'People are getting very resigned to another winter and spring here. Feeling goes right up and down according to the news. Jim Rogers says the place should be called Hotancolditz.

During October I heard that my brother David, who had been wounded in Italy when commanding the 3rd Battalion, Welsh Guards, had been successfully evacuated and was in a Birmingham hospital, well and cheerful but with his leg in a bit of a mess. I also heard the very sad news that Ronnie Littledale had been killed when commanding our 2nd Battalion in France. I wrote, 'It's curious that Mike and Ronnie, who escaped and spent so much time together, should have been killed so near to each other in time and so far away in distance.'

The attempt in August by the Polish Home Army to drive the Germans out of Warsaw had naturally occupied my close attention. I had agonized at the way the Russians, deliberately as it turned out, had held back on their side of the Vistula to allow the Germans to destroy the Polish insurgents, and I had worried intensely over the fate of the brave Polish fighters, some of whom I must have known. The Polish Commander-in-Chief of the Home Army, General Bor-Komorowski, together with members of his staff, were however held by the Germans and granted prisoner of war status, in the hope that they would throw in their lot against the Russians. Having refused to do so they eventually joined us in Colditz.

On 21 October I noticed in one of the papers a nice chivalrous comment by a German war correspondent at Arnhem. 'The enemy,' he had written, 'fought with unusual stubbornness. The English Colonel Fock (Presumably a reference to Lieutenant Colonel John Frost whose paratroopers seized the end of Arnhem bridge and held it until the battle ended) was the soul of resistance. There were cases of paratroops, cornered by our flame-throwers and machine guns, jumping out of the first story windows of houses and, if uninjured, continuing to fight from other points of vantage.'

My diary, from which I shall be quoting a number of extracts, gives a full account of our time as the winter closed in and food became scarcer.

Friday, 27 October: Last night was the coldest since last winter, and today is cold and grey. Attended one of the historical lectures in the evening ('The Forging of the Entente'). A new arrival from the Brunswick camp brought verbal messages and two photos from my brother John.

Wednesday, 1 November: Cold, wet, and a slightly hungry day. Four 'Super Prominentes' are arriving tomorrow. The various speculations are General Urquhart (GOC 1st British Airborne Division), Lord Lascelles, General Bor, Admiral Horthy (*Regent of Hungary*), Lieutenant Colonel Churchill (caught in the Balkans) and John Elphinstone, nephew of the Queen.

Thursday, 9 November: I spent the morning preparing my lecture on the Palestine Campaign for our historical course. No breakfast these days and, by lunchtime, I was ravenous, but lunch only consisted of two mouthfuls of carrot, one potato, a very thin slice of bread with a touch of fish paste on it and half a cup of German *ersatz* coffee. During the afternoon I collected wood with Alan in the park, but our meagre diet makes me feel too slack even to enjoy walking. There is a great disappointment in the camp about the delayed end of the war. We had pinned our faith on being home this year.

Early in November two of the long expected Prominente arrived: they turned out to be John Elphinstone and a chap called de Hamel who, I think, was a godson of Churchill. A day later came Lord Lascelles (the present Lord Harewood, eldest son of the Princess Royal) and Earl Haig (son of the Field Marshal), the former being allocated to our mess.

As food became scarcer most of us were affected, often in different ways. In particular George Lascelles, being several years younger than most of us, and a prisoner for several years less, was continually gnawed by the pangs of hunger, and John Arundel (Holder of the oldest Viscountcy which ceased with his death) got TB and later died from the illness, which was undoubtedly aggravated by our increasingly poor conditions. A few others became, to a lesser or greater degree, mentally unstable, and I began to suffer from what our doctor said was neuritis in the hips (we called it 'prisoners' hip') from which I have suffered intermittently ever since.

Friday, 24 November: A representative of the International Red Cross visited the camp today and told us that it was doubtful whether any food parcels would reach us for some time. It was hoped that a few might reach us before our supply gave out, which will be at Christmas time on our present strength, but he could not promise it. All ports in France are being used for supplies and munitions, so it is understandable that no parcels can get through.

Friday, 1 December: We are getting fed up with a continual feeling of hunger. The German rations are quite edible but totally insufficient. In order to build a reserve our mess of six is only drawing two parcels per week. I had three letters today, one from Gwynedd in France (My sister was among the first batch of VADs to land in Normandy). She is roughing it but thoroughly enjoying herself and says she would not have missed the experience for anything.

Saturday, 2 December: After continual air activity in this area yesterday, today has so far (6 p.m.) had no air alarms, but we usually get one during supper which means eating in the dark. I am working very hard at my lectures for next week. The problem of keeping warm at night is a tricky one. It is essential to have windows open owing to the numbers in the room and the tobacco smoke which accumulates during the day. I have one thickness of blanket and the bottom half of the German sheet under me: over me I have the other half of the sheet, six blanket thicknesses and a great coat and my short greatcoat over my feet. In addition I wear one pair of pyjamas, a shirt, a second thick pyjama top and have stockings pulled up to my knees. I am thus tolerably warm. I suppose that on such reduced rations one's circulation is bad and one's blood thin. I had the second of Gwynedd's letters from France today: she is no longer under canvas.

During this period my diary refers almost daily to our deteriorating food situation and mentions that my weight (eleven and a half stone pre-war) had dropped to eight and three quarters stone.

We had managed, however, to save up enough food to have fairly lavish Christmas fare.

Monday, 25 December: On the whole most of us agree that this, the quietest of all our Christmases in prison (practically no-one had any alcohol) was the happiest we have spent. All the wonderful food which we ate, including some of the German rations, had been diligently saved up from our very short rations, and there was a real feeling of friendliness about the whole day.

The cold this winter was intense. Our feet would feel like blocks of ice all day and we seldom took off our greatcoats, scarves and, if we had them, balaclavas. No room was really warm enough to sit in until after teatime when the stoves would be lit so that something could be cooked for supper. Despite the way the war was going and the near certainty that our long imprisonment was coming to an end, it was for us a pretty bleak New Year. Snow fell heavily during January, while our basic fuel and food ration was cut and our supply of parcels dwindled. The reduction in our bread and potato issue was particularly serious, and German supplies by now consisted mainly of over-ripe pumpkins, Swedes, turnips and kohlrabi. The diary records:

> A most sordid scene always takes place when the vegetable carts come into the yard, with turnips etc. filthy from the fields, and deposit them in the cellars. They are not weighed out till later and are therefore fair game for pinching. They are heavily guarded by armed sentries and NCOs, but nevertheless some are usually secured by the hungry officers standing round, with the aid of the orderlies unloading them. It ought to make the Germans ashamed to see how hungry their prisoners are – that they will grovel on the ground for this food at the risk of being shot or clubbed with a rifle butt, yet they seem to take it as a matter of course. But one is so hungry one will do almost anything for food. The diet is occasionally varied by the introduction of sauerkraut (very nasty) and dried millet.

These food carts coming into the yard gave me the opportunity of talking to the horses and their drivers, and I noticed that, while one cart was pulled by two very nice, healthy-looking chestnut draught horses, the other had two miserably thin and wretched looking animals. My curiosity was aroused. 'Why,' I asked the driver of the thin pair, 'when the other horses are in such good condition yours look like skeletons?'

'Those,' he replied, 'are German horses, mine are Polish.'

At first I did not understand.

'Do you mean,' I asked, 'that German horses generally do better than Polish ones?'

'Not at all,' he answered, 'but Polish horses are not given as much to eat as German ones.'

So, I thought to myself, as well as the '*Untermensch*', we now have the '*unterpferd*' as well!.

Throughout all this our splendid SBO, Colonel Willy Tod, was marvellous. He not only set us a splendid example of fortitude but did all he could for our well-being and kept the German authorities under constant pressure, especially over the shortage of fuel for our stoves. Unfortunately our determination to have some fresh air in our rooms at night both annoyed and mystified the Germans, so that Colonel Tod's complaint fell on deaf ears.

'My soldiers report,' said the Commandant, 'that you British open your windows at night. When this practice ceases completely then I will see what can be done about the fuel.'

On 20 January six French Generals arrived. It transpired that there should have been seven, but one had been shot en route, officially 'while attempting to escape' though his comrades insisted that he had been murdered. In fact the SS officer responsible was identified some years later and I believe shot himself to avoid arrest.

Then, suddenly, we had parcels, 500 American ones, through Red Cross channels and 350 Canadian, the latter a present from a nearby Stalag (Other Ranks Camp) which had heard of our plight. This act of enormous generosity left themselves with only a tiny reserve.

> **Monday, 5 February:** I have just heard that the Polish Generals have arrived and amongst them the Warsaw revolt leader Bor-Komorowski. We now have as our Colditz celebrities George Lascelles, John Elphinstone, Charlie Hopetoun (son of Lord Linlithgow), a French Corps commander and now the leader of the Polish Underground Movement.
>
> **Tuesday, 6 February:** The Poles have now arrived – six Generals, seven officers and seven soldiers. They were all taken at the end of the Warsaw uprising.

It is hardly surprising that the morale of our guards was just about rock bottom, and even the newspapers were beginning to reflect the growing German gloom.

> **Thursday, 8 February:** The SS Standard Leader, Police President of Bromberg, by name von Salisch, together with the

Mayor of Bromberg and the head of the Bromberg City Council have all been shot by Himmler's order on account of cowardice and failure in duty. No, I'm wrong, Salisch was shot, the other two got penal servitude as did the *Bromberg Kreisleiter* (Kreisleiter was the local Nazi leader's title).

Wednesday, 14 February: 'Every German,' says an article, 'must be asking how we shall be able to achieve victory. The answer is the prevention of the enemy's military objective which is a big break-through: when the enemy sees he cannot achieve this objective he will give up the struggle.' I think this is the first time that all hopes of a positive victory has been officially discarded.

The war was now rolling rapidly on, and an air of unreality descended on the castle. Martin Gilliat and I were actually invited to visit Mike's grave in the town! For this we had to give our parole which, at this stage of the war, seemed a reasonable thing to do. It made me feel I was no longer a fully-fledged POW but existing in a kind of twilight situation:

Friday, 16 February: Martin and I were taken down on parole, under the supervision of Long Tom (our name for Capt. Püpcke), to see Mike's grave. It was a lovely springlike morning, and it felt really wonderful, almost unbelievable, to be 'outside' and to see normal life in progress – children playing in the streets, women washing their doorsteps, shop windows being cleaned and so on. Mike's grave had been marked with a wooden cross painted white, his birth and death dates inscribed with the words 'Leutnant Michael Sinclair'. The next door grave was that of a Belgian Commandant (or Major) who had died in the camp during 1940. Mike's was still covered with evergreen but looked untidy. Long Tom explained that it would be tidied up and photographed when the winter was definitely over. Long Tom then asked if we would like a small walk, so we crossed the river by a footbridge and came back along the railway and the main town bridge. The fresh air and sunlight, the smell of spring and the sound of birds singing made me feel ten years younger. We had left the camp at 9.30 and were back at 10.15.

Then suddenly we heard that 1,500 French officers, being marched from a camp near Bautzen to the east of Dresden, were about to arrive. Consequently we were uprooted from our own little patches, to which in some curious way we had become almost attached, and moved into much more crowded quarters. At the same time the Germans started laying down straw in all the passages and even in the lavatories. Then we were warned that we might be moved away altogether, so most of us started frantically making haversacks and sorting out the kit we might be able to take with us. A week later hordes of French poured into the camp in an utterly exhausted state and bedded down in the rooms allotted to them or wherever there was straw on which to lie. The poor wretches had been on the move for two weeks, maybe more, and they were in the most terrible state – unshaven, unwashed and smelling to high heaven in their filthy clothes. The lavatories became quickly blocked, and an over-powering stench settled on the camp.

Thursday, 1 March: St David's Day. Again no papers, so we are cut off from the news of the great events which must be happening at this very moment. (My diary could not, for obvious reasons, betray the presence of our wireless set.) The air-raid sirens go pretty frequently now, and we are regularly plunged into darkness after supper. Some of the French smell so strong that one almost vomits when one passes near them. No insult or criticism of the French is intended, as it was not their fault. I do think the Germans might have arranged hot showers for them after their march. Poor devils, they are like a lot of aimless, dirty animals, wandering or standing about bored, hungry and uncomfortable. The drains are still almost perma-nently blocked, and water runs in all the taps spasmodically if at all. Roll calls are chaotic. The German ration for today was four slices of bread, one twenty-seventh of a margarine packet, a plate of very thin soup and two cups of *ersatz* coffee. As we have to share with all the extra French, our parcel reserve is almost exhausted.

Saturday, 3 March: Colditz is beginning to smell worse and worse. Lice have been found amongst the French and identified as the typhus-carrying kind. Colder weather has tickled up our appetites.

Sunday, 4 March: We have just heard the story of Bigavitz, a French White Russian who used to be here. He escaped from the officers' camp at Lübeck and fell into Gestapo hands. The Commandant of Lübeck professed to know nothing about him (no doubt fearful of admitting he had lost anyone) and he remained with the Gestapo for four months in solitary confinement. He was allowed neither reading nor smoking materials and kept on a starvation diet. He spent one month, using a pin, making himself a pack of cards from the cardboard cover of the prison regulations and played 'Patience' for the next three months. Finally he managed to get a message out to his friends (how, I have no idea) and was returned to Lubeck in a very frail condition. But he was luckier than Giraud, who had also been in Colditz; he too escaped from Lubeck and was shot by the Gestapo. Giraud was one of the nicest Frenchmen here.

It was now becoming very clear that the war in Europe would be ending during the next few weeks but, in some ways, it was difficult for us long-term prisoners to visualize what being free again would really be like. Yet the old routine of day following day without great meaning was forever gone. Indeed the war had actually arrived in Colditz!

Tuesday, 20 March: Great excitement last night: a plane swooped down while the floodlights were still on and machine gunned the German headquarters wing. Bullets broke the windows of one room and embedded themselves in a table. Rumour has it that the plane was shot down nearby. Unfortunately I slept through it all.

As by now there was virtually no heating fuel available to us the Germans agreed that POW parole wood-collecting parties could be conducted into the forest beyond the town. Once again I saw no good reason to refuse parole with the war so near its end.

Thursday, 22 March: Today was the best I have spent since leaving England. The Colonel had arranged with the Germans a parole wood-collecting party. Alan was going, and I watched him enviously as he got up early, dressed and ate his breakfast, but he was continually bobbing about between bites and mouthfuls of coffee. It was a perfect spring morning. At the last minute the party was enlarged, and I was told I could go if I liked but must be ready in ten minutes. I flung on some clothes, snatched at some breakfast, while Bertie and Charles cut me a few sandwiches to take with me. I can't describe on paper the joy of walking away from the smells and crowd of the castle into the fresh, early morning spring sunshine. We had a glorious five kilometre walk up the hill beyond the river into the big forest, leaving all the sordidness of prison life behind us, right in amongst all the smells of wood and field and earth. We did a very little wood-collecting, and then Alan, Pembum and I wandered off by ourselves. In a clearing on the top of the hill we sat down and ate our picnic – we might have been on holiday at home – and we spent the afternoon meandering about or sitting in the sun. I felt strong, energetic, mentally alert, all my prison inertia swept away. I was thrilled to see Camberwell Beauties flying around, and we revelled in the song of birds. To be away from Germans, away from barbed wire, away from all the petty little problems even for a few hours – I thanked God for all the happiness that was flooding over me. At 3 o'clock we assembled and, protected by our two guards, walked slowly back to prison. As we walked into the yard the prison smell hit us in the face.

The Red Cross managed to get some food supplies through to us as April succeeded March, and a number of French officers were moved away, so food-wise, by being extremely careful and economical, we were managing to hang on, still maintain some reserve and even, on very rare occasions, to give a small party. In this way, our mess was able to entertain General Bor-Komorowski on one occasion and the French General de Boisse on another.

Throughout the first ten days of April we waited, almost breathlessly, for the Americans to arrive. Only a few weeks earlier it had looked as though the Russians would reach us first, and we were most anxious over the fate that would then be in store for our Polish friends. Plans had even been made to hide them, and Colonel Tod had asked the Commandant, without success, to have them moved further to the West. Now Eisenhower's armies had crossed the Rhine and were driving rapidly eastwards.

Thursday, 12 April: According to today's rumours, which seem to be reasonably trustworthy, allied forces have reached Magdeburg on the Elbe, and Halle, twenty-five miles from Leipzig. There is great excitement in the camp tonight. American troops are rumoured to be getting quite close, the best, and perhaps least likely, tale being that they are only twenty miles away. It is said that the German officers here have already sent their families and belongings away, but few of us believe that! People are constantly staring out of windows in a westerly direction, others are busy packing!

A few hours after I had made that entry, actually at midnight in the middle of an air-raid blackout, the Germans suddenly marched a lot of soldiers into our part of the camp, placed sentries on the entrances from our quarters to the yard and then removed all the Prominente including General Bor and his staff. There was absolutely nothing any of us, barred as we were in our quarters, could do to prevent the Prominentes' removal. It was disgracefully unfair, if true, as I understand it was, that Colonel Tod, our superb SBO, should have later been blamed for allowing the Prominente to be taken away.

Friday, 13 April: No-one knows what will happen to the Prominente, whether they will be held as hostages or what.[1] We reckon it is 50/50 on all of us being moved today if they can get us away. There are rumours that the Americans have entered Leipzig and Jena, that parachutists have been dropped twenty-seven kilometers from Berlin and that Marshal Shukov has started his offensive. The Germans here expect the Allies to arrive at any moment. Great but restrained excitement here! I spent the morning getting my belongings together, and our mess drew three parcels on the strength of the rumours: we now have six left. It seems absurd not to eat up everything. It is now midday.

Feeling suppressed excitement, not about being freed, that is too unreal an idea to be excited about – it is almost outside one's imagination – but about the possibility of being evacuated to the south of Germany. We feel that this would mean further weeks of prison under unpleasant conditions, though with some reasonable possibility of escape. Most people believe it will happen today or not at all, or at latest midday tomorrow. It is now nearly teatime. There has been no air-raid alarm yet today which is strange.

6 p.m. No word of a move as yet (touch wood!). Spent some time tidying up the belongings of George Lascelles and Michael Alexander (both Prominente) which they have left behind, and completing my own preparations for evacuation or liberation. Had cheese soufflé, bread and butter and jam and two really good cups of tea at 4 p.m. Distant gunfire can be heard at this moment ('Oh, they listened dumb and breathless and they caught the sound at last.' *The Pipes at Lucknow* by J. G. Whittier) from the direction of Leipzig and Halle.

8.30 p.m. Darkness is falling! The floodlights have come on. Still nothing about an evacuation. Gunfire to the West continues. Two columns of brown-clad troops (probably *Volksturm* local militia) have marched through the town and can be seen digging on the high ground behind the castle. A very light was seen to go up some miles away.

In this situation, part anxious, part euphoric, we bashed into our reserves of food. Supper in our mess on that Friday evening consisted of 'soup, cold salmon with potato soufflé, fried spam with fried potatoes, French beans and turnip, chocolate prune pudding and a delicious cup of coffee'.

Few of us could have slept well that night with so much to think about, anticipate and look forward to, and with the difficulty of coming to terms with a situation which we had dreamt of and yearned for during the long years which had now passed. At all events I was fast asleep at 7 o'clock the next morning when Colonel Tod stalked into our room.

'You're on the road at 10 o'clock,' he said.

The diary recorded:

We got up, washed, shaved, dressed, sorted out the stuff we wanted to take and then sat down to a huge breakfast-as much bread, butter, marmalade, spam, coffee and cake as we could possibly eat, for who could know how and when we might eat again? At 9.30 our last reserve of parcels (in the case of our rather provident mess it was six and a quarter) were brought into the yard and handed out. Next we heard news that

219

American troops had bypassed Leipzig and were forty miles from Dresden with no opposition in front of them. The Colonel then gave orders to get ready but said we would only move under threat of force.

Most of us made such plans as we could to escape from the column if we were marched away. No opportunity would, I am certain, have been missed, the motive partly to achieve some sort of triumph during the last moments of the war and partly to avoid further imprisonment elsewhere, possibly as hostages in the Bavarian mountains.

Meanwhile a major drama, as we later learned, was being enacted in the office of the Commandant, Lieutenant Colonel Prawitt, who was being confronted by Colonel Tod with his interpreter, Lance Pope and, I think, the senior French and senior American officers. Prawitt had presented them with an ultimatum. All prisoners would parade at 10 a.m., ready to move. He was persuaded, however, to postpone the parade until 11 a.m. to provide the time for final preparation which Colonel Tod insisted was required.

At 11 a.m. Prawitt, observing no signs of the parade, summoned Colonel Tod before him. He and Lance Pope went across once more to the *Kommandantur*.

'Why is the parade not ready?' asked Prawitt.

'I have changed my mind,' said Colonel Tod. 'We are not prepared to leave the castle after all.'

'Then the prisoners will be moved by force.'

'By force?' exclaimed Colonel Tod. 'Have you no idea of what is happening out there in the countryside? Don't you realize that the Americans are only twenty miles from here, advancing against virtually no opposition? They will be here in a few hours.'

'That is not our information,' replied Prawitt with some dignity.

'Then you have no information,' said our Colonel. 'We on the other hand have the BBC on our wireless which we have had, hidden in the camp, for two and a half years.' The German officers standing behind Prawitt's chair looked at each other in astonishment. They apparently had no idea that we had been enjoying BBC news. Prawitt however, said nothing for a moment, so Colonel Tod continued, 'If you attempt to use force, then I must warn you that we shall resist, and then there will be bloodshed. How will you explain this bloodshed when the Americans arrive?'

Again Prawitt said nothing. He then lifted his phone and asked to be put through to his General in Dresden.

'Hullo, yes, is that you, General? This is Prawitt speaking from Colditz.'

The general's voice could not be heard by others in the room.

'Yes, General. Certainly, General. I have already given the order. Yes, General, but they refuse to obey . . . Yes, General, that is what I said, they refuse . . . Colonel Tod, the SBO, . . . Yes General, I have him before me now. . . Yes, General, I have indeed warned him, but it makes no difference. The prisoners here are very obstinate, very determined. There will undoubtedly be bloodshed . . . I understand, General.'

Then, very slowly and clearly Prawitt spoke down the phone, 'General, will you accept responsibility for what will happen here? . . . Neither will I.' said Prawitt and put down the phone.

This was the moment, as he replaced the receiver, that Prawitt finally surrendered his authority and that of the German Army over Colditz Castle. He turned to Colonel Tod.

'What,' he asked, 'do you wish me to do.'

Note:
1. The Prominente were taken as hostages to Bavaria and, after many adventures, released unharmed.

18

FOR THIS RELIEF
MUCH THANKS

Colonel Tod was in a difficult position. Although he had told Prawitt that the Americans (US Cavalry to the rescue) would be arriving at any moment, it was partly bluff. From our latest information on the BBC and from talking to the German sentries, we did not seriously expect them until, at the earliest, next day. Personally I found it difficult to visualize their coming at all; it was beyond imagination, or so I felt. The Colditz Germans under Prawitt might be willing to cooperate, but the SS Company, which Prawitt said had recently arrived to organize the town's defence, most certainly would not. Indeed SS reaction to any takeover of the castle by the prisoners would undoubtedly be extremely violent. Prawitt's genuine anxiety on this score was shared by Colonel Tod.

A compromise was therefore reached. Sentries round the castle would remain on duty in the normal way, armed but without ammunition, and none of Prawitt's men would take any part in the defence of the town against the Americans. It was a delicate situation for all concerned.

Amidst the excitement I continued to maintain my diary and guarded closely all the seven notebooks which contained it. The entry for Saturday, 14 April, which has recorded the events so far described, continued:

As the morning wore on it became pretty clear that if we were moved it would only be outside to the woods. Distant explosions could be heard all round. Just before lunch the Colonel

222

had an interview with Prawitt, the Commandant, and was informed that the Americans were reported twenty kilometres to the south of us and on the river, and that there was no question of moving us at the moment. We had a very good light lunch.

It is now 2 p.m. The Colonel is about to have another interview with Prawitt. No more news of the Americans' whereabouts. An occasional shell has been seen to burst in the distance. Trains have been running as usual and there is no sign either of troop movements or aerial activity. The camp is naturally very excited, but not much noise. I suppose this is one of the greatest days of my life, but I merely feel rather exhausted and as if a great burden which has been on my back for nearly five years has suddenly slipped off! The guards are still on duty round the camp.

At 6.30 p.m. A lovely evening. Just heard John's camp near Brunswick has been relieved!! Smoke on the horizon and now continual gunfire. We hear the Americans are only a few miles away. Groups of *Volksturm* are in defensive positions in the town and fields round about. We have so much food lying around – it's amazing to lash jam and cheese and butter all over the place – haven't done that for years. 'Enemy Armoured Units' warning has gone this afternoon. Everyone here remains calm – we are speculating on the possible arrival of the Americans tonight.

Next morning most of us were up at the crack of dawn to gaze out of the windows towards the west. It was a beautiful day, but there was no sign of the war.

The early Communion service was sparsely attended, about seven or eight of us turning up. At about 8.45, just as we were reaching the climax of the service, there came a sudden roar of planes low overhead and the sound of loud explosions and bursts of machine-gun fire. Discipline, however prevailed and we remained motionless on our knees. Dickie Heard completed the service with almost indecent haste, and we rushed for the nearest windows.

What we saw seemed utterly unbelievable, and for several moments I was totally unable to take it in: for American planes (Thunderbolts, I believe) were circling and diving over the town and letting fly with machine guns and cannon. We watched fascinated: one plane dived right past and slightly below my window and I could see the pilot quite clearly. This went on for nearly twenty minutes until the planes suddenly vanished, and all was quiet again.

The diary jogs my memory sufficiently to enable me to recount the remainder of this amazing day.

At 11.30, having had some breakfast, I returned to the attics to obtain the best possible view, though every west-facing window was crowded and one had to shove and push to get a place. The countryside looked quiet and peaceful enough except for some smoke from burning buildings in the town. Then quite suddenly someone shouted, 'Look! Tanks!' and sure enough, round the end of the great wood, some two or three miles away, came five of them, moving slowly and spreading out into a cornfield where they stopped.

I was smoking a pipe at that moment, and the sight of the tanks so excited me that my mouth gaped open and my precious pipe, which had come in my mother's last clothing parcel, fell all the way down onto the terrace below and landed at the feet of a sentry. A few moments later I retrieved it from him at the main courtyard gate. A small segment had broken off from the round top of the bowl, and as the pipe remained in use for several years I was constantly being reminded of that dramatic moment when the American tanks first came into view.

The tanks could, in fact, have been German, and there was considerable argument among our 'experts' about their identity, but Americans they proved to be. Meanwhile then more Thunderbolts appeared and subjected the town to further strafing. Was it all really happening?

Strangely, as the tanks moved no further, we who had waited so very patiently all these years now became ridiculously and unreasonably impatient. For heaven's sake, why don't they move? Don't just sit there, come on, get cracking! What on earth do they think they're doing? The silly words echoed round the attic. I suppose we were all light-headed with the prospect of imminent release.

At all events we had not long to wait. At 1.30 the tanks suddenly began to move along the edge of the wood, and, now joined by others, subjected the southern part of the town to some intense fire. We could see their gun-flashes quite clearly. At 2.30 (according to my diary) two shells landed close to the *Kommandantur*, and Colonel Tod ordered us all down to the ground floor. Shortly afterwards some shell splinters penetrated the roof above the attic we had left. The general sounds of battle steadily increased.

Clutching my precious notebooks, which contained my diary, I retreated with some others into what had once been the medical room which was on the side of the courtyard furthest from the town. Even so an occasional shell came over us and landed somewhere behind. One of these, or possibly a mortar bomb, burst just outside while Bertie Boustead was sitting on the loo; the blast came through the window behind, blowing open the door, and his trousers, wrenched from his legs, disappeared with great velocity down the passage!

Suddenly a particularly loud bang announced an unsuccessful German attempt to blow the large bridge which spanned the River Mulde in the centre of the town. At about the same time one Frenchman, still in an attic, was wounded by a shell splinter in his ankle, and Colonel Tod's two lookouts, which he had stationed at an upper window, had several narrow escapes.

By teatime our flags were hoisted on the clock tower, one Polish, one French and a Union Jack, and these may have been partly responsible for the noise abating. Indeed it became quite quiet, and we began to wonder what was going on. Two of us from each mess were allowed to go back to our quarters to make some tea so Bertie, now happily reunited with his trousers, and I went up and had a good look from the windows. We could not see very much owing to smoke from a number of fires. Someone said that American infantry had been seen crossing the river to the south of us, and Püpcke confirmed that the Castle was almost completely surrounded.

We had supper, still downstairs, to the accompaniment of spasmodic explosions, and then the noise all seemed to die away. 'Who has won?' we wondered.

Colonel Tod allowed us back into our own quarters for the night but, after so much excitement, I found it difficult to sleep. There were still some occasional bangs and crumps and, at one moment, shells came whistling unpleasantly close overhead.

At dawn all was quiet. In the early light we could see the American soldiers moving about quite casually on the far side of the river; actually Americans, our Allies, our friends and about to be our rescuers! At one moment we noticed a German civilian, with his hands above his head, walking across the bridge towards the Americans at the far end. Then suddenly he seemed to lose his nerve, hesitated and ran. A burst of fire from the Americans cut him down. No one seemed very interested in us or the castle, so Colonel Tod sent David Walker and Eggers to contact the Americans and report that the Commandant wished to surrender the castle. Although they could have been targets for either side, they accomplished their mission safely and successfully.

I went down to the courtyard which was full of prisoners waiting for something to happen. After a while the great gate into our courtyard opened and through it, muddy and filthy from battle, steel-helmeted and armed to the teeth, came the first American GI most of us had ever seen. He stopped, looked nervously around him and, as one or two prisoners started towards him, shouted, 'keep back' and threatened with his rifle. Then two or three others came in and joined the first, the tension relaxed and the oh-so-long awaited moment had arrived. Suddenly we were all shouting and cheering and making friends with our liberators. We even invited them to breakfast, and one came up to our mess. He was quite exhausted and utterly famished, so we fed him well. He did not say much but we gathered that his unit had been continuously in action or on the move since they had crossed the Rhine. My diary noted, 'We are free at last. From 26 May, 1940 to 16 April, 1945 I have been a prisoner of war, 1,785 days!'

Too much excitement inevitably clouds the memory, and I must increasingly rely on my diary to recall all those wonderful moments of the next few days. One or two flashes of memory do however remain vividly with me. There was Alan, released from his pledge, opening up a bottle, most of which was avidly consumed by a GI! There was the rather smashing American female war correspondent who wanted to interview Bader and eventually took him away with her to have him flown home. There was the sight of all our guards being paraded to be marched away into their imprisonment. In particular I remember seeing one rather elderly German soldier, whom we knew quite well, appearing with his bicycle and his belongings strapped on its carrier, only to have it seized by an American and thrown over the drawbridge into the moat. Others were kicked and shoved; one felt sorry for them.

Meanwhile Colonel Tod was busy taking over the castle, liaising with the Americans and commandeering an adequate supply of rations. I remember we had an extremely good lunch, after which I was sent down to the town with Alan on patrol, the idea being to see that only prisoners of war with passes were down there. The diary continues, 'Fancy being able to walk about the town! On

226

the way back three rather ancient-looking German soldiers were handed over to me for escort back to the castle.'

The dramatic change in our fortunes, which had come about, with such suddenness, was so exciting that it dulled our senses and produced, certainly in me, a feeling of total unreality. This was increased when, a little later, I was invited by an American officer to look at two survivors from the local concentration camp, all but four of the inmates having been shot by the SS guards just before the Americans arrived. I was shown two living skeletons, though I understand they did not long survive, lying on a bed, quite unconscious, arms and legs like matchsticks and bodies covered with sores and bruises. One of them, I was told, was believed to be an eminent Budapest doctor. It was a terrible sight and one I shall never be able to forget.

An American soldier dined with us in our mess, and we had quite a party.

The next morning I spent with Charles Elwell, a RNVR Lieutenant and a member of my mess. We looked all round the *Kommandantur*, then walked down into the town and visited Mike's grave, (moved later to the Imperial War Graves Cemetery, West Berlin). We had a long talk with the woman in charge of the churchyard. She seemed very nice, and while we were chatting a heavy bombardment started up from the direction of Leipzig.

'The fools!' cried the woman, 'Why do they go on resisting? There is no further point.' She went on to say how thankful everyone was in Colditz that it was the Americans and not the Russians who would be occupying their area. Alas, she was to be terribly disappointed as the Americans eventually withdrew and let the Russians in, according to the agreement reached at the Yalta conference.

My diary for 17 April continues:

On the way back we searched the town for some eggs and eventually ran some to earth in an outlying village with the help of some British soldiers. After lunch walked with Martin in the woods, and only a mile away we were stopped by an American soldier and warned that German patrols were in the neighbourhood. Four French officers, exceeding the two mile limit from the castle, were recaptured yesterday! One later escaped and returned to tell the tale.

I gathered the following about the local military situation. The troops which captured Colditz consisted of two depleted companies supported by a few tanks. They came from the 69th Infantry and 9th Armoured Divisions of the First Army and had orders to clean up as far as the river. They had had no idea that the Castle contained prisoners and were about to open fire with some field guns that had come up when information about us arrived and orders given to cross the river, if the opposition was not too great, and rescue us. Thus the bridgehead which they established was only two miles deep and very precarious.

Later at night we were informed that we would leave in lorries at 8 a.m. for an aerodrome beyond Naumburg.

Sure enough the next morning we left Colditz Castle for good. We could only take with us what we could carry, and what we left behind was probably very useful to the French who remained. It was a funny feeling to walk through the main gate and down the hill, leaving behind so many memories, mostly unhappy ones of boredom and frustration but also some of good comradeship, laughter and occasionally excitement. I could only wish that Mike Sinclair had been talking there beside me as we left.

A convoy of American trucks awaited us below, all driven by black soldiers, and into them we piled. I do not remember looking back at the castle or having any wish to do so, being only thankful to be rid of the wretched place for ever. Our destination was seventy miles to the west near Weimar. My diary reads:

Wednesday, 18 April: A crowded journey in lorries to Kolleda aerodrome near Erfurt. On the way we nearly ran into a pocket of enemy resistance, and I was told that a burst of machine-gun fire was directed at one of our lorries. At one halt we watched a battery of 105 mm field guns firing on some enemy positions over the hill. In the evening we arrived at a hutted camp on Kolleda aerodrome. We were issued with American rations and I had a wonderful night's sleep, sharing a room with Alan and Bertie.

The American rations were excellent, and I was so anxious to open a tin of meat quickly that I cut a finger to the bone.

Next morning we were assembled near the runway at 9 a.m., but no planes arrived, so we spent the morning strolling about, chatting excitedly, trying to calm our impatience and every now and then gazing hopefully into the sky. Alan was not with us; he had always said that once he was free he never wanted to see any of us again, as we would remind him of so many things he wanted to forget. Now I could see him, a solitary figure, all alone on the other side of the runway. Sure enough it would be thirty-five years, at a Colditz reunion, before I would see him again. He went to Canada soon after the war, married and became a Doctor of Forestry in British Columbia.

It was while waiting thus that I was approached by David Stirling. David was a Scots Guards officer who had invented the Special Air Service and was generally regarded with a certain amount of awe and reverence due to his daring exploits in North Africa. Now he invited me to become his Adjutant in a new SAS regiment which he hoped to form for operations behind the Japanese lines in China. Martin, Phil and Tony Rolt had, he told me, already agreed to join. As it had been worrying me for some time that the Army and my Regiment might not be interested in us long-term prisoners, this offer by David seemed to come like a saving grace and I jumped at it. It seemed too good to be true (and indeed so it turned out).

At last at 2 p.m. a number of Dakotas suddenly appeared and swooped down onto the runway. We had never seen such graceful and modern looking planes. 'Ooh! Monoplanes!' several of us exclaimed.

We were off without any further delay. Most of us had never flown before and I had only had two ten shilling trips, one from Eastleigh in 1935 and one from Shoreham in 1939. There were twenty-five of us in our plane, which bounced about a bit, and some of my fellow passengers were sick. I soon got used to the motion and, as we flew quite low, there was plenty to look at. We passed over the Remagen bridge, then north to Aachen, where there were impressive signs of the recent fighting, and landed at Liege. Here there was no petrol, so three of our planes, including mine, went to an aerodrome south of Abbeville, the remainder proceeding to Brussels.

Then we flew on, and suddenly below us was the English Channel, my first sight of the sea for very nearly five years. Even more exciting was the coast as we flew over Eastbourne, and I recognized the big chalk-pit on the downs near Lewes. Finally, in fading light, we put down at Westcott near Aylesbury. We were on English soil again. I still could not quite believe it.

We were greeted with great acclaim, showered with cigarettes and disinfectant and taken into a large hangar where a sumptuous tea was spread before us and actually English newspapers. One of the first things I saw therein was a picture of Bader who had arrived the previous day. Also paraded on our behalf were some very pretty WVS girls but, unluckily for them, we had appeared later than expected, and the dark yellow lights of the hangar had to be turned on, so that the girls' faces looked green and their lips pitchblack, which rather spoilt the effect! In any case sex was far from my mind and would remain so until I had been home for a bit, when good food and renewed health had had a chance to work on me, and at this precise moment *The Daily Mirror* and white bread and butter were fully occupying my attention.

We were then driven off to a large country house near Amersham. There we filled up masses of forms, were individually debriefed and had an excellent dinner. I was even able to telephone and actually speak to my mother and finally went to sleep on a spring bed with real sheets in a pair of issued pyjamas and with a new toothbrush, toothpaste, flannel and soap! Was it all nothing but one long fantastic dream?

I woke to find it had not been a dream after all.

The final entry of my long diary reads as follows:

Friday, 20 April: After a wonderful breakfast, spent two hours filling up forms, seeing the MO, QM and getting pay and rations. Travelled to London with Martin Gilliat and Pat Campbell-Preston, of the Black Watch, saw Mr Welsh, (of Welsh and Jefferies, our Regimental tailors) looked in at my club and then took a taxi to Victoria. It was quite a thrill to be able to say, 'Victoria, Brighton Line' after so long!

Had a pork pie and a cup of coffee at the station buffet, rang up Mummy and said I was catching the 2.28, caught it and was met at Shoreham Station by her with Margaret.

It was the end of a very long journey.

Epilogue

As we grow older Time seems to quicken, and five years can pass just like an evening gone.

Certainly my five years spent as a prisoner of war sliced away a substantial part of my youth. When I was captured I was but twenty-one, just 'come of age.' When I came home I was nearly twenty-seven.

They were for the most part wasted years, years 'eaten by the locust' and gone for ever with the wind. They could not be reclaimed. Yet, on the credit side I had at least survived and learnt such things as patience, fortitude, some measure of resourcefulness and the ability to improvise and look after myself. Now, like so many others at that time, I would have to be picking up the pieces and starting all over again.

The family home, Annington, near Steyning in Sussex, seemed much the same, just the shrubs and trees in the garden grown bigger, and old Nanny Bridge, who had received my first prison postcard, the one I wrote from the hospital in Calais, was still there, waiting to welcome me back.

It took me some time, of course, to catch up on all the news of family and friends, and I was shocked to find how many of the latter had been killed. There was, however, one piece of exceptionally good news. As my mother drove me home from Shoreham station she told me that Mrs M had escaped from Poland and had arrived, miraculously and safely, in London. Within a week I had run her to earth and listened to her tales of adventure and escape. It was marvellous to see her safe and sound in England as she had always been in danger when I had known her before.

She wished to be known as Miss Jane Walker, with the MBE awarded her for her wartime work in Warsaw. She lived to a ripe old age and died in Bexhill ('Breezy Bexhill', as she liked to call it) in 1963 at the age of eighty-six. I wrote her obituary in *The Times* and, to this day, my wife and I go annually to tend her grave. It is often raining when we go there and, if she ever watches, she will certainly be laughing at us. She had a great sense of fun.

I was able fairly quickly to find out about my old platoon from Calais. Nine of them, less than I feared, had been killed, including Sergeant Wall, Corporal Gorringe and Lance Corporal Smith. Three had been seriously wounded early in the battle and been successfully evacuated home. The remainder, of whom a number had been wounded, were taken prisoner. My faithful batman, Smith, had survived and we met again in London.

At first, I was none too well and was even suspected (wrongly, I am glad to say) of having TB. But I was soon busily involved with the formation of David Stirling's new SAS regiment, though the atom bombs and Japan's subsequent surrender put paid to that.

I have never managed to learn very much about the fate of my brave Polish friends, partly because Poland was behind the Iron Curtain and party because, with a few exceptions, I had never been told their real names. Most of what I did discover only came gradually to light. I believe Mr Olszewski (my dear 'Puffy') was killed or died in a concentration camp and that several of the resistance groups, including those in Posen, Lodz and Warsaw suffered casualties and were broken up.

In 1951, however, when I was soldiering in Germany I discovered that the Kotyllas were living in a West German Displaced Persons camp. Diana and I visited them there and I was able to recommend them to our Control Commission as suitable people for immigration into Britain or the USA.

Charles Whitehead, or Karol as we knew him, who had helped us so much in Warsaw and, in whose empty flat, I had resided while in the care of Mr R was arrested by the Russians; it was something to do with his mother's chocolate firm which had been taken over by the Germans during the war. Despite strong British protests he was imprisoned for eight years but managed to survive.

Many years later I made contact with a Mrs Lutostanska, whose husband's family had sheltered me during the war and, with the help

232

of one Josef Hlebovicz, who had been a Polish officer in Colditz with me, I also contacted Charles Whitehead, Mr R and one Zygmunt Klichowski, who, as a boy, had been the link between the Posen camp and the local Resistance. Zygmunt had been imprisoned by the Germans but had survived to become a Colonel in the Polish Airforce.

During a visit to Poland in 1991 I was able to meet up with John and Lucy Lutostanski, Zygmunt and his wife Janeczka, and with Karol Whitehead, but unfortunately Mr R, now over ninety, was unable to see me. Karol and I had much to talk about and, before saying goodbye, I stood with him for a few moments on the great bridge across the Vistula near Saska Kepa at the exact spot where I had stood on the old bridge (destroyed in the war) feeling lonely and very far from home, one evening long ago.

I had hoped my visit would give me an opportunity to repay in some small way the wartime hospitality I had received. I was not allowed to do so. Once again Polish hospitality overwhelmed me. The old song of my prep school days came back into my mind.

> *In Poland stands an inn,*
> *In Poland stands an inn,*
> *In Poland stands a Polish inn*
> *And there the people all go in,*
> *For nothing all their food they win,*
> *They do not pay a pin.*

Within three months of my return to England in 1945 I became heavily involved in courting, slightly inhibited by my intended's sensible caution while the war was still going on. Then came the atom bombs, and suddenly it was Peace. I was staying at the time with my eldest brother and his wife at Esher. Learning of Japan's impending surrender, I rang Her-who-had-become-the-light-of-my-life, making use of an A, D and C call (*Advise, Duration and Cost*) and explained that the new situation had removed all barriers to our immediate engagement. Encountering what I considered to be some regrettable lack of spontaneous enthusiasm at the other end of the line, I expounded my case with gusto and passion. It took me three-quarters of an hour to settle matters satisfactorily.

A few minutes after I had replaced the receiver the operator phoned back and mentioned an unexpected high figure of cost for my call.

'Preposterous,' I gasped. 'Surely, it cannot be so much.'

'Well, I dunno,' he replied. 'It was worth it, wasn't it?'

It certainly was.

ADDENDUM

As thirteen years have passed since this book was first published, it is not surprising, that a number of my links with the people and places mentioned in the book have now been severed.

Of the officers who fought with me in the 2nd 60th at Calais in 1940, for example, only Peter Parker and I remain.

In the Epilogue I describe my return to Poland in 1991 to visit those, still alive, who had helped and sheltered me when on the run in 1941/42. Sad to relate, Karol Whitehead died in 1993; Witold Romanski (Mr R) in 1995 and Zygmunt Klichowski in 1998. My only surviving links with Poland now are John and Lucy Lutostanski, Janeczka Klichowska (Zygmunt's widow), Josef and Hanka Hlebowicz (he was with me in Colditz) and Georgi Romanski, a senior executive in Polish television and nephew of 'Mr R' who visited us in England shortly before his uncle's death.

Of the original party of six officers (including Pat Reid) who made the first escape from Laufen in 1940, were recaptured and sent to Colditz, only Kenneth Lockwood is still with us. He and I took part in the *Escape from Colditz* documentaries shown in January/February 2000 on Channel 4.

Of the seven members of my little mess at Laufen only Tony Rolt and I are still around.

From my own family my elder sister Gwynedd, and both my brothers, David and John, all of whom are mentioned several times in my book, have now died – all three in their eighties. My younger sister, Margaret still survives.

A well known hymn tells us:

Time like an ever-rolling stream
Bears all its sons away;
They fly, forgotten as a dream
Dies at the opening day.

I have never thought that true, as people are by no means always forgotten. As far as those of whom I have written are concerned, I hope this book will help to keep their memory alive.

June 2004   G.D-S.

Index

239